The Opacity of Narrative

The Opacity of Narrative

Peter Lamarque

ROWMAN &
LITTLEFIELD
INTERNATIONAL
London • New York

Published by Rowman & Littlefield International, Ltd.
16 Carlisle Street, London, W1D 3BT
www.rowmaninternational.com

Rowman & Littlefield International, Ltd. is an affiliate of Rowman & Littlefield
4501 Forbes Boulevard, Suite 200, Lanham, Maryland 20706, USA
With additional offices in Boulder, New York, Toronto (Canada), and Plymouth (UK)
www.rowman.com

British Library Cataloguing in Publication Information Available
A catalogue record for this book is available from the British Library

ISBN: HB 978-1-78348-016-6
ISBN: PB 978-1-78348-017-3

Library of Congress Cataloging-in-Publication Data

Lamarque, Peter.
The opacity of narrative / Peter Lamarque.
pages cm
Includes bibliographical references and index.
ISBN 978-1-78348-016-6 (cloth : alk. paper) — ISBN 978-1-78348-017-3 (pbk. : alk. paper) —
ISBN 978-1-78348-018-0 (electronic)
1. Narration (Rhetoric) 2. Opacity (Linguistics) I. Title.
PN212.L36 2014
808—dc23
2013048453

∞™ The paper used in this publication meets the minimum requirements of American National Standard for Information Sciences Permanence of Paper for Printed Library Materials, ANSI/NISO Z39.48-1992.

Printed in the United States of America

Contents

Preface vii

Acknowledgements xiii

1 Opacity, Fiction and Narratives of the Self 1

2 Narrative and Invention: The Limits of Fictionality 33

3 On Not Expecting Too Much from Narrative 51

4 On the Distance between Literary Narratives and Real-Life Narratives 67

5 Fiction and the Nonfiction Novel 83

6 Wittgenstein, Literature and the Idea of a Practice 105

7 Literature and Truth 121

8 Thought, Opacity and the Values of Literature 141

9 Aesthetics and Literature: A Problematic Relation? 169

10 On Keeping Psychology Out of Literary Criticism 185

Bibliography 201

Index 211

Preface

I suspect that few enter the field of narratology without some trepidation. So extensive are the outpourings about narrative from so many perspectives—linguistics to clinical practice, literary theory to jurisprudence, sociology to historiography, psychoanalysis to theology—that any one intervention in some corner can seem insignificant in the vaster realm. My own perspective is that of the philosophy of literature. I don't believe this is an insignificant niche; however, I am under no illusions that it leaves untouched many important questions that practitioners from elsewhere want to press.

One need not be apologetic, though, about giving focus to literature in a study of narrative. Arguably, the great literary works provide some of the finest examples of narratives; they exemplify storytelling at its very best. Needless to say, there are narratives that are not literary works (even in the broadest sense of the term that includes works of history, biography, autobiography and philosophy), and some of these can impinge deeply on people's lives, not least narratives of self. But novels, sagas, myths and narrative poems have a special place in human self-consciousness. They provide a frame of reference for cultures at large and for personal reflection. They are admired not just as feats of the imagination but also for skills of expression. They show how language can be elevated well beyond the mundane practicalities of day-to-day exchange to something sublime and almost magical in its ability to conjure images and transport the mind to distant worlds.

The values of narratives, sometimes implicitly, often explicitly, play a crucial role in this study. Precisely what values do literary narratives exemplify? What makes them special? What is it about them that draws us back to them and makes them exemplary among stories told and enjoyed?

Not all that emerges from the discussion will be uncontroversial. In fact, a strong undercurrent of scepticism towards received opinion will be prominent throughout.

For example, a common, one might say commonplace, view about the great works of literary fiction is that they reveal truths—about human motives and desires, the dark recesses of the mind, tangled human transactions in social, political and personal spheres—that are profound and largely unrecoverable elsewhere, in social science or philosophy. But on closer inspection, this appeal to literary or "poetic" truth yields rather less than it promises (chapter 7). The relevant conception of truth is hard to pin down and other ideas like vision or clarification or "enriched understanding" jostle for attention without being especially illuminating and serving only to weaken claims to truth. The "truth" idiom itself, it will be argued, sets up all the wrong expectations about the achievements of literary fictional works and is largely unhelpful as a touchstone of literary value.

Scepticism is one thing, but is there nothing more positive on offer to accommodate perfectly familiar intuitions about "cognitive" gains from the works in question? This is where the idea of the "opacity" of narrative can contribute (explained in chapter 1). Rather than supposing that a fictional narrative presents a transparent glass through which a world—fictional or real—is revealed to us, somehow beyond or independent of its narrative vehicle, we should think of the narrative as absorbing us in its own fine-grained details, its "world", its characters, incidents, setting and structure, seen in, not through, the glass. Attending to these aspects *in their own terms* triggers thoughts and images that can lodge in the mind more securely than mere items of knowledge, serving sometimes to "shape" the mind or change its inner landscape in more or less permanent ways (chapter 8). This is how the great novels stay with us. They linger in the mind not as truths or moral precepts, but rather as fine-grained memory-like thoughts that could, but need not, be a resource useful in multiple ways in negotiations with our own world, even when we don't notice this happening.

The truth issue about literature emerges in other contexts as well. One of these concerns the model that literary narratives are sometimes thought to provide for narratives in ordinary people's lives. It is said that works of literature can directly aid our own self-conception: in exemplifying genres like tragedy, romance or comedy, they can supply patterns to the narratives of self; in offering paradigmatic character types, they can guide behaviour and help substantiate a self-image; and through their structures of meaningfulness, their plots with beginnings, middles and ends, with closure and teleology, they can promote shape in a life in which shapelessness otherwise prevails. But again, scepticism is in order (chapter 4). If we think of literary works as essentially just plots and characters somehow "mirroring" real lives, then perhaps they can, in superficial ways, serve as models for self-narratives. This is to read them "transparently", as works to look through but not at. But when we attend to them as literature or as works of art (i.e., "opaquely", in the terms of this book)—remarking those features in virtue of which they make a claim to literary greatness—parallels with ordinary lives begin to seem strained and unhelpful. Although from an internal perspective characters often act and live their lives according to ordinary principles of choice and cause, when viewed, externally, as artefacts in a work of art they become subject to radically different kinds of explanation. Why do they act as they do? Perhaps because they *must* act that way to meet aesthetic, structural and genre-based demands for works of that kind. Perhaps their actions have a symbolic function or a function connected with the development of a theme or because they represent a "polarity" with another character.

Literary constraints differ hugely from the retail constraints on human action in the real world. All this is plain enough for those used to attending to literature with an eye to structure and meaning. But there are dangers for those who seek to model their own life-narratives on the narratives of literature: dangers of seeking meaning where no meaning exists, of letting formal structures rather than rational choice dictate action, of aestheticising lives, of imposing a false teleology. To look to literature as a guide to life is not quite the anodyne activity sometimes supposed.

Truth crops up again in a different way when we turn to those genres of writing that seem to lie somewhere between the fictional and the nonfictional. Chapter 5 discusses the puzzling case of the so-called "nonfiction novel" or "faction". These are works that purport to stick rigidly to the facts—as a kind of journalism, "New Journalism", exploring real lives—but use novelistic techniques that owe more to the traditions of the novel than to conventional history. What is the correct classification for works of this kind? Do these cases weaken the distinction between fiction and nonfiction? Again, caution is recommended. Serviceable distinctions should not be jettisoned. But it puts the spotlight once more on the very idea of fiction and what makes a work fictional.

The broad proposal here is that rather than looking to semantics (word-world relations) or form (styles of writing), we should look to the notion of rule-governed practices as the framework for a satisfactory account of fiction (chapter 2, chapter 6). The contrast with history (chapter 1) is instructive. Some works of fiction look like works of history and history can sometimes read like fiction; yet there are familiar constraints on both genres that point out the differences that matter: constraints on reading, aims, expectations, modes of evaluation, focus of attention, inferences permitted and so forth. Sometimes no-doubt individual constraints (the "rules") might be more salient, or less so, in particular cases, allowing for genuine borderlines or puzzlement. But if we want to retain a reasonably clear view of fiction (to provide a useful contrast with other kinds of writing), we must look in the right places:

not, surprisingly, to "truth", or to rhetorical modes, but in effect to the rules of the "game" being played.

The idea of a practice is useful also, returning to our earlier discussion, in characterising the values of literary narratives. To attend to works of literature as works of art involves a particular kind of focus. But it is important not to be reductive in characterising what that focus should be (chapter 9). It should not give exclusive priority to formal aspects, highlighting factors like "fine writing", over broader matters of content, theme or character. To do so is to downplay what gives literary works their primary interest. In fact, narrative opacity suggests that, in the literary context, form and content are better viewed as indivisible (chapter 8), in the sense that "content" be thought of as *constituted* by the modes of its presentation. To attend to the fine-grained aspects of narrative language is not to resort to an arid formalism or to endorse styles of "practical criticism" that seem merely pedantic but can open up intricacies and richness in the narrative worlds presented (chapter 8). And this, in turn, affords a far deeper hold on the imagination than coarse-grained summaries of plots or characters could ever achieve.

Other forms of reduction are also to be discouraged: for example, over-emphasising grasp of propositional or utterance meaning in responding to literature at the expense of more literary modes of "appreciation" (chapter 9) and overestimating the place of emotional response among the values of literature (chapter 10). A general observation is important here, distinguishing between features that are merely contingently associated with particular works and features that are at the core of the value of literature. Take two examples: the potential of works to impart facts about their setting and their potential to stir emotions in readers.

There is no denying that readers can learn facts from novels and that they can react emotionally to novels. In both cases, these might be valuable to the readers concerned and count as reasons for them to value the works. This might be sufficient to give the works value. But is it the kind of value that marks off the great works of literature? Picking up facts from novels might make them intriguing and informative. But this is rarely used in support of stronger "truth" theories that seem to be looking for something deeper, more substantial and more universal. It is not usually the acquiring of facts that is claimed to be behind the more distinctive values of literature. And what about emotion? Admittedly, Aristotle saw part of the value of tragedy in stirring the emotions of pity and fear, leading to a cathartic purging of those emotions. But it is at least arguable—perhaps even consistent with Aristotle—that the actual emotions aroused in audiences are not the crucial element in an effective tragedy (resting too much on local psychological dispositions). What matters is that the tragic portrayal be *pitiable* and *fearful*. The measure of that is in the intensity and effectiveness of the writing, not in actual effects on actual audiences. Then we are back to values of a more intrinsic, less instrumental, kind and thus to more inherently literary values.

Let us return once more to that strand of scepticism that runs through the book—at least scepticism about received views. It seems to be nearly universally acknowledged that narrative is central to most aspects of human social and personal life. Let's set aside the value of *literary* narratives, which is explored and, I hope, established throughout the book. But I wonder if the more general claim hasn't been exaggerated by narrative enthusiasts. I am drawn to two lines of thought here. One is to suppose that it has indeed been exaggerated and that narrative is not as important in human life as supposed. The other is to concede that narrative is central but to observe, given the nature of narrative, how unsurprising that should be and how little it actually amounts to (the theme of chapter 3). A word on each of these, which are not really at odds.

On the first, that narrative (literary exemplars aside) is not that important in human life, I am inclined to appeal to introspection and personal reflection. Here then, briefly, are some homely facts about myself. I don't find that narrative is especially prominent in my own experience (in this I am similar to Galen Strawson [2004]). I am not a natural storyteller—about myself or anything else—and in particular I don't attend to my life through narratives. For example, characteristically, I bring memories to mind not through narratives (even mini-narratives) but through images and not even image sequences that might take a narrative form. My memory images tend to be discrete snapshots of events. No doubt, if asked to recall events, I will use the story form. But it doesn't come easily to me. I don't find that I have recourse often to what Peter Goldie calls "narrative thinking" either (Goldie 2012), although I recognise it in others through the vivid examples he offers. Of course, all this is just personal. But when I read Strawson's similar reflections, I did wonder, at the least, whether people might differ considerably in their narrative proclivities and, while I am not in a position to deny that for many people narrative does provide just the kind of sense-making facility claimed for it, maybe narrative is not *essential* to living a fulfilled human life.

My second thought, not, I think, at odds with the first, is the acknowledgement that narrative is widespread, but unsurprisingly so. Underlying this thought is the recognition of how trivial a thing narrative can be. To say that *this happened as a consequence of that* is a minimal narrative. But, of course, narrative at that level of simplicity is bound to be common, for the very reason that made Kant see causation as one of the fundamental categories of thought. Maybe not all narratives involve causal connections but all causal connections look like a potential subject for narrative. If narrative is so closely linked to explanation and humans are so tied to the imperative to explain, then it is of no surprise at all that narrative should be ubiquitous. But this is a hollow victory for the narrative enthusiast. Such a person wants so much more from narrative—and narratives of so much more interest. For them, the narratives that bind lives together, that ground a sense of self, that ascribe purpose and meaning to actions and provide a foundation for the moral life are not little snippets of explanation but something altogether richer. And it is those rich narratives that seem absent or rare in certain lives (maybe mine and Strawson's).

All this simply carries on the theme of the values of narrative. Not all narratives are of equal interest. It might be deflationary to point up the existence of paltry narratives—trivial things that come and go barely recognised—but that should not deflect from the potential power of narrative at the other end of the scale. The principal focus for this study, as emphasised above, are the great narratives of literature, and if an advertisement were needed for what narrative can achieve, it surely lies there. So although there is a sceptical undertone about some of the claims made for narrative, there is no doubting the values, properly located, of the very best narratives.

Acknowledgements

I have been thinking and writing about the broad themes of this book for so many years that it would be nearly impossible to list all the people who have helped and influenced me and with whom I have debated. There are just too many. But, of course, I am hugely grateful to them in recognition that none of us can just go it alone.

I do, though, want to extend special thanks to the organisers of a number of conferences over the past ten years for their invitations to give papers or lectures. These meetings have proved invaluable for working out some of my ideas on these topics. The relevant conferences are as follows: "Narrative: Art and Mind", Cumberland Lodge, Windsor, UK, May 2003; American Society for Aesthetics, San Francisco, USA, October 2003; American Society for Aesthetics, Houston, Texas, USA, October 2004; "Philosophy and Literature", University of St Andrews, Scotland, December 2004; "Art and Cognition", Erfurt, Germany, June 2005; "Narrative and the Self" (Royal Institute of Philosophy), University of Hertfordshire, UK, July 2005; American Society for Aesthetics, Providence, Rhode Island, USA, October 2005; Oberlin Colloquium, Oberlin College, USA, April 2006; British Society of Aesthetics, Oxford, UK, September 2006; "Aesthetics and Knowledge", Nancy, France, November 2006; "Aesthetic Psychology", University of Durham, UK, September 2007; American Society for Aesthetics, Los Angeles, USA, November 2007; Logos Colloquium, University of Barcelona, Spain, November 2008; University of Rijeka, Croatia, March 2010; "Wittgenstein Reading" (Ghent Conference on Literary Theory), University of Ghent, Belgium, June 2010; "Knowledge and Meaning in Literature", University of Regensburg, Germany, June 2011; "How to Make Believe: The Fictional Truths of the Representational Arts", Lund University, Sweden, March 2012; "Interpretation and Meaning: Exploring the Theory of Interpretation", University of Utrecht, The Netherlands, June 2012; "Understanding Value", University of Sheffield, UK, July 2012; "Semantics of Fictional Discourse", Gottingen, Germany, March 2013; Programme in the Theory of Literature, University of Lisbon, Portugal, March 2013; "Art and Belief", University of York, UK, October 2013.

Personal thanks, too, to my son Hugh for his painstaking work in formatting the bibliography, and to Mary, my wife, for doing the index. And thanks finally to Sarah Campbell at RLI for her encouragement and support from the very start, and to Patricia Stevenson for her efficient production work.

The bulk of the chapters (excluding chapters 1 and 5, which are new) have appeared in more or less similar form in other publications. The sources of the papers are given below. All have been edited and revised to some extent.

Chapter 2: "Narrative and Invention: The Limits of Fictionality", in *Narrative in Culture: The Uses of Storytelling in the Sciences, Philosophy and Literature*, edited by Cristopher Nash (London: Routledge & Kegan Paul, 1990), 131–53. This paper dates back much further than any of the others and represents an early attempt of mine to reflect on fiction and narrative. I have included it here because I still hold to its central claims, still believe that the distinction between kinds of fictions (logical, epistemological and make-believe) is important, and I think it gives a succinct and useful outline of views that are developed in Peter Lamarque and Stein Haugom Olsen, *Truth, Fiction, and Literature: A Philosophical Perspective* (Oxford: Clarendon Press, 1994), and in subsequent work. Towards the end, I have made some fairly substantial changes to bring the terminology into line with other parts of the book.

Chapter 3: "On Not Expecting Too Much from Narrative", *Mind & Language* 19, no. 4 (September 2004): 393–408.

Chapter 4: "On the Distance between Literary Narratives and Real-Life Narratives", in *Narrative and Understanding Persons*, edited by Dan Hutto, Royal Institute of Philosophy Supplement (Cambridge: Cambridge University Press, 2007), 117–32. I have drawn on some material from this paper in my book *The Philosophy of Literature* (Oxford: Blackwell, 2008). But the contexts are quite different and the polemical aspects of the paper do not appear in that book.

Chapter 6: "Wittgenstein, Literature, and the Idea of a Practice", *British Journal of Aesthetics* 50 (2010): 375–88.

Chapter 7: "Literature and Truth", in *A Companion to the Philosophy of Literature*, edited by Garry L. Hagberg and Walter Jost (Malden, MA: Wiley-Blackwell, 2010), 367–84. This is an outline (I hope in a clear, accessible form) of arguments against truth-theories of literature that are developed in Peter Lamarque and Stein Haugom Olsen's *Truth, Fiction, and Literature*, and in other writings of mine. The arguments have appeared in this form only in this paper itself.

Chapter 8: Draws on "Thought Theory and Literary Cognition", in *Understanding Fiction: Knowledge and Meaning in Literature*, edited by Jürgen Daiber, Eva-Maria Konrad, Thomas Petraschka and Hans Rott (Münster: Mentis, 2012), 67–80, and "Thought, Make-Believe and the Opacity of Narrative", in *How to Make Believe: The Fictional Truths of the Representational Arts*, edited by Alexander Bareis (forthcoming, DeGruyter). This chapter is pivotal in the book, as it illustrates in detail how the idea of "opacity" applies in actual cases. It draws on material in the two papers listed but goes substantially beyond them in giving a clearer working out of just what opacity amounts to and how it relates to another view of mine dubbed "thought theory".

Chapter 9: "Aesthetics and Literature: A Problematic Relation?" *Philosophical Studies* 135 (2007): 27–40. Scattered bits of this paper have also appeared in *The Philosophy of Literature*, but again the context is different, and in its entirety the paper fits well into the polemic of this book showing where the values of literary narrative do and do not reside.

Chapter 10: "On Keeping Psychology Out of Literary Criticism", in *The Aesthetic Mind: Philosophy and Psychology*, edited by Elisabeth Schellekens and Peter Goldie (Oxford: Oxford University Press, 2011), 299–312.

I am most grateful to the publishers of these papers for permission to reprint them here.

Chapter One

Opacity, Fiction and Narratives of the Self

There is no need to start with a definition. That can come later and the difficulties explored. At the beginning, it is sufficient to think of narratives as stories.[1] This can be helpful because there is much less pressure to find a *theory* of stories. Stories vary immensely from one to another, in kind and quality, in length and complexity, in genres—novels, histories, poems, songs—and in degrees of seriousness, from bedtime stories to the Story of Art or the Story of Civilisation. But on the whole, we know a story when we see it (or hear it). To seek to define "story" could seem unduly pedantic. In contrast, "narrative" has become a technical term used across multiple academic disciplines and also in journalism, politics and elsewhere (the "narrative of welfare", the "narrative of human rights"). It even has its own branch of enquiry: narratology. As such, it cries out for a definition because it is far from clear what is meant in these different contexts: narratologists themselves disagree. It might well turn out that there is no single concept that spans every usage. The view I shall advance in this book is that the best way to proceed in so complex a topic is to settle on a common core of meaning that is minimal in its commitments and then account for differences as they emerge in terms of enrichments of the core for different purposes and in different practices. That common core need be little more than the intuitive notion of a story. What is that notion? Minimally, just this: the representation of two or more events, real or imaginary, from a point of view, with some degree of structure and connectedness.

In fact, the focus in what follows will be less on trying to nail down a definition and more on finding satisfactory ways of drawing distinctions between items that all would agree are narratives: those of history, philosophy, biography or the novel, for example, as well as those simple conversational narratives that animate social interactions and those more elusive narratives that individuals create for themselves to help make sense of their lives, perhaps to justify actions, enliven memories or aggrandise mundane existence. Distinctions can be important here because the purposes, achievements and norms of evaluation can differ radically in these contexts and to blur boundaries that matter can have serious consequences both in understanding and at a disciplinary and even personal level. Just how the appropriate distinctions should be drawn can be a subject of contention, in particular that between "fiction" and "nonfiction". A central aim of this book is to propose a basis for how to draw lines here that are not arbitrary or gratuitous.

The place where a definition of "narrative" might be useful is not in drawing distinctions between narratives but in distinguishing narratives from modes of discourse that are not narratives. Again, it is only in some cases that disputes might occur. Historians can agree that annals that merely list facts by date are not examples of "narrative history" (White 1980), and no one supposes that botanical classifications, mathematical proofs or *Tractatus Logico-Philosophicus* are narratives. But sometimes what is and is not a narrative is not so clear. As we shall see, in discussions of personal narratives or narratives that supposedly shape or constitute our identity as selves, there is unclarity about just what counts as a narrative. Can lives be narratives? Can thinking be a narrative? We shall return to this issue.

If narratives are first and foremost stories, it is not unreasonable to attend to stories that stand out as exceptional or of the highest quality. It is not that value judgements as such will be prominent in what follows, but particular focus will be given to narratives that aspire to be *works of art*: narratives that we call "literature". Needless to say, "literature" is a contested term itself, no easier to define than "narrative". But again, definition is not the exercise that matters. It is better to take works that are uncontroversially works of literature and ask what distinctive features they possess in virtue of being literature. In fact, the enquiry will be even narrower than that because the works to be examined are works of fiction, in contrast to those literary works that are nonfiction (such as history or biography). It is important not to beg any questions, and these terms will need to come under scrutiny, as will the distinctions themselves. Nor is there any implication that works of so-called "imaginative literature" or of "literary fiction" are of a higher quality or more worthy to be classed as *works of art* than their nonfiction counterparts. But it is the combination of their literary and their fictional qualities that is of special interest. What is it that sets them apart as stories or narratives that merit special attention, that seem to reveal the human mind at its most acute and most inventive? Is it the power of the imagination? The fineness of the writing? The skills of plot construction and character delineation? The vision or truths imparted? No doubt bits of all of these. Yet the key to literary fiction lies elsewhere, as we shall see: not least in the kinds of pleasures and rewards that readers gain from them.

OPACITY AND TRANSPARENCY

A prominent feature of literary fictional narratives, I shall argue, is their *opacity*, so a preliminary exploration of that notion will be helpful. The idea at its simplest is that the content of literary fictional narratives stands in a peculiarly intimate relation to the manner in which it is presented. Put like this, the point is virtually a truism. Of course, readers of novels are not indifferent to the actual descriptions that present the fictional worlds they are imagining and enjoying. The descriptions matter and novels are praised or denigrated for the quality of the writing, its vividness, power, resonance, expressiveness, clarity, wit and so on, through the familiar multiplicity of positive attributes (different ones no doubt being more apt in different cases). But narrative opacity says more than just that descriptions matter—although it does say that. In the literary fictional case, the events and characters that make up the content are *constituted* by the modes of their presentation in the narrative. Their identity is determined by the narrative itself such that they are not merely contingently but essentially connected to the descriptions that characterise them. Rather than supposing that narrative descriptions are a window through which an independently existing (fictional) world is observed, with the implication that the very same world might be presented (and thus observed) in other ways, from different perspectives, we must accept that there is no such transparent glass—only an opaque glass, painted, as it were, with figures seen not *through* it but *in* it.

Narratives in poetry provide clear examples of the phenomenon. Consider the first stanza of Thomas Hardy's poem "The Darkling Thrush" (1900):

> I leant upon a coppice gate
> When Frost was spectre-grey,
> And Winter's dregs made desolate
> The weakening eye of day.
> The tangled bine-stems scored the sky
> Like strings of broken lyres,
> And all mankind that haunted nigh
> Had sought their household fires.
> (Hardy 1994, 134)

The lines are presented as part of a small but intense narrative: the poem represents a speaker outside on a cold, desolate winter evening who hears a thrush's song ("An aged thrush, frail, gaunt and small, / In blast-beruffled plume, / Had chosen thus to fling his soul / Upon the growing gloom") and infers "[s]ome blessed Hope, whereof he knew / And I was unaware". In this stanza, the mood of wintry melancholy is reinforced in the succession of negative images: "dregs", "desolate", "weakening", "tangled", "scored" (i.e., cut or scratched), "broken". The ghost-like quality of the scene is given in "spectre-grey" and "haunted". Alliteration in each couplet—gate/grey, desolate/day, stems/strings, haunted/household—together with the ballad-like metre and rhyme scheme increases the hypnotic intensity. To bring to mind the requisite images, these epithets must play an essential, not merely contingent, role. It is not as if other ways of capturing the scene would be just as effective, for the scene itself derives its very identity (including its mood and character) through these exact lines.

Of course, many questions about opacity defined in this way need to be addressed. What about fictional narratives that describe essentially the same fictional events—that tell the same story—but in different ways? Should we not say in such cases that there is indeed an independently existing world not constituted by any one narrative but accessed by several? And what about novels grounded in real events, such as *War and Peace*, *For Whom the Bell Tolls*, a long list—surely these do not constitute the events they describe? To answer these questions, we need an account of the "content" of a work, in particular some criterion for sameness and difference of content. And is content the same as "subject matter"? What is it for two works to share a subject matter?

Before pursuing these questions directly, it is necessary to sharpen the characterisation of narrative opacity. We need a few more resources to tackle the all-important issue of content-identity. There are two contexts elsewhere in philosophy in which parallels with the relevant kind of opacity can be usefully invoked.

Referential Opacity

The first is with *referential opacity*, as characterised by W V O Quine (e.g., Quine 1956; Quine 1960, §30; Quine 1961). Quine noted, as Gottlob Frege had done before him, that in certain contexts names or singular descriptions do not act in a "purely referential" or "transparent" manner. In these contexts, an "opaque construction" is generated and this can arise from different sources:

> An opaque construction is one in which you cannot in general supplant a singular term by a *codesignative* term (one referring to the same object) without disturbing the truth value of the containing sentence. In an opaque construction you also cannot in general supplant a general term by a *coextensive* term (one true of the same objects), nor a component sentence by a sentence of the same truth value, without disturbing the truth value of the containing sentence. All three failures are failures of *extensionality*. (Quine 1960, 151)

The criterion for a "purely referential position" is "substitutivity of identity" (Quine 1960, 142). Although Quine spread the net of opacity widely, he was most concerned with referential opacity involving singular terms. He offered different kinds of cases. The most familiar arise from propositional attitudes such as belief. Take the sentence "Cicero denounced Catiline". In normal contexts in which the sentence is used to make an assertion, the name "Cicero" is purely referential and substitution of the codesignative name "Tully" for "Cicero" does not, as Quine puts it, "disturb the truth value" of the assertion. Nevertheless, as he points out, we might affirm "Tom believes that Cicero denounced Catiline" while denying "Tom believes that Tully denounced Catiline" under the circumstance that Tom is not aware of the identity of Tully and Cicero. The name "Cicero" in this latter context is not purely referential, so the context itself (following the operator "Tom believes that") is opaque.

It is not just propositional attitude contexts that generate opacity. Quine gives other examples. Thus quotation blocks "pure" reference. In the sentence "'Tully was a Roman' is trochaic", again the name "Tully" cannot be changed to "Cicero" without changing the truth value. And in spite of the identity of Giorgione and Barbarelli, the substitution of "Barbarelli" for "Giorgione" in "Giorgione was so-called because of his size" does not preserve truth. A further example from Quine involves singular descriptions rather than names: "The commissioner is looking for the chairman of the hospital board". Suppose the chairman of the hospital board is, in fact, the dean, but the commissioner does not know this. Then, at least on one way of construing the sentence, substituting "the dean" for "the chairman of the hospital board" seems again not to preserve truth.

We need not dwell on the details of Quine's exposition nor on the complex issues it generates.[2] Suffice it to say that Quine himself sought in his "regimentation" of language to minimise occurrences of opaque contexts and maximise extensionality. His programme was to seek, when possible, paraphrases into extensional formulations. Thus "Giorgione was so-called because of his size" is easily paraphrased into "Giorgione was called 'Giorgione' because of his size", in which the first occurrence of "Giorgione" is purely referential and the second, in quotation marks, refers not to the person but to his name. Extensionality is preserved and opacity removed. Quine was anxious not to follow the Fregean route of postulating "intensional" entities, such as senses, as referents of names within opaque contexts.

For our purposes, only some elements of Quinean opacity have a bearing on narrative. Needless to say, referential opacity in Quine's sense can occur in narratives, just as it can in discourse of any kind. Propositional attitude judgements as well as quotation are not unusual in narratives. But that is not the key to the opacity of narrative as it concerns us. In fact, narrative opacity has little to do with reference and little to do with extensionality. The key lies more in what is and is not preserved under substitution of identities. Something *like* "failure of extensionality" arises when substitution of alternative means of characterising, or picking out, items in a narrative is blocked because different ways of picking out those items are not equally permissible. Opacity occurs when the narrative is not indifferent to how the items are identified or characterised. In the extreme case of literary fictional narratives, as was suggested earlier, the very content of the narrative is constituted by the linguistic forms used to present that content. If other descriptive forms had been used, the content (and thus the "world" presented) would have changed. I say it is only "like" failure of extensionality because what matters is not preservation of *truth* under substitution but preservation of the narrative itself. Opacity of narrative occurs when substitutions of co-extensional terms are impermissible if the content of the narrative (in a sense to be explained) is to be preserved. Likewise, transparency occurs when the very same content can be accessed in different ways (i.e., the content is not dependent on some specific mode of presentation). Examples will be given in chapter 8.

Representational Opacity

These points will be consolidated after we have introduced a second philosophical context in which the idea of "transparency" is invoked and which again has a bearing on narrative opacity of the relevant kind. This is a discussion in which photography is compared to painting particularly with regard to the kinds of "representation" involved in each. For want of a better term, I will label this kind of opacity *representational opacity*.

The idea, in some version or other, that photographs are "transparent" to their subjects has been around virtually since photography was invented. It has been the focus of intense philosophical debate at least since Kendall Walton's well-known intervention.[3] Walton sought to demonstrate that transparency—photography's "remarkable ability to put us in perceptual contact with the world" (Walton 1984, 273)—is the key to understanding photographic "realism". Here is Dominic McIver Lopes's account of transparency in photographs, largely following Walton:

> To say that photographs are transparent is to say that we see through them. A person seeing a photograph of a lily, literally sees a lily. She does not see a lily face-to-face, for there is no lily in front of her; nor is the photograph a lily—it is an image of a lily. Rather, her seeing a lily through a photograph of a lily is like her seeing a lily in a mirror, through binoculars, or on a closed-circuit television system. As in all these cases, seeing a lily through a photograph is indirect seeing in the sense that the lily is seen by seeing the image; even so, indirect seeing is seeing. (Lopes 2003, 438)

The Walton/Lopes view of transparency is a strong claim: that in seeing a photograph of a lily, we literally see a lily. But it is important not to misunderstand its implications, as Lopes points out. For example, it is not to claim that photographs involve a kind of illusion, in which someone looking at a photograph must be unaware that it is a photograph. Nor is there any implication that being transparent photographs cannot engender false beliefs about the object photographed. In one sense, photographs "cannot lie" because of the causal relation between image and object, but they can misinform in numerous ways—for example, by suggesting what is not the case. And transparency in photographs does not imply that there is no role for the intervention of the photographer in what is seen or how it is seen. The photographer selects and even manipulates the objects seen. But if the transparency thesis is right, it is still the objects themselves that are seen.

The contrast with photographic transparency that is relevant in a discussion of narrative is with a kind of "opacity" in paintings. It is a familiar claim that while photographs stand in a causal relation to their subject matter, paintings stand in an intentional relation to theirs. Roger Scruton develops that distinction in his influential paper "Photography and Representation" (1983). He describes the difference succinctly:

> If a photograph is a photograph of a subject, it follows that the subject exists, and if x is a photograph of a man, there is a particular man of whom x is the photograph. It also follows, although for different reasons, that the subject is, roughly, as it appears in the photograph. (103)

In contrast:

> If a painting represents a subject, it does not follow that the subject exists nor, if it does exist, that the painting represents the subject as it is. Moreover, if x is a painting of a man, it does not follow that there is some *particular* man of which x is the painting. Furthermore, the painting stands in this intentional relation to its subject because of a representational act, the artist's act. (103)

Although a portrait of Winston Churchill might look very similar to a photograph of him, nevertheless, on Scruton's account, they are fundamentally different kinds of depiction: only the former counts as a "representation", partly because it expresses a thought about the subject, whereas the latter, however much pre-planning it involved, is merely the end product of a mechanical (causal) process.[4]

Interestingly, a connection is already emerging between the two kinds of opacity. Given transparency and the causal relation in photography, a report of a photograph's subject will be fully extensional (transparent). If it is true that this is a photograph of O, and O is identical to S, then it follows that this is a photograph of S. However, under at least one familiar construal, reports of what a painting is of are not fully extensional (therefore they are opaque) because if this is a painting of O and O is identical to S, it does not follow that this is a painting of S. To use a fictional example, a painting of Dr Jekyll will not count as a painting of Mr Hyde. The non-extensionality of "is a painting of" is also shown in the failure of existential generalisation noted by Scruton. In terms we used earlier, we might say that in a painting the way an object is depicted *matters* as much as mere denotation.

These issues about photography and painting have given rise to many strands of debate. One source of contention is whether Scruton is right in saying that there can be little or no aesthetic interest in a photograph that is not an interest in the subject of the photograph (i.e., the object being photographed), while aesthetic interest in a painting can be directed to the painting itself as a representation. Of the latter, Scruton writes:

> [I]t could not be said that the painting is being treated as a surrogate for its subject: it is *itself* the object of interest and irreplaceable by the thing depicted. The interest is not in representation for the sake of its subject but in representation for its own sake. And it is such an interest that forms the core of the aesthetic experience of pictorial art. (1983, 110)

Many philosophers, including Lopes, have sought to challenge Scruton on this point about aesthetic interest.[5] But the point itself, whether true or not about photography, seems to have a bearing on the kind of interest we have in literary narratives and in the possibility of an aesthetic interest in them. Indeed, the idea of giving attention to a representation for its own sake looks like another instance of opacity.

Other issues, of course, also remain in contention, perhaps none more so than the claim in Walton and Lopes that photographs are transparent. Happily, for our purposes, we do not need to take sides on this. Although I have appropriated the term "transparency" from this way of thinking about photography, nothing in the argument to come hangs on the truth of the transparency thesis. We need only grant sufficient plausibility to the idea of transparency in photography and the idea of pictorial representation as "intentional" to provide a resource highly suggestive in thinking about narrative. The weaker thesis about photographs—that they stand in a direct causal relation to their subjects in a way that is not true of paintings—is all that is needed to provide a powerful analogy with the opacity of narrative.

Generalising from the particular parallels we have explored, from the philosophy of language and the aesthetics of photography, we can say that opacity can occur in (at least) two contexts: the non-substitutivity of identities and the non-transparency or intentionality of representation.

The Opacity of Narrative

The first thought, then, that I want to propose, arising from these broader contexts, is that narratives are "opaque" somewhat as paintings are opaque.[6] They have the same kind of intentionality, not just as products of intentions but also, in different ways and to different degrees, through expressing thoughts or a point of view on what they represent. This seems to be true of all narratives, not just those of literary fiction. At its simplest, the expression of thought or point of view comes in the choice of linguistic form in which the narration is presented. Being artefacts and also representations, narratives have a purpose and their design is in service of that purpose.[7] Design can be more or less elaborate, more or less self-conscious. Even simple conversational narratives have formal features, but the storyteller might invest little effort in these, happy to substitute alternative narrative forms to achieve the same end. In contrast, writers of literary fictions invest form, design and artifice with the utmost significance.

If we grant the intentionality of narrative representation, somewhat in the mould of Scruton on painting, it seems to follow all too easily that narratives cannot be "transparent" in the way that it is claimed photographs are transparent. This means that they do not represent simply in virtue of standing in a causal relation to their subjects. Although this might seem obvious, it is an important preliminary finding as it can be tempting in certain contexts to postulate an "ideal" kind of narrative (unadorned, immediate, unbiased, fact-stating) that reveals its accuracy and reliability in virtue of a kind of unmediated "mirroring" of the reality it represents.

However, there is no narrative that stands in such an unmediated relation to its subject, so no narrative that is transparent in the way that, according to the transparency thesis, a simple photograph is transparent. But something of the intuition behind the purely transparent narrative might be captured by appealing to referential rather than representational opacity. The key to opacity of the referential kind is substitutivity. I suggested earlier that the equivalent of transparency-as-extensionality in narrative is not the preservation of truth under substitution but the preservation of narrative content itself. Consider, to return to Quine's example, a narrative about Cicero. If the narrative content is unaffected by the substitution of "Tully" for "Cicero", then the narrative counts as more transparent than a narrative in which that substitution is not permissible, perhaps because it changes the purpose or character of the narrative in ways that are deemed significant. Again, a link between the two kinds of opacity is in evidence. We have seen that referential opacity arises commonly in propositional attitude contexts, notably in contexts in which beliefs or thoughts are reported. One reason why substitutions of codesignative terms are not licenced in such contexts (preserving truth) is that the person whose beliefs or thoughts are being reported might not be aware of the identities (i.e., the items might figure non-extensionally in the thoughts reported). If narratives express a narrator's thoughts or point of view on a subject, as suggested by the analogy with painting, then we would expect that substitutions within the narrative, unlicenced by the narrator, would also be impermissible (preserving content).

A similar point emerges about *reporting* a narrative, which is like reporting speech or a belief. To report that in Jane Austen's *Persuasion* Anne Elliott accompanied a family party to Lyme Regis might be open to extensional, *de re* construal permitting codesignative substitutions for the name "Lyme Regis" (in other words, it is true *of* Lyme Regis that in Austen's novel it was the town that Anne visited and where Louisa Musgrove suffered a bad fall), but if faithfulness to Austen's narrative is paramount, the report should be construed opaquely and the substitutions not permitted. On the opaque construal, for example, the substitution of "Lyme Regis" for "the town that is the setting for John Fowles's novel *The French Lieutenant's Woman*" does not preserve content. Further discussion of this point is in chapter 8.

To deny that narratives can be transparent in the way that photographs might be transparent has no implications for truth or falsity. The distinction between transparency/opacity in narrative cuts across the distinction between truth/falsity. Opacity does not imply falsity any more than transparency implies truth. Referentially opaque sentences (e.g., about someone's beliefs) can be true, just as purely extensional sentences can be false ("Cicero denounced Cleopatra"). Similarly, paintings, as intentional representations, can be true, even if "opaque", and photographs can at least lead to false beliefs or give a false impression. It should be noted also that opacity does not imply "obscurity", in the sense of being difficult to interpret. No doubt some narratives are obscure in this sense, but that is not in virtue of their opacity alone.

What might be meant by "preserving a narrative" under substitution? We must return to content identity and ask under what conditions two narratives can have "the same content". Here an important but intriguing complication arises. My suggestion is that there is never an absolute answer to the question of whether this narrative has the same content as that one. The answer is always, as I shall put it, interest-relative—that is, relative to the interests of the questioner.[8] The answer will depend on the degree of specificity demanded in the characterisation of content. Imagine two historical treatises on, say, the Wars of the Roses. In some contexts, relative to some interests, it would be acceptable to assert that they have the same content merely in virtue of sharing this broad subject matter. They refer to the same period of history. Of course, the narratives might differ in many ways, in emphasis, in facts and personalities highlighted, in historical theses propounded, in the perspective taken. Where these aspects are deemed to matter, the narratives can be said to differ in their content. Suppose, though, the narratives broadly agree in these respects; then, relative to an interest in the commonalities, criteria for sameness of content become increasingly demanding as more aspects are covered and more similarities and differences taken into account.

My general claim is that the opacity of a narrative increases to the extent that the content of the narrative is deemed—under certain interests and no doubt under increasingly fine-grained specification—to be dependent on the manner of its presentation. We can think of this in terms of the substitutivity criterion. Return, a final time, to Quine's example and the substitution of "Tully" for "Cicero". Suppose we ask, assuming for the time being an intuitive, non-theoretical conception of "content":[9] Does "Tully denounced Catiline" have the same content as "Cicero denounced Catiline"? I suggest that we can view this question, too, as interest-relative. If our interest is, as it were, purely extensional, concerning just the facts of the matter, then we will judge the content to be the same. If our interest is more fine-grained and it matters, for whatever reason, what name is used to denote Cicero (without necessarily invoking Fregean senses), then we will say that the two sentences differ in content. In the latter case, the content is more opaquely specified than in the former, being more dependent on the mode of its presentation.

However, the example is purely illustrative because narrative is not the same as isolated sentences. Narrative is more complex, involving structure and connectedness and crucially involving a narrator's point of view. Suppose we now ask: Under what conditions can narrative A be substituted for narrative B, "preserving the narrative" (i.e., preserving narrative content)? Under certain interests, A might be substitutable for B if all that matters is merely sharing a broadly specified subject (the Wars of the Roses). In this somewhat implausible scenario, in which mere sameness of subject matter is the only criterion of content identity, the narratives attain more transparency than when finer criteria are applied.[10]

Another way of putting the claim is that the less exacting the demands of specificity on content, the more a narrative moves towards transparency. Both substitutivity and intentionality come into play. If the same content (defined under some degree of specificity) can be accessed in multiple ways and is less bound by constraints on a narrator's own perspective, then transparency is increased. Thus if someone is interested merely in reading about the Wars of the Roses but is not concerned about the perspective taken or any thesis advanced, then they could be recommended any number of works indifferently. These works, under these weak constraints on content, stand more transparently to that content than would works in which more specific constraints are applied. In these cases, how the content is presented is less important than mere identification of the subject matter presented.

If content identity is interest-relative in this way, and transparency and opacity are defined in terms of the relation between narrative content and the mode of presentation of that content, then an interesting consequence follows. Transparency and opacity in narrative are not intrinsic qualities of a text but ultimately rest on the interests brought to the text. We can read (or interpret) a narrative transparently or opaquely relative to the interest we bring to it and the kind of attention we give to its linguistic form.

We have seen that in the case of literary fictions, opacity arises because the content is not merely loosely or contingently connected to its mode of presentation but is partially constituted by it. One familiar way of putting this is that a literary narrative's content is largely indivisible from its form. But now we see that rather than supposing this to be a simple fact discovered about literary narratives, it is instead a demand imposed on them when a certain kind of interest is brought to them. The indivisibility of form and content in works of literature is sometimes expressed in terms of paraphrase. Literary works are unparaphrasable, it is claimed, because of the density and fineness of the writing. But that gets things entirely the wrong way around. We do not discover that certain fine writing is unparaphrasable, but we insist that no paraphrase of a literary work is substitutable for the original because of the importance we attach to that precise fineness of expression in identifying the work's content. We read for opacity. In fact, paraphrases of literary narratives are all too easy to effect if we loosen the demands on "content". Plot summaries of novels are perfectly adequate paraphrases for certain purposes. Relative to certain interests ("what happens in the novel"), a good plot summary has the "same content" as the novel itself. Of course, relative to other interests ("the literary qualities of the novel") the plot summary is not substitutable and its content is not the same.

Translation is a special case of paraphrasability. The ambivalent attitude that readers have towards translations of literary fictional narratives reflects the view we have taken about the interest-relativity of narrative content. For some, a good translation is indeed substitutable for the original such that to have read the translation counts as having read the work itself. For others, however good a translation, it is never substitutable without loss. Those in the former camp are satisfied that a fairly stringent criterion of "sameness of meaning" will preserve the content that needs to be preserved. Their interest in the narrative as, in effect, propositional content will be served if propositional meaning is retained. Those in the latter camp make even stricter demands of narrative content. Propositional meaning matters, as do far more fine-grained aspects underlying the precise way that meaning is conveyed, including nuance, connotation, tone, character and so on. Their reading maximises opacity.

We asked earlier about different works of fiction that treat the same fictional subject matter in different ways. Does this not suggest that this subject matter is somehow independent of its presentation in the different forms? Cannot the "same" fictional world be accessed in different ways, in which case the world cannot be constituted by a mode of presentation? Perhaps renderings of Dr Faustus, Robin Hood or even James Bond might be simple examples. But if content identity is interest-relative, we must insist again that although the renderings have the same content under certain interests, they have different contents where more fine-grained attention to expression is demanded. No one would suppose that Christopher Marlowe's rendering of Dr Faustus is somehow substitutable for that of Goethe in virtue of having the "same content", but that is only because it seems obvious that we are likely to have an interest in the precise descriptive modes in each case: an interest, in other words, in more finely specified content. Note that the original "worlds" of Faust or Robin Hood are not independent of narrative any more than are the subsequent renderings.

More interesting cases of sameness and difference of fictional content are those in which a single work presents the "same" events from different perspectives. Examples might include Lawrence Durrell's *The Alexandria Quartet*, John Fowles's novel *The Collector* or, in an even more intriguing case, Raymond Queneau's *Exercises in Style*, with its ninety-nine renderings of the same story. Here, though, the "world" depicted is not independent of any one perspective but rather is a unified, if complex, construct from the different perspectives.

The case of historical fiction is slightly different because the world depicted is the historical world of fact, not, or not all, a made-up world. But the principle is the same. To the extent that readers are interested primarily in the historical facts, then the novels can, as it were, be read "transparently" if thought of as having the same content as works of history on the same topic and if readers are broadly indifferent to the finer details of the presentation. But readers taking a literary interest in the novels will indeed attend to such detail and reject substitutions or paraphrases that lose the specificity of the presentation. As such, their reading will give priority to the "opaque" nature of the writing. In practice, no doubt readers of historical fiction find some compromise between the two kinds of interest.

A final point is needed in this preliminary look at narrative opacity before turning later to applications. It might seem that in stressing the relativity of opacity to readers' interests and to modes of reading we have lost any substantial connection between opacity and literary fiction. Yet that connection seemed to be at the heart of the earlier characterisation of literary fiction. In fact, the connection is important, as we shall see, but it is not threatened by the thesis of interest-relativity. The reason is that the connection between literary fiction and modes of reading is not an arbitrary one. The fact that readers of the great works of literature give special attention to the precise manner in which the content is presented is integral to the practice of reading literature as literature. What is at issue is the value of literature and that value is deeply involved with the intricacies of linguistic artifice. The form in which a literary work is constructed is not a merely contingent fact about it; it is absolutely essential to both its identity and its value as literature. So a reader who is indifferent to the fine-grained linguistic presentation and attends to the content only as broadly specified plot and character, who is open to alternative forms of expression, including summaries or character sketches, is not a reader who is showing an interest in the work as literature.

A major strand of argument in the chapters that follow is that a special kind of attention to literary works, rooted in a familiar and ancient practice of reading, gives priority to opacity as earlier outlined. What gives value to these works is not their extractable "truths" (chapter 7) or even the emotions they evoke (chapter 10), but rather the way their content is shaped by their linguistic form and the way that attention to that content can have a bearing on a reader's own thought processes and outlook on the world (chapter 8). The focus is on the narratives of literary fiction, but in order to establish what makes these stand out, we need a secure basis for drawing distinctions among kinds of narrative. This, as we shall see, proves more difficult than might be predicted. The distinction between "fictional" and "factual" narratives is obviously central, but equally so is the distinction between the former and the narratives of history and the narratives of personal lives. To prepare for the discussion to come, we need to attend to some of the issues that arise in characterising these kinds of narratives and in drawing defensible demarcations between them.

HISTORY AND FICTION

On the face of it, there is a world of difference between a novel and a work of history. Naturally, one starts with paradigm cases: *Joseph Andrews* and *England Under the Tudors*, *The Castle of Otranto* and *The Making of the English Working Class*, and so on. Novels, we say, are works of the imagination, involve made-up characters and events and are mainly written to give pleasure. Historical works are in pursuit of truth, seek to explain actual events and the actions of real people and are judged for accuracy and informativeness. Both paradigmatically use narrative form—they tell stories—but there is usually little chance of confusing one with the other.

It is important to hold on to these paradigms but equally important to recognise how far each category can stretch from them. Novels are often about actual people and events, about which they strive for accuracy, and can be useful sources of information on periods and places. Historical works can seek to give pleasure, are themselves products of imagination, use many of the devices of novels and, in certain cases, can be indistinguishable in appearance from novels. Some novels are even called histories: *The History of Tom Jones*, *Historia de Mayta*. Does that mean that, deep down, there is no genuine distinction between novels and histories? That doesn't seem right, or helpful, but upon closer inspection the natural places to look for grounding that distinction—reference, truth, real versus imaginary worlds, "correspondence to the facts"—come to seem inadequate.

History

Even setting particular cases aside, it is remarkable that there should be a serious strand of historiography that itself seeks to weaken the distinction between history and fiction. The favourite provocateur in this context is the historian Hayden White, who puts the case at its most eloquent and also most explicit. Here is a typical passage, often cited:

> Stories are not lived; there is no such thing as a real story. Stories are told or written, not found. And as for the notion of a true story, this is virtually a contradiction in terms. All stories are fictions. Which means of course that they can be true only in a metaphorical sense and in the sense in which a figure of speech can be true. Is this true enough? (1999, 9)

For all its provocation, there is much to agree with here, notably that "stories are not lived . . . [and] . . . not found". The world itself does not consist of stories. Stories have to be told. But why state that "all stories are fictions"? The motif of historical narrative as *fiction* is recurrent in White's writing: "[N]arration itself has been shown to be *inherently* fictive, whatever its subject matter" (2010, 202). Additionally,

> there has been a reluctance to consider historical narratives as what they most manifestly are: verbal fictions, the contents of which are as much *invented* as *found* and the forms of which have more in common with their counterparts in literature than they have with those in the sciences. (1978, 82)

But what does he mean by "fiction"? Not surely just "true only in a metaphorical sense". To say that historical narrative is fiction is, for White, primarily to say that historical narrative is an artefact; it is constructed, designed, a product of the mind, not an entity in the natural world. The point is entirely right and innocuous. It is important to remind ourselves of this basis in White's account because his ideas are often dismissed as hyperbolic and even dangerous (undermining the aspiration of history to truth, opening the door to "anything goes" relativism and so forth). No doubt some of the ways he presses the parallels of history and fictive literature can seem extravagant, such as his emphasis on the "figural" nature of historical truth or his insistence that historical narrative must fall into generic plot structures like romance, tragedy, comedy and satire. But he does a service to historians by reminding them of certain important truths: that their narratives are constructions that share features with literary works; that the world itself is not made of stories; that history doesn't simply copy or "mirror" reality but rather puts structures on it; that making a story out of events, with a beginning, middle and end, is not an entirely neutral process but is grounded in certain demands and desires;[11] that events do not simply "speak for themselves"; and also that an over-simple distinction between what is "real" and what is "imagined" is not especially useful in understanding the difference between histories and novels.

In a word, White holds that historical narratives are not "transparent" in at least one sense we have explored, the sense in which a photograph is thought to be transparent to the facts it records: "[I]t is wrong to think of a history as a model similar to a scale model of an airplane or ship, a map, or a photograph" (1978, 88). In place of transparency, he proposes for history just the kind of opacity we have identified in literary fiction, an opacity in which content is constituted by mode of presentation:

> This means that the *shape* of the *relationships* which will appear to be inherent in the objects inhabiting the field will in reality have been imposed on the field by the investigator in the very *act of identifying and describing* the objects that he finds there. The implication is that historians *constitute* their subjects as possible objects of narrative representation by the very language they use to *describe* them. (95; italics in original)

If White is right that historians, through their narrative descriptions, somehow *constitute* the subjects they are writing about, then the parallel with literary fictions will be strong and the claim that history is a kind of fiction will be more substantial than the claim that stories are artefacts. The distinction between the novel and history begins to look tendentious. But is he right? If historians literally create the subject they are writing about, then they do indeed look like novelists, but they also cease to look like historians. Much will depend on what exactly is being "constituted" on White's account. It takes us back to "content" and "subject matter". It is central to historical writing that it is answerable ultimately to the facts on the ground, to evidence available, to empirical testing and falsification. In this, novels are different, being not open, in anything like the same way, to falsification or refutation; they might be implausible, lacking in verisimilitude, incoherent, inaccurate in their settings. But it is not appropriate to demand of their content evidence or proof. Why not? Because in the paradigm cases, the content has no existence independent of its presentation in just this form. That is, of course, to identify the content under its most fine-grained specification. And that, as argued earlier, is the way that literary fiction invites us to attend to its content.

We must be careful, though, not to misread White's claims about historical narratives. He is not saying that historians simply make up facts or that there are no (objective) facts:

> This is not to say that a historical discourse is not properly assessed in terms of the truth value of its factual (singular existential) statements taken individually and the logical conjunction of the whole set taken distributively. For unless a historical discourse acceded to assessment in these terms, it would lose all justification for its claim to represent and provide explanations of specifically real events. (1987, 45)

The point is that there is a difference between listing facts and telling a story. White is quite right to insist on that distinction and to explore what telling a story does (or can do) that listing facts does not do.[12] So far in this chapter, I have not pressed the question, in any detail, of what a "story" or "narrative" is, letting an intuitive conception carry the discussion forward. Even now, I am reluctant to enter the definitional exercise, as I think it would be a distraction in this context (the context of laying out some of the parameters in this book as a whole). But the intuitive—and minimal—conception offered earlier does mark the distinction that White insists on. To say that something is a story might not say much: it makes no commitment to truth or falsity, to a real or merely imaginary subject matter, to any particular purpose or any particular style. But it does bear a commitment to connectedness and to structure. An atomistic fact is neither a narrative nor a list of unrelated facts. A narrative must connect events, causally or temporally or teleologically. The fuller the narrative, the more it helps to explain or make sense of the subject of the narration. Narrative is also from a point of view, purposive and selective in the items connected.

When White talks of historical narrative constituting its subject, he is speaking, in his more cautious moments, not of constituting the facts themselves but constituting the structures that bind the facts into a narrative, what he calls "the *shape* of the *relationships*". Yet there is often some tension in how far he wants to extend the scope of the "constituting". Consider the example he uses in this context—interpretations of the French Revolution:

> [T]he different kinds of historical interpretations that we have of the same set of events, such as the French Revolution as interpreted by Michelet, Tocqueville, Taine, and others, are little more than projections of the linguistic protocols that these historians used to *pre*-figure that set of events prior to writing their narratives of it.

He refers to "the same set of events" (in the French Revolution) as if these are independent of the narratives themselves. Yet these events are "prefigured" by the historians in the sense of being identified and characterised, prior to the narratives, by the different "linguistic protocols" used. There is a hint of anti-realism about the events themselves:

> [I]t seems possible that the conviction of the historian that he has "found" the form of his narrative in the events themselves, rather than imposed it upon them, in the way the poet does, is a result of a certain lack of linguistic self-consciousness which obscures the extent to which descriptions of events already constitute interpretations of their nature. (1978, 95)

But even if it is not facts so much as larger structures that are constituted by historical narrative, there should be no denying their answerability to the facts they purport to explain and organise, subject, that is, to familiar kinds of historical scrutiny, not just accepted as imaginative (essentially novelistic) reconstructions of events.

The historian Richard J Evans puts up a spirited "defence of history" against "postmodernists" such as Hayden White. He offers numerous examples of how the actual practice of historians involves procedures for challenging, testing, revising and evaluating narratives. One such example is a narrative concerning the decline of the aristocracy and the rise of the gentry in seventeenth-century England, a narrative that is offered as a strong explanatory factor among the causes of the English Civil War. It was a hypothesis advanced by the historian Laurence Stone, who had argued that, in Evans's words, "English aristocratic landowners in the early seventeenth century were extravagant, financially inept, and declining in economic power" (Evans 2000, 122). This sparked a major controversy, one of whose instigators was Hugh Trevor-Roper:

> Trevor-Roper . . . pointed out that Stone had confused different generations of aristocrats with the same title, got many if not most of his sums wrong, and altogether misunderstood the nature of landownership at the time. In arguing that aristocratic ownership of manors had declined, for instance, Stone took county samples without realising that aristocrats owned land in many different counties, and would readily sell their holdings in one to build up their estates in another; moreover, manors differed substantially in size, a factor Stone ignored completely, so that his figures showing a decline in the number of manors held by aristocratic landowners in some cases concealed an actual growth in the acreage and quality of land they possessed overall. (122–23)

The argument might not be a knock-down refutation of Stone, but it shows that historical narratives are not immune to empirical testing. Evans is uncompromising about the role of facts for historians: "[T]he vast majority of the historian's efforts are devoted to ascertaining them [the facts] and establishing them as firmly as possible in the light of the historical evidence" (127).

However, Evans is under no illusions about the "transparency" of a historian's access to facts or to the evidence that might be cited:

> The language of historical documents is never transparent, and historians have long been aware that they cannot simply gaze through it to the historical reality behind. Historians know, historians have always known, that we can only see the past "through a glass, darkly". It didn't take the advent of postmodernism to point this out. (White 2000, 104)

So where does this leave the opacity of historical narrative? White, at least in his early work, argues for a strong opacity: not just that historical narratives do not mirror a given story-like world but also that the narratives constitute their subject matter somewhat as novels do. At its extreme, I have suggested, such a conception serves to eliminate just the sort of empirical grounding that the practice of history demands. But weaker versions retain the constraint of fact and locate the "constituting" only in larger "shapes" and structures. Notions like the Middle Ages, the Renaissance, and the Hundred Years' War are indisputably artefacts of historical narrative. A kind of transparency is important in history even if it is not of the photographic kind. For one thing, historical narrative should aspire to extensionality in its references, or, put in another way, readers of these narratives should read for extensionality. Additionally, it cannot be the case that there is just one way of characterising historical events. There will be different ways of capturing the "same content" even when that content is quite finely delineated, which is to say that the content is suitably independent of any particular mode of its presentation.

But the kind of opacity we associated with paintings does seem to apply to historical narrative. For the latter also are representations from a point of view. They express thoughts on their subject, they do not merely "reproduce" it, although this need not compromise their truth, and they are still constrained by facts. It is always reasonable to ask of a historical narrative what point of view on its subject it takes, whether there might be biases of a personal or cultural kind in the narration, and if the structures imposed on the facts clarify or distort.

Strictly speaking, the question "Is historical narrative opaque?" is ill conceived. No narrative, it was argued earlier, is intrinsically opaque. We read narratives opaquely or transparently in relation to the coarseness we permit or the fine-grainedness we demand of content. And appropriate modes of reading will be grounded in practices. Historical narrative belongs in a practice in which appeal to evidence and empirical support is a major constraint on evaluation. When the perspective of the historian dominates evaluation of the narrative so that opacity becomes the natural mode of reading, and such that alternative perspectives are excluded and non-substitutable, then history becomes like literature and is a form of fiction. But when attention to historical content allows that the very same reality is accessible in different modes and from different perspectives, and yields to constraints of fact and evidence, then a more transparent reading is encouraged and questions of objectivity and truth gain purchase.

Fiction

What about fiction itself? In the chapters to come, it will be argued that the heart of the distinction between fiction and nonfiction, including but not restricted to history, is the idea of different "practices". The relevant idea of a practice is examined in detail in chapter 6, but in brief it is the thought that those engaged with works of fiction (or nonfiction)—both storytellers and audiences—are governed by certain simple and usually familiar conventions relating to intention, response, understanding, evaluation, reasoning, expectation, even emotion. These conventions are rarely spelt out in explicit ways but are taught by example (often, in the case of fiction, at an early age). Both those making up fictions—storytellers—and those responding to fictions are subject to the same broad presuppositions and protocols. One advantage to seeing fiction in this way is that it avoids appeal to either semantic relations (truth, reference) or inherent syntactic or structural conditions that might be claimed as definitive. At its most basic level, it merely stipulates an intention on the part of a storyteller to engage the conventions of the practice. More specifically, this is an invitation to an audience (reader) to attend to the story with a reader protocol that can be dubbed the "fictive stance". For an audience to adopt the fictive stance is, at its most general, for the audience to recognise, as it were, the terms of engagement and make-believe (or imagine) that it is being informed about particular people or objects or events, regardless of whether there are (or are believed to be) such people or objects or events. This is the "game" that is played. There is no deception involved.[13]

It is important to add a small rider. If a narrative is offered as fiction, then the fictive stance is taken to the whole narrative, not merely to parts of it. In effect, the narrative itself is offered in the fictive mode. Even if a fictional narrative appears to have components consisting of authorial assertions aiming at truth, these should not be thought of as somehow separable from the narrative itself. It is integral to the fictive stance that inferences to what an author believes or intends to assert are standardly blocked; they are licenced only when circumstances external to the narrative are invoked.[14]

If some such account of fiction is right and that what distinguishes fictional from nonfictional narrative are at root differences in rule-based conventions within practices, and if the practice of fiction is roughly as described, then the distinction between fiction and history is plain. Works of history do not invite the fictive stance, they do not block inferences back to the author, and they do not involve make-believe in the manner just outlined. They are also constrained, as discussed, by the facts and they lack the strong opacity of literary fictions (in the sense that they do not encourage the opaque mode of reading). This is not to deny that historical narratives might be excellent prompters of the imagination, and intended as such, or that they use literary devices and sometimes have all the appearance of a novel. The difference between historical and fictional narratives does not lie either in surface appearance or in reference or in truth or falsity. A history might involve egregious error but still be history; a fiction might include descriptions largely true (of the real world) and still be fiction.

Needless to say, characterising the "practice" of history in any more substantial way is difficult and controversial; it might be useful to postulate more than one such practice for different kinds of history (not all history is narrative). But that need not undermine the value of drawing the distinction in this way. In fact, we shall see that even within the category of fiction, there are different practices. Literary fiction, which is our focus, has elements that go beyond the account of fiction per se. And characterising literature in terms of practices is itself controversial. Both chapters 7 and 10 make claims about the practice of literature—about truth and about psychology—which are not accepted universally, even if, as is argued, they conform to familiar assumptions among readers who value literature as art.

The account of fictionality briefly sketched here and developed in later chapters is again to be seen as involving minimal theoretical commitments. It is based on a simple idea of a kind of mutual understanding (complicity) between storytellers and audiences as to what—under the broadest headings—are appropriate and inappropriate ways of responding to a narrative offered and recognised as fiction. Thus, in familiar examples, to ask what evidence a storyteller has for the private thoughts of a fictional character or to ask why a tough Moorish general speaks in sublime poetry is to miss the point of the fiction "game".

Many similar accounts of fiction have been proposed, and although details are important, stressing core commonalities can help to reinforce a picture of the subject which is illuminating and towards which one can detect signs of convergence.[15]

Richard Walsh, for example, has developed a sophisticated account of fictionality based on a "rhetorical" and "pragmatic" definition, in which "the criteria are not ultimately inherent in the narrative itself, but are contextual": "The rhetoric of fictionality is brought into play whenever a narrative is offered or taken as fiction, regardless of issues of form, style, or reference" (Walsh 2007, 44). "The distinction between fiction and nonfiction", he writes, "rests upon the rhetorical use to which a narrative is put, which is to say the kind of interpretative response it invites in being presented as one or the other" (Walsh 2007, 45). Because of his emphasis on rhetoric rather than reference or ontology, Walsh allows some credence to Hayden White's conflation of fictionality and narrativity: "[T]he categorical difference between real and imagined events is overwhelmed by the artificiality of narrative representation: all narrativity, from this point of view, shares in the properties of fictionality". But that does no more than endorse the view outlined earlier, emphasising the artifice in all narrative and the residual opacity in historical narrative as representation rather than reproduction of the world. Walsh is far from collapsing the distinction between fiction and nonfiction:

> Fiction is no longer seen as narrative with certain rules (of reference) in abeyance. Rather nonfictional narrative is seen as narrative under certain supplementary constraints (connoting historicity, objectivity, etc.) that serve to establish a rhetoric of veracity. (39)

The pragmatic driving force behind Walsh's theory is very congenial to my own, even if his theoretical idiom is different. He draws on the vocabulary of pragmatics in linguistics, notably relevance theory, presenting what might be called a "naturalised" picture of fiction as continuous with other communicative functions, as distinct from the more "conventionalised" picture, in terms of rules and practices, advanced in this book. While there might be some merit in Walsh's approach in explaining fiction per se, with the outcomes not significantly different from those of the practice-based approach, I suggest that a more "institutional" account is preferable in the context of literature.[16] This idea is expanded in chapter 6.

I take it that another broadly similar view is that of Stacie Friend, who has proposed that we think of fiction as a "genre", along the lines of Kendall Walton's categories of art (Friend 2012). The idea is intriguing and is motivated by a rejection of attempts to define fiction in terms of necessary and sufficient conditions. She targets "fictive utterance" theories, notably those of Gregory Currie and David Davies, which she thinks are open to counterexamples. However, her arguments are less effective against the version of the fictive utterance view presented here, and I wonder if the common elements between her account and mine are not more significant than the differences. Thus she claims that "the right way to distinguish between fiction and non-fiction focuses attention . . . [on] how the whole work is embedded in a larger context, and specifically in certain practices of reading, writing, criticizing, and so on" (Friend 2012, 187). That seems exactly right, but instead of proposing necessary and sufficient conditions along these lines, she offers only "a cluster of non-essential criteria" or "standard features". Here are some such features:

> If we take a text to be fiction, for example, we will expect it to engage us imaginatively through narrative; to deploy certain literary devices; to include invented elements, such as descriptions of what has never happened and names that fail to refer; to make claims that are not assertions by the author; and so on. If we take a work to be non-fiction, on the other hand, we will expect an

> effort to be faithful to the facts; references to real people, places and events; assertions that convey the author's views; and so forth. (189)

What matters, it could be argued, is not whether any of these (or others) are individually or jointly necessary or definitive of fiction (and nonfiction), but rather that they should be typical "expectations" brought to a narrative by readers under the assumption of the narrative's status. They help to characterise the "fictive stance", which itself can consist of a cluster of elements. What Friend brings out particularly well is the fact that even the broadest classification of "fiction" and "nonfiction" makes a difference to appropriate "reading strategies", including modes of interpretation and evaluation. The distinction has consequences.

I infer, then, that hers is also a kind of practice-based account, even if again the theoretical idiom is different. My own insistence that a storyteller's intention to engage the relevant practice is at least a *necessary* condition of fictive utterance, as mentioned previously, might mark a difference from the genre account. It is partially motivated by the thought that it is important to retain a distinction between *being fiction* and being read *as fiction*. But Friend does recognise a place for intention: "Though fictive utterance theorists are correct to recognize the importance of authorial intention, it is the intention that a work belong in a particular category, along with contemporary practices regarding categorization, that helps to determine classification—not the intention that certain parts of a work be believed or imagined" (Friend 2012, 203). Maybe, but the intended category brings with it implications for belief and imagination.

LIFE NARRATIVES

It is an obvious truth that on occasion (perhaps frequently) we tell stories about ourselves to ourselves and to others. We recount memories, we chat with friends, we run through events to reassure ourselves about what actually happened, we make excuses by elaborating on why we were late, why we didn't reply to an email or why we cannot attend a meeting. Such mini-narratives are commonplace. Is there more to this than meets the eye? Is something more serious going on?

One familiar thought is that these and similar narratives somehow serve to constitute ourselves as selves, they consolidate an identity for us that otherwise we would lack. We find claims like these: "[M]y self-understanding necessarily has temporal depth and incorporates narrative . . . we understand ourselves inescapably in narrative" (Taylor 1989, 50, 51); "We constitute ourselves as persons by forming a narrative self-conception according to which we experience and organise our lives" (Schechtman 2007, 162; see also Schechtman 1996); or "Let me . . . note another property of Self as we encounter it in ourselves and in others. It is 'storied', or narrative, in structure" (Bruner 1994b, 43). Even more interesting from our point of view is a connection sometimes drawn between these self-constituting narratives and works of fiction or literature. Thus "we are all virtuoso novelists . . . We try to make all of our material cohere into a single good story. And that story is our autobiography. The chief fictional character at the centre of that autobiography is one's self" (Dennett 1988, 1029); "[a] self is probably the most impressive work of art we ever produce, surely the most intricate" (Bruner 2002, 14).

There is a huge number of different accounts on offer, and it is unreasonable to conflate them and generalise too indiscriminately. I do believe, though, that many of the more prominent claims about the role of narrative in self-identity exaggerate the importance of narrative and that some of them, in which too close a link is postulated to fiction, can even have dangerous consequences. Marya Schechtman, herself an advocate of a "narrative self-constitution view", has helpfully identified a spectrum of narrative-based views. Thus, on what counts as a "life narrative", we find at one end "nothing more than a sequential listing of events in one's history"; somewhere in the middle is not just a listing of such events but also "an account of the explanatory relations among them", while at a more extreme end a life narrative becomes "an account of a life that approximates as much as possible a story created by a gifted author . . . [possessing] a unifying theme and direction". As for "having a narrative", the spectrum runs from a "requirement that a person's narrative must somehow operate to impact his current experience . . . [but] need not be in any way accessible to consciousness", to a middle view under which a person must be able, "at least sometimes, to become conscious of her narrative and make it explicit", to a strong view whereby "to have a narrative in the relevant sense, a person must actively and consciously undertake to understand and live her life in narrative form". Finally, there is a spectrum of implications: from "having a narrative is necessary to function at all" to "having a self-narrative is necessary for engaging in certain sorts of complex, person-specific activities . . . [e.g.,] autonomy, moral agency, prudential reasoning, [etc.]", to the more extreme end, in which "a narrative self-conception is essential to leading a good or meaningful life" (Schechtman 2007, 160).

Schechtman finds the strong views in each case "too strong" and the weak views probably true but not worth defending. Hers is the middle way. Her target here is the extreme scepticism of Galen Strawson, who rejects as false both a "psychological Narrativity thesis" (the empirical claim that ordinary people experience their lives in narrative terms) and an "ethical Narrativity thesis", which states that conceiving one's life as a narrative is a good thing and "essential to a well-lived life" (Strawson 2004). I share much of Strawson's scepticism about life narratives. However, I do not need in this context to engage his primary concern, which is to promote what he calls an Episodic life, which does away with any sense of an enduring "Self" binding together past, present and future experience, over a Diachronic life, which gives primacy to such a self—indeed, the very kind of self that either is constituted by or finds its identity through narrative. Strawson makes the case against the two narrativity theses, and in favour of the Episodic life, largely in terms of his own autobiography: "I have absolutely no sense of my life as a narrative with form, or indeed as a narrative without form. . . . Nor do I have any great or special interest in my past" (Strawson 2004, 433).

The puzzle is what becomes of *narrative* either in Strawson's rejection of narrativity or in Schechtman's defence. It is inconceivable that Strawson does not, at least on occasion, tell stories about himself, at the simple level of recounting events, recalling memories or making excuses. There is no reason for him to deny that, although he would no doubt insist that these first-person mini-narratives make no assumption of an enduring self of some especially intimate kind. It is not the existence of actual narratives that he is rejecting—nor that Schechtman is advocating—but something more mysterious: experiencing life "as a narrative". What is puzzling is the suggestion that one could experience life as a narrative without there being any such narrative.

Recall Schechtman's weak conception of "having a narrative", one she endorses but thinks trivial: this is a narrative that "need not be in any way accessible to consciousness". Even on the middle view, which she promotes, a person's having a narrative involves only "at least sometimes . . . becom[ing] conscious of her narrative and mak[ing] it explicit". The implication is that there is some kind of narrative there, but it is not, and need not be, consciously articulated. Even Strawson spells out the view that he rejects, not in terms of actual narratives but in terms of "tendencies". To experience life as a narrative is to have three tendencies: first, a "form-finding" tendency ("relatively large-scale coherence-seeking, unity-seeking, pattern-seeking"); second, a "story-telling" tendency ("think[ing] of oneself and one's life as fitting the form of some recognized narrative genre"); third, a tendency to "revision" ("to engage unconsciously in invention, fiction of some sort—falsification, confabulation") (Strawson 2004, 441–43). The tendency to revise is not necessary, he thinks, for narrativity, but widespread. The storytelling tendency is sufficient for narrativity. Needless to say, Strawson finds none of these tendencies in himself and does not believe them to be integral to or even desirable in a human life.

I believe there is a damaging tension in narrative views of the self. They insist on the importance of narrative in our self-conception, and yet they allow that there might be no actual narrative. Schechtman is clear on the latter: "[C]onstructing a self-narrative is . . . not conceived as something that must be undertaken as a conscious and active project" (Schechtman 2007, 163). But then what is the "constructing"? Anthony Rudd is another defender of the narrative view. The tension is there in his account, too. On the one hand, he says that "having a more or less coherent narrative to tell myself . . . is a part of what is involved in living my life as a self-conscious agent" (2007, 62), but concedes that "I don't have to be constantly reciting the story of my life to date in order to have an essentially narrative conception of who I am as a temporal being". He goes on to say, "The existence of that self-conception is what gives meaning to what I am doing now, and is the basis for my capacity to formulate narratives about myself when I do so" (63). This seems to imply that it is not the narrative that provides the self-conception but the self-conception that makes it possible to formulate a narrative.[17]

It is helpful to remind ourselves of Hayden White's dictum: "Stories are not lived. . . . Stories are told or written, not found" (1999, 9). Narratives are representations, they are not events, even connected events, in the world; they need to be narrated to become narratives. There is a crucial ambiguity in "life narrative": it is either a narrative of a life or a life that could be the subject of a narrative. Life and narrative should not be conflated. The idea of an unconscious narrative makes little sense. There might be tendencies to narrate or desires to live an ordered life, but lives themselves are not narratives.

Peter Goldie is a narrative theorist who is anxious to keep hold of a distinction between a narrative itself and the subject matter of a narrative, such as events in a life. But his notion of "narrative thinking" might seem to oscillate between being a kind of narrative that occurs in thought and being a kind of thinking, about oneself, that is narrative-like but possible in the absence of any articulated narrative (e.g., just a "single spontaneous moment of thought, without any conscious intention") (2012, 5). He distinguishes between "narratives that are just thought through" and "narratives that are publicly narrated", the former often more "indeterminate", but it is not clear how committed he is to there being actual narratives at the heart of narrative thinking. In fact, he is more interested in the perspectival reflections we have about our past and the "branching possibilities" we project about our future. Sometimes "narrative" is prominent, with appeals to notions like "free indirect style"; sometimes merely temporal structure is involved. Goldie goes on to postulate a "narrative sense of self", insisting it is not equivalent to a "sense of a narrative self" and does not involve the kind of strong narrative continuity that Strawson rejects and Schechtman promotes. The self is merely the subject of narrative thinking and a subject that allows for radical discontinuities (142ff). But now the link between narrative and self-identity is very modest. Is narrative necessary?

What many narrative theorists want to capture is a perfectly reasonable and familiar conception of human life: humans seen as more or less autonomous agents, acting for reasons, with goals and plans, with an enduring identity extended across time, often concerned with the image they project to the world, even anxious to be consistent. However, it is not clear what appeal to narrative (particularly a narrative that need not be consciously formulated) adds to this, how it consolidates a conception of a person as an agent living a life. The life itself can be lived and enjoyed, a person identified, self-consciously so, without being driven by any narrative imperative. Of course, we might capture the sense of a meaningful life by telling stories about ourselves that rationalise our actions and ground our outlook on life. But this is not needed and there are other ways as well.

Take the case of lyric poetry.[18] Sometimes poetry is in the form of narrative and reveals a life or part of a life. But sometimes no narrative is involved, but an image of a life—and a search for its meaning—emerges as sharply delineated as any narrative. Many of Emily Dickinson's small, poignant, fragile poems reveal a self-conception in condensed form:

> If I can stop one heart from breaking
> I shall not live in vain;
> If I can ease one life the aching,
> Or cool one pain
> Or help one fainting robin
> Unto his nest again
> I shall not live in vain.
> (Dickinson 1924, poem VI)

Sometimes the self-image comes in self-deprecating humour:

> I'm nobody! Who are you?
> Are you nobody, too?
> Then there's a pair of us—don't tell!
> They'd banish us, you know.
>
> How dreary to be somebody!
> How public, like a frog
> To tell your name the livelong day
> To an admiring bog!
> (Dickinson 1924, poem XXVII)

Thomas Hardy is another poet who often probes his own self through poetic image:

> I am the one whom ringdoves see
>   Through chinks in boughs
>   When they do not rouse
>   In sudden dread,
> But stay on cooing, as if they said:
>   "Oh; it's only he".

I am the passer when up-eared hares,
    Stirred as they eat
    The new sprung wheat,
    Their munch resume
As if they thought: "He is one for whom
    Nobody cares".

Wet-eyed mourners glance at me
    As in train they pass
    Along the grass
    To a hallowed spot,
And think: "No matter; he quizzes not
    Our misery".

I hear above: "We stars must lend
    No fierce regard
    To his gaze, so hard
    Bent on us thus,—
Must scathe him not, He is one with us
    Beginning and end".
("I Am the One", Hardy 1994, 777)

R G Collingwood has famously argued that the poetic expression of emotion not only articulates but also clarifies, and to a certain extent serves to shape, the emotion expressed, the nature of which the poet might not know in advance: "Until a man has expressed his emotion, he does not yet know what emotion it is. The act of expressing it is therefore an exploration of his own emotions. He is trying to find out what these emotions are" (1938, 111). It is not implausible that poetry can serve in this way as a kind of self-exploration, clarifying and shaping emotion not just for the poet but also for a reader. So when Coleridge in the following poem expresses despair, he is, in Collingwood's view, also finding out something about his own state of mind:

I have experienc'd
The worst, the World can wreak on me—the worst
That can make Life indifferent, yet disturb
With whisper'd Discontents the dying prayer—
I have beheld the whole of all, wherein
My Heart had any interest in this Life,
To be disrent and torn from off my Hopes
That nothing now is left. Why then live on?
That Hostage, which the world had in its keeping
Given by me as a Pledge that I would live—
That Hope of Her, say rather, that pure Faith
In her fix'd Love, which held me to keep truce
With the Tyranny of Life—is gone ah whither?
What boots it to reply? 'tis gone! and now

> Well may I break this Pact, this League of Blood
> That ties me to myself—and break I shall!
> (S T Coleridge, *Lines from a Notebook*, 1810)

This is not a narrative, but rather a different kind of probing into whether life is worth living in this state, whether the pact we all make with life really has any effect in holding back the tyranny that life subjects us to or offers any escape from hopelessness. The questions in the poem are not just rhetorical but also self-directed.

Examples could be multiplied. It reminds us how important images can be in grounding a sense of self, even a self across time. Memories often take the form of mental images, sharp or blurred, in sequences or isolated, without anything like the structure of a narrative. Indeed, trying to construct a coherent story out of the images can often destroy their integrity as memories. Poetry can show how non-narrative patterns of thought can entrench a deep sense of personal self-awareness.

It seems likely that at the back of the mind (in some cases at the forefront) of many narrative theorists stands the paradigm of the rich, detailed narratives of biography, history and the nineteenth-century realist novel, for in those cases lives are indeed presented as coherent and "rounded", featuring unified selves, actions explained, morals drawn and usually closure at the end. In the case of novelistic fiction, with its strongly opaque narrative, the characters are literally constituted by the narrative. With biography and history, constrained as they are by fact, there is a conscious effort to find meaning in the real lives of people, to see overarching themes displayed and worked through, even to present the whole within some more or less recognisable genre. But this is where the dangers of the narrative view emerge. Strawson is forceful: "Narrative self-articulation is natural for some . . . but in others it is highly unnatural and ruinous. My guess is that it almost always does more harm than good—that the Narrative tendency to look for story or narrative coherence in one's life is, in general, a gross hindrance to self-understanding" (2004, 447). Samantha Vice takes up the theme: "Thinking of ourselves as if we were characters in stories presses us to think of ourselves in ways that are potentially dehumanising and falsifying" (2003, 105).

What are the dangers exactly?[19] One is self-deception. Not nearly enough is said about truth and falsity in narrative views of the self. If my life narrative constitutes my self, then it might seem that the narrative couldn't be false about that self, any more than *Bleak House* could give a false picture of Lady Dedlock. But that seems plainly wrong, not least given the tendency to "revision" that Strawson identifies. In fact, one might suppose that those who cultivate a life story most assiduously are most given to falsification (Zahavi 2007, 183). Seeing themselves as characters in a plot already indicates a degree of self-aggrandisement. There are other dangers associated with seeing oneself as a fiction-like character. It can put a constraint on action and undermine the sense of being in control of one's life, for example, by forcing one to act in a way that seems to be demanded by the "plot" but otherwise might have little to commend it. It can encourage the thought that situations have "meaning", as they might if they were in a novel, while in fact they are largely a matter of chance. Lives are just not "designed" in the way that novels are. It can artificially impose genre expectations on a life: if I see my life as shaped like a tragedy, I will expect it to end badly, whatever I do. It might also lead me to see myself as a character-type of some recognisable kind, the tragic hero, the anti-hero, the buffoon, the picaresque wanderer, the Don Juan lover, the recluse. Again, by identifying myself too closely with these literary archetypes, I can find myself cut off from the mundane realities of the actual world I live in, forcing me into patterns of action determined by the "part", not necessarily by my own interests. Finally, most lives lack the "closure" that a good narrative demands, a completeness that rounds out and makes sense of the whole (although biographers might try to impose this). Lives are more like medieval chronicles than completed histories. As Hayden White describes it, a chronicle "does not so much 'conclude' as simply terminate; typically it lacks closure, that summing up of the 'meaning' of the chain of events with which it deals that we normally expect from the well-made story" (1980, 20). Lives in reality just "terminate", quite often *in medias res*. Those obsessed with their life narrative might seek closure where it has no natural place.

To see oneself as a character is not quite the same as seeing oneself as an author.[20] As a character, I might or might not conceive myself as my own creation. Often people think of their life stories not as self-created but as written by someone else, perhaps God, or Fate, or some malignant agency. But for others, we are authors of our narratives (Alasdair MacIntyre [1985, 213] says we are "co-authors") in the sense that it is we who put a perspective on our lives, shape them and organise them into some kind of coherent whole. We do not make the facts in our worlds, except those that directly involve our actions, but we give the facts meaning in our story. Nevertheless, the dangers of this self-authorship conception are as much as before. If we make our lives into novels, we "aestheticise" them—think of them as works of art, with artful designs. But that is another form of distortion, promoting quite the wrong kinds of explanations, finding meanings in mere coincidence, finding teleology where there is mere cause and elevating genre over brute fact.

If these points about the dangers of self-narration have purchase, then they amount to a strong argument against what Strawson calls the ethical narrativity thesis, that a worthwhile life is necessarily one lived under these precepts. But curiously, as noted by Peter Goldie (2012, 172), the dangers, in spite of being real enough, point up something deep, perhaps disturbing, and yet true, about human life: the existence of that very "fictionalising tendency" which many succumb to, not perversely, but because there is an urge to impose structure and meaning where there appears to be nothing but chance and contingency. Maybe that urge accounts for the enduring place of fiction in human life and the enduring love of those works of fiction that excel at creating imaginary worlds that seem so much more entrancing than our own.

NOTES

1. Gregory Currie distinguishes narrative from story, calling the former "the representation" and the latter "the represented" (i.e., the *content* of the representation) (2010, 24; see also Gibson 2011, 71f). But rather than supposing there are separate concepts here, it might be better to think of this as two aspects of narrative: as object (text) and as product (see chapter 3). "Story" has the same dual aspect.

2. For illuminating critical discussion, see, for example, Bell (1973); Recanati (2000); and Orenstein and Kotatko (2013).

3. Walton (1984); criticisms have been raised in Warburton (1988); Currie (1995); and Friday (1996). Walton has replied in Walton (1997).

4. Significantly, one of the examples that H P Grice uses to illustrate "non-natural meaning" rests on the difference between showing someone a photograph of two people "displaying undue familiarity" and showing a drawing of such behaviour. Only the latter, Grice argues, possesses non-natural meaning, because it, unlike showing the photograph, conveys the message about what is going on through the recognition that this is the intended meaning. The photograph conveys the message merely causally (1957). Note that Grice's point does not rest on the transparency thesis about photographs but only on the weaker thesis about direct causation.

5. See, for example, King (1992); Phillips (2009); and Davies (2009). Friday (2012) criticises both Scruton and Lopes on the aesthetic interest argument.

6. Roger Scruton also makes a connection between narrative and painting:

> A painting does not merely present a point of view on a world: it presents that world, unfolds it before us in an imaginative thought that it invites us to share. Understanding the painting involves grasping the narrative content. . . . Although there are paintings of real people and real scenes—where we can, so to speak, "quantify in" to the narrative content—we understand figurative paintings as we understand narratives in language: they tell a story, and their aesthetic success does not as a rule depend upon the literal truth of that story. They also convey a point of view; they are 'about' many things other than their subject-matter; and they express emotions, moods, and attitudes. But the story-telling part comes first; it is the sine qua non without which nothing else in the painting can be understood. (2009, 453)

7. Gregory Currie also views narratives as both artefacts and representations (Currie 2010, ch. 1) but insists they are "intentional-communicative artefacts" (26), which is more contentious, not because they might be non-intentional but because they might not serve to communicate (self-narratives being a case in point).

8. I have applied this notion to poetry in Lamarque (2009a). A slightly different application is to the identity of fictional characters: see Lamarque (2010), ch. 9.

9. It is not helpful in this context to introduce intensions, senses, connotations and so forth to explain the options for content-identity. It is more illuminating to stick with a notion of interests taken to a narrative and a largely intuitive conception of what a narrative is about.

10. The notion of subject (or subject matter) owes something to a similar notion proposed in Bradley (1926). Bradley states that the "subject" of a poem is "outside" the poem in the sense

that it is not exclusive to the poem and could be shared with other poems. In contrast, he postulates a highly fine-grained notion of a poem's "content", which he thinks is indivisible from its form and unique to the poem; the content is the realisation of the subject in the poem. Bradley, however, does not adopt the interest-relativity of content identity.

11. "The demand for closure in the historical story is a demand, I suggest, for moral meaning, a demand that sequences of real events be assessed as to their significance as elements of a *moral* drama" (White 1980, 24).

12. His essay (White 1980) is particularly illuminating, if still controversial, on that theme.

13. Stein Haugom Olsen and I have spelt out this characterisation of fictive utterance as follows:

> (1) A Gricean intention that an audience make-believe (or imagine or pretend) that it is being told (or questioned or advised or warned) about particular people, objects, incidents or events, regardless of whether there are (or are believed to be) such people, objects, incidents, or events;
> (2) The reliance, at least in part, of the successful fulfilment of the intention in (1) on mutual knowledge of the practice of storytelling; and
> (3) A disengagement from certain standard speech act commitments, blocking inferences from a fictive utterance back to the speaker or writer, in particular inferences about beliefs. (1994, 45–46)

14. Kathleen Stock (2011a) tackles this issue but still seems to regard fictive utterances atomistically in a narrative, which at least gives sense to the question of whether any individual sentence in a narrative is fictive (rather than asking, as I think is better, whether the whole work is presented in the fictive mode). She also thinks that fictive utterance involves an audience imagining that *p*, rather than imagining that it is being told that *p*.

15. For example, Peter Goldie rather casually endorses the practice-based conception (2012, 152–53). But he adds, without further argument, "Thus the question of reference and of truth simply does not arise within the 'fictive stance': it is just irrelevant" (153). That seems too strong, as is argued in Lamarque and Olsen (1994), ch. 5.

16. Gregory Currie, who also appeals to relevance theory, takes me to task for seeking too sharp a distinction between the conventions of literary interpretation and "pragmatic inference". As he recognises, though, I do not want to deny any place at all for the latter in our responses to fiction; rather, I want to emphasise the often peculiar, even recondite, procedures of the literary interpreter and the differences between these and inferences that are made in ordinary conversational exchanges. See Currie (2010), 16–18.

17. John Gibson introduces the idea of "thick narrative" to show how a self-conception can grow out of a narrative of the self, in which the narrative does more than just relate items in a life but finds a deeper significance in the life as a whole (2011). But the question arises again as to whether the self-conception is somehow constituted by the narrative or whether the choice of narrative presupposes a particular self-conception.

18. I am grateful to John Gibson for encouraging this thought.

19. Peter Goldie helpfully identifies several "fictionalizing tendencies": in summary, "we see ourselves as plotting out the course of our lives; we find agency in the world where it is not; we seek narrative closure where it cannot be found; and we transport notions of genre and character from fiction into real life" (2012, 171–72).

20. Marya Schechtman separates different roles we can play in relation to our narratives—character, author or critic; see Schechtman (2011), 412–14.

Chapter Two

Narrative and Invention

The Limits of Fictionality

In the most general terms, to narrate is to tell a story. The focus in this chapter is on fictional narration—the telling of stories that are "made up", "invented", "products of the imagination". There are other kinds of stories, or narratives, of course. Historians, biographers, journalists and psychoanalysts are all involved in narration, as are, at least some of the time, lawyers, scientists, sports commentators and people in pubs. One of my aims is to keep some basic distinctions intact, to resist the tendency to collapse all storytelling into a single category.

A brief word, first, about what I take to be common to all narrative. Narration of any kind involves the recounting and shaping of events. Description is not enough. A mere catalogue of descriptive sentences does not make a narrative. For one thing, there must be *events* described, not just things. Narration has an essential temporal dimension. The descriptions in botanical taxonomy, for example, do not constitute a narrative. Furthermore, the events must be shaped or ordered. Narrative imposes structure; it connects as well as records. In some cases, it even defines the events it connects (e.g., the Hundred Years' War and the Middle Ages owe their identity to historical narrative). Finally, for every narrative there is a narrator, real or implied or both. Stories don't just exist, they are told—more specifically, told from some perspective or another. Already, we have four basic dimensions of all narrative: time, structure, voice and point of view. Under "structure", I include the idea of "plot"; a plot is a structured concatenation of events.

Narrative per se is a formal feature of a text. It is indifferent to subject matter and to discursive ends. Narratives might amuse or instruct, philosophise or theologise. Some philosophical works, but not all, are in narrative form: Descartes's *Discourse* is; Spinoza's *Ethics* is not. Nor is narrative identical with literature. For one thing, "literature" is an evaluative term, while "narrative" is not. Furthermore, some literary works, like much lyric poetry, lack the narrative form, and some narration, like much sports commentary, lacks literary merit. Above all, narrative per se is indifferent to truth and reference. The appearance of a sentence or a name in a narrative has no implications for the truth-value of the sentence or the denotation of the name. Narratives can be about real people or fictional characters and their descriptive content can be true or false.

The relation between narrative and fictionality is complex. There is a strong temptation to conflate the two concepts, or at least to suppose that in talking about narrative one is talking about fiction. For example, to focus exclusively on the narrative features of a text involves laying aside questions about referentiality. Yet the latter is also a characteristic of our attitude to fiction. At a deeper level, it is clear that we are not going to be able to distinguish fictional narratives from other kinds merely, as suggested earlier, in terms of what is "made up", "invented" or "a product of the imagination". After all, we have seen that all narration involves making or structuring, and it would be hard to deny a prominent role for the imagination in the narratives of science, history or philosophy.

The distinctness of fictionality from narrative is open to challenge from different directions: from literary narrative as well as from issues deep within metaphysics and literary theory. Let us begin with these challenges.

A LITERARY EXAMPLE

Here is a literary example that nicely brings home the difficulties we face: the novel by the Nobel Prize–winning, Peruvian author Mario Vargas Llosa, entitled *The Real Life of Alejandro Mayta.*[1] In fact, its original Spanish title, *La Historia de Mayta*, is more teasingly ambiguous. *Historia* covers both "history" and "story". One striking feature of the book, reflected in the title, is that few readers will have any clear idea as to how many (if any) of the events narrated actually took place and how many (if any) of the characters are real. It is offered as a novel and we read it as "fiction". The crucial question is: What does that mean?

The narrative tells of a writer (maybe Llosa, maybe not) trying to piece together the life of an obscure would-be revolutionary, a Trotskyist, who was at the centre of an abortive, even ludicrous, insurrection twenty-five years earlier in the Peruvian mountains. The narrator, intrigued by the thought that he'd been at school with the revolutionary, painstakingly delves into the records, examines old newspaper cuttings and interviews anyone who had any connection with the event. Inevitably what emerges is a fragmented, partial, often contradictory, account. The participants interviewed are either wilfully forgetful or resentfully deceitful. Seemingly, the facts behind this pathetic debacle of history are unrecoverable. "One thing you learn", the narrator remarks, "when you try to reconstruct an event from eyewitness accounts, is that each version is just someone's story, and that all stories mix truth and lies" (118).

An added twist is that the narrator admits to us, and to his interviewees, that he is not trying to write a history but only a kind of fiction: "Not a biography, but a novel. A very free history of the period, Mayta's world, the things that happened in those years" (15). The clear and serious suggestion is made that only a novelistic or literary narrative is possible for recounting events in a country like Peru, full of deception, turmoil and incompatible perspectives.

The complex time frame of the narration reflects the fragmentation of history. There is a narrative present and a narrative past bounded, as it were, by the real (or external) present and the real (or external) past. The narrative present sees the narrator cross-examining the participants (even, finally, Mayta himself). But the dialogue is indissolubly interwoven with dialogue from the narrative past, twenty-five years earlier. Twenty-five years might separate the facts from the distorted recollections, but fact and report simply blur into one. The narrative "I", the investigator, even merges, momentarily, into the persona of Mayta, the investigated. Meanwhile, this narrative time frame is located in the wider frame of real time. The real past of Peru is obliquely evoked, part mirror, part explanation: a visit to the Museum of the Inquisition reveals cruelty and corruption as somehow integral to the country's history. The real present is evoked in the slums and garbage of present-day Lima. To round it off, this present embodies a nostalgia for a more naive past and a gloomy prognosis for the future.

The novel revels in the complexity of its formal features—time, structure, voice and perspective—and it plays unceasingly with the ambiguity of history and fiction. Using all the artifice of literary form, it gives us a sharply focused, pessimistic insight not just into the turmoil of modern Peru but also into the revolutionary sensibility.

Do novels like *Mayta*, either in formal structure or in theme, give us reason for blurring fact and fiction, truth and invention, fictive and historical narrative? In the end, I think not. But the issue calls for philosophical investigation.

SOME AIMS OUTLINED

As the discussion that follows has many strands, let me briefly outline the direction I want to take. Much of the focus of this chapter will be on fictionality. Through the identification of different kinds of fiction—notably logical, epistemological and "make-believe" fiction—the central purpose is to establish constraints on the tendency to "fictionalise" our narratives or to see the world as "invented" rather than "discovered". From the metaphysical point of view, my intuitions are realist. I believe that objects exist independently of what we think about them. I do not believe, to use Goodman's expression, that the world is "man-made". I will not be defending these intuitions as such, but I will try to keep my conclusion consistent with them.

When it comes to distinguishing kinds of narrative, I hold a "pragmatic" view. Fictional narrative *is* distinct from historical (or scientific or philosophical) narrative, but the distinctness, I will argue, does not reside either in formal features—time, structure, voice, perspective—or in semantic features—truth, correspondence with the facts, reference. A narrative like *Mayta*, which I will show is "fictional" in the "make-believe" sense, can contain true sentences and even references to real objects. It can convey truths of both a particular and a universal kind. Its fictionality, I will argue, lies elsewhere: in pragmatic, conventional features, such as context, attitude, intention and response. In the relevant sense, fictionality resides in a special kind of practice-based and rule-governed relation between writer, text and reader.

A common mistake, which I will try to combat, is to suppose that what we say about narrative must affect our metaphysics (i.e., what we say about the world), and that our metaphysics must inform our view about narrative.

THE CHALLENGE FROM METAPHYSICS AND LITERARY THEORY

It is easy to see how discussions of metaphysics get drawn into discussions of narrative. The starting point is the reasonable-sounding attempt to distinguish fictional from nonfictional narratives in terms of what they are about. A fictional narrative, so the thought goes, creates an imaginary world with imaginary characters, while a nonfictional narrative is about the real world and the real things in it. To find out which is which is just a matter of checking for "correspondence with the facts".

It is precisely the implied link with contentious metaphysical conceptions that I want to sever, not by proposing an alternative view of truth or the world but by producing a much sharper account of narrative and fictionality.

Let us, however, briefly recall the issues, both metaphysical and literary-theoretical, which make the simple picture problematic. At the heart of the matter is the distinction between a world constructed (by the imagination, by the mind) as against a world discovered ("out there", independent of the mind).

Any undergraduate can rehearse Descartes's seductive sceptical challenge: what we call the real world might be just a massive illusion, just a figment of the imagination. Although we can perhaps shrug off talk of illusions and demons, we should take seriously Descartes's challenge when stated in terms of belief. In effect, Descartes tries to convince us of the thought that we could have beliefs indistinguishable from those we now have about the world even though each one is false, either because the world is quite different from how we believe it to be or (in the extreme case) because there is no world at all. This sceptical challenge is a perennial issue for philosophers examining the nature and content of belief.

The analogue with narrative might be this: If it is impossible to tell with any logical certainty which, if any, of our beliefs correspond with a world "out there", then why should one suppose that narratives will reveal their referential commitments with any greater conviction? Narrative-content is as susceptible as belief-content to something analogous to "methodological solipsism".[2] Maybe all our narratives are, as it were, Cartesian narratives describing different aspects of an inner world. No intrinsic features, if Descartes is right, can guarantee correspondence.

Doubts about the distinction between what is "made up" and what is "out there" are only compounded if we take the Kantian route out of Cartesian scepticism. Kant showed, or purported to show, how you could be an "empirical realist", holding on to an objective world independent of the mind, and at the same time a "transcendental idealist", insisting on the ultimate ideality of objects. Objects, he thought, can be "out there" empirically and yet "made up" transcendentally. Ordinary things can be mind-independent from the empirical point of view, in contrast to illusions and fantasies, while at the same time mind-dependent from the transcendental point of view, in contrast to unknowable things-in-themselves. From the transcendental viewpoint, we have knowledge only of appearances; from the empirical viewpoint, we can readily distinguish how things appear from how they really are.

Kant's Copernican revolution, with its complex equivocating on the ideas of "object", "appearance", "reality", "inner", "outer" and so on, encourages a conception of the world as a "product of the mind" or a "construction". More than that, Kant seems to have identified something like a narrative process, the temporal structuring of experience unified by a "transcendental" subject, at the heart of epistemology. Against this background, along with subsequent refinements of idealism, we at least become wary of trying to distinguish narratives in terms of "worlds".

Then there is the contribution from literary theory. There was a time when sceptical poststructuralists instinctively put quotation marks (or scare quotes) around such words as "reality", "existence", "the world", "objective", even "truth". They viewed as naive philosophers who still retained the old hankerings for a world "out there", independent, something to ground and validate our thoughts, something to make our true propositions true and our false ones false. In their own terms, in the literary context, these theorists were surely right. One of the enduring insights in twentieth-century literary theory was that so-called realism in literature is a convention, a genre: a kind of writing, not a kind of relation (think of Barthes's "reality effect" [1986]). The realistic novel, contrary to the claims of its early French proponents, has no privileged status in representing the world "as it really is". Indeed, and this is the point of those inverted commas, the very idea of representing the world either better or worse has to be handled with extreme care in the context of literary criticism.

The whole modernist movement in art amounted to a challenge at a fundamental level to the idea of representing reality. At its best, modernism exhibited the plurality of worlds, private and public, in contrast to some single "objective" world given in experience. Once representation itself had been exposed as a kind of artifice, it was natural for artists to highlight the artifice of their own media. In the literary case, this became an obsession with drawing attention to the fictionality of literary writing, one clearly manifested in Mario Vargas Llosa.

In response to modernism, there arose various attempts by certain literary theorists to generalise the lessons learned from literary fiction. The generalisations are far from implausible. All writing involves some degree of artifice; there is no pure unmediated representation of extra-linguistic fact; there are other purposes served by words than merely describing how things are in the world. It is a short step, so it seems, from these modest claims to stronger, more anti-realist conclusions. Just as the idea of a single objective reality seems to crumble away in the literary case, perhaps it crumbles away in any case. Perhaps there is a lesson to be learned from literary realism about realism *tout court*.

Out of all this, an argument might be mounted from the grounding of literary realism in literary convention to some kind of metaphysical anti-realism. By "anti-realism" here, I mean the view, which takes many forms, that the world itself is in some way or another dependent on the mind (or language, or concepts, or theories or verification-procedures).[3]

My interest is with an argument of a slightly different kind, going in the other direction. This is the appeal to varieties of anti-realism, drawing on the metaphysical and poststructuralist challenges just outlined, to try running together different kinds of narrative, those of the novelist, the historian, the scientist and so on. Such a move, which I will criticise, partly explains the common inclination among poststructuralists and others to see all discourse as a kind of fiction.[4]

Schematic Arguments towards the "Fictionalising" of Narrative

I suggest there are two arguments, with particular appeal in certain literary theoretical circles, which evoke versions of anti-realism in the service of "fictionalising" narratives. The following are abstract and schematic renderings. Although the arguments are stated in general terms, they can be applied directly to narrative. The first (A) goes like this:

1. The distinction between fictional and factual discourse (or narrative) ultimately depends on a correspondence conception of reference and truth. Factual discourse makes reference to, and corresponds with, what is "out there" (objects and facts), while fictional discourse concerns only what is "made up".
2. But the correspondence conception of reference and truth is untenable. Anti-realist and pragmatist arguments in philosophy of language show this, not to mention Kantian-type arguments in metaphysics.
3. Therefore, there is no ultimate ground for the distinction between fictional and factual discourse (or narrative).

The second argument (B) goes like this:

1. Fiction is whatever is man-made (conceptually or linguistically).
2. Truth is man-made (conceptually or linguistically).[5]
3. Therefore, truth is just a species of fiction.[6]

Although I think the conclusions follow from the premises, I don't think the premises are true. I have doubts about the second premise in each argument, but I will be concentrating only on the two first premises. By identifying different conceptions of fictionality, along with the different kinds of "making" involved, with different referential commitments, I hope to show that no widespread "fictionalisation" is going to be licenced along these lines.

FICTIONALITY IN OBJECT AND DESCRIPTION

One difficulty with our discussion is the looseness with which terms like "fiction" and "narrative" are often used. In literary contexts, "fiction" can simply mean "novel", or even "story", and in that way becomes virtually synonymous with "narrative". If we are to distinguish fictional narratives from other kinds, we will need finer discriminations. The etymology of "fiction" reveals it roots in the idea of making, fabricating or feigning, but on closer inspection we will see different kinds of making connected with different conceptions of fiction.

First of all, we need to note an ambiguity between the object and the description sense of "fiction". We speak of fictions sometimes as *things*—Pickwick, average families—sometimes as kinds of descriptions—*Pickwick Papers*, John's statement to the police. To say of a thing that it is fictional is to suggest that it doesn't exist. To say of a description that it is fictional is to suggest that it isn't true. The object sense of fiction gives us the contrast between what is fictional and what is real, the description sense the contrast between what is fictional and what is true.

An ontological enquiry will show whether we can retain a distinction between an invention of the mind and a real object. A semantic enquiry will show whether we can retain a distinction between the truth of a description and the fictionality of a description. I hope to lay the groundwork for retaining both distinctions in the discussion that follows.

The second ambiguity, if that is the right word, is between positive and negative connotations of "fiction". On the positive side, fiction is constructed or imagined. On the negative side, it is false, fabricated, contrary to fact, nonexistent.

The two ambiguities cut across one another. A fictional object may be praised as a product of the imagination or denigrated as nonexistent. Likewise, a fictional description can elicit favour for being imaginative (e.g., *Pickwick Papers*), or invite censure for being false (e.g., John's statement).

The term "narrative" carries clear connotations of making, or structuring, but without the ontological implications of "making up" or "fabricating". Within narratives, there can be fictions in both the object and the description senses. But narratives are not limited to fictions in either sense. In addition, narratives, fictive or otherwise, can be subject to praise or blame. Yet when we praise a narrative for its imaginativeness we make no assumptions about its truth-values, and when we denigrate it for unreliability with regard to the facts we might nonetheless applaud its inventiveness. As earlier stated, narrative in itself is indifferent to both semantic and ontological constraints. Only further classification of narratives, relating to genre, intent, convention and so on, will reveal the criteria appropriate for other forms of assessment.

FICTIONS IN PHILOSOPHY

It is time to pursue some of the different kinds of fictions that arise in philosophy. The acknowledgement by philosophers of fictions deep within our ordinary descriptions of the world as well as in our knowledge of the world might seem a further irresistible argument for the blurring of distinctions among narratives. Logical fictions, on the one hand, have a venerable place in semantic theory, as do epistemological fictions, on the other hand, in ontology and epistemology. It is worth giving some attention to these conceptions before returning to narrative per se so we can see exactly what support there might be here for the schematic arguments given earlier.

Logical Fictions

The concept of a logical fiction connects with naming and analysis. The core idea is this: a logical fiction is the purported referent of an eliminable syntactic name. Such a conception probably originated with Jeremy Bentham. It found its fullest expression in Bertrand Russell's logical atomism. I will say a bit about both.

Bentham thought that our ordinary language was unavoidably committed to what he called "fictitious entities". He didn't think that mattered—indeed, he thought it often advantageous, as long as confused inferences weren't drawn about what is real. Bentham argued, for example, that all of the following were fictitious entities: motion, relation, faculty, power, quantity, form, matter and, more notoriously, duties, obligations and rights.

While his contemporaries in the French and American revolutions used the existence of rights as their rallying cry, Bentham kept insisting that rights were mere fictions. What did he mean? After all, he saw the danger that denying the existence of rights would appear to give "*carte blanche* to tyranny" (Ogden 1951, 121). He meant two things: first, that the word "right" as a noun doesn't stand for any real entity; second, that sentences containing "right" as a noun can be paraphrased into sentences containing only nouns that do stand for real entities.

So Bentham's theory of fiction has two parts: a theory about what is real and a theory about paraphrase. The first is a thoroughgoing empiricism: a real entity is an "object the existence of which is made known to us by one or more of our five senses" (Ogden 1951, 114). The theory of paraphrase is more interesting, although, of course, it connects with the theory of the real. It has been hailed, notably by C K Ogden and John Wisdom (and later by Ross Harrison), as a clear forerunner of twentieth-century logical analysis. Bentham's breakthrough was to move from the level of the single term to that of the sentence. Locke had offered a compositional view of complex ideas and mixed modes in terms of the concatenation of simple ideas. Vestiges of the Lockean view remain in Bentham (as they do in Russell), but the step to the level of sentences allows for a much richer analysis of a concept. For example, Bentham wants to explain rights and duties in terms of the omissions for which someone is liable to be punished in law; in turn, punishment is explained in terms of pain. Bentham is not claiming that rights and duties are somehow constructed out of pains, like Lockean complex ideas. He is rather explaining the conditions under which someone can correctly be said to have a right or a duty.

The connection of logical fictions with names, sentences and analysis by paraphrase also appears in Russell. Russell's theory of logical fictions is more complex than that of Bentham (not least because it changed), but, like Bentham's, it presupposes a conception of what is real and a mechanism of analysis. It also involves a theory of meaning. Russell conceived of what is real as what we are acquainted with. This idea connects with the theory of meaning, which has two parts: first, a realist view of meaning itself (i.e., the meaning of an expression is the entity for which the expression stands); second, the principle of acquaintance (i.e., the view that understanding the meaning of an expression involves acquaintance with the entity which is its meaning). The atoms of logical atomism are precisely the entities which, according to the realist view, are meanings and, according to the principle of acquaintance, are the basis of our understanding. Russell held that only these entities—simple sense-data, for example—are "genuine entities"; everything else is a "fiction" or "construction". That leaves all material objects as fictions.

Logical analysis, for Russell, is the process that takes us from ordinary sentences to sentences conforming to the principle of acquaintance (i.e., those that are immediately understandable). But it also has ontological implications. Russell says that if you analyse the statement "Piccadilly is a pleasant street", "you will find that the fact corresponding to your statement does not contain any constituent corresponding to the word 'Piccadilly'" (1956, 191). The theory of descriptions provides the paradigm of analysis. But its connection with what is real and fictional was perhaps originally misunderstood by Russell. Russell seems to have thought that because he could eliminate descriptions by translation into propositional functions, this was equivalent to showing that there was nothing real, or no "genuine entity", answering to the description. He called descriptions "incomplete symbols", a term with just that connotation according to the realist theory of meaning. But, in fact, that conclusion requires further premises from logical atomism. The theory of descriptions itself remains neutral as to whether any object is designated by a description. All it shows is that the syntactic form of a sentence containing a definite description doesn't require the existence of a designated object for it to be meaningful.

W V O Quine went on to argue that the theory of descriptions, or any elimination of singular terms, shows not what exists or is real but only what a person is committed to accepting as real in what he says. Logical paraphrase, for Bentham and Russell, cannot in itself give a direct answer to the question of what is real. It shows only how we can avoid apparent (syntactically based) commitments to types of entities. In both cases, to say that something is a logical fiction is to say that its existence need not be assumed in order to make sense of a particular sentence. The fact that objects for Russell and rights for Bentham turn out to be logical fictions is a product of other features of their theories.

Even with these qualifications, it still might seem that logical fictions offer support for the conclusions of each literary theorist's argument: in effect blurring fact and fiction. After all, the suggestion is that quite ordinary descriptive sentences, by means of which we convey factual beliefs, turn out to be shot through with talk about fictions. Logical fictions also seem to offer some confirmation of the first premise of argument (A), which grounds the distinction between fact and fiction in correspondence. Both Bentham and Russell see meaning itself in referential and correspondence terms.

But I don't think there is much to be gained here for the literary theorists, at least not for their general ambition of running together different kinds of writing: literary fictional, philosophical, historical and so forth. For one thing, logical fictions belong in the object, not the description, category; they concern reference rather than truth. It is not a sentence or narrative that is fictional in the logical sense, only a kind of name, even though the removal of the fiction takes place at a sentential level.

Furthermore, the dichotomy between what is "made up" and what is "out there" is not obviously applicable to logical fictions. For Russell, what is real is not what is "out there" but what is "in here" (i.e., sense-data). Yet this affords no blurring of the distinction between what is real and what is "made up" (sense-data are not "made" but "given"). The positive connotations of construction or imagination are also absent from logical fictions. The focus is on eliminability, not creativity. Finally, as I will go on to show, there is a marked difference between logical fictions, defined in terms of elimination by paraphrase, and literary or "make-believe" fictions.

Epistemological Fictions

Whereas logical fictions relate to naming and paraphrase, the central idea being the elimination of reference, epistemological fictions emphasise not elimination but construction. Perhaps the term "fiction" is tendentious here, but only if we stress the negative connotations. Constructivist theories of knowledge with which I am concerned see objects (indeed, the empirical world itself), not as *given* in experience, but rather as constructed out of it. The theories, which take many forms, stress the active role of the mind in the construction of an ordered and unified world.

Epistemological fictions arise from two kinds of constructivist theory: foundationalist and anti-foundationalist. Locke, Kant and Russell were foundationalists in the sense that they distinguished between a "given" and a "construction"; what is constructed in knowledge is constructed out of a given that is not itself constructed. It would be wrong, though, even for foundationalist theories, to associate the given exclusively with the real.

Although Locke had reservations about the reality of things corresponding to at least some complex ideas, Kant was in no doubt that the synthetic world of objects was real; that's the point of empirical realism. Russell, in contrast, did associate the given exclusively with the real. "All the ordinary objects of daily life", he wrote, "are extruded from the world of what there is" (Russell 1956, 273). And he spoke of "the unreality of the things we think real" (Russell 1956, 274). It is far from clear why Russell couldn't admit his logical constructions to be real or genuine entities. Part of the answer is that he thought of objects as classes or series and he held an anti-realist view of classes. But part also rests on the doctrine of logical fictions and the mistaken belief that to eliminate a syntactic name is to eliminate any entity named.

Epistemological fictions also appear in anti-foundationalist theories of knowledge. Quine's idea of objects as posits belongs in this category. The overt connection with fiction is made in Quine's famous comparison of physical objects with the gods of Homer. He spoke of the "conceptual scheme of physical objects" as "a convenient myth" (1961, 18). Quine, of course, in relativising ontology, wouldn't hesitate to accept his posits as real. Reality, too, is relativised. Quine agrees enough with Carnap to reject so-called "external" questions of existence. There is no contrast for Quine between what is real and what is posited nor ultimately between what is posited and what is given.

Such, too, is the position of Nelson Goodman, another anti-foundationalist. In his view, we make worlds by making world-versions. There is no single world but a plurality of worlds. And we make a world-version not out of an experiential given but out of other world-versions. Goodman describes his view as "irrealism" partly to pour scorn on the very idea of a real world. Yet although he thinks the world is man-made, and he rejects the idea of truth as correspondence, he insists in the end on quite strict rules for good and bad makings. Not all versions are right versions. To be right is to be deductively and inductively valid and to consist only of "right categorisations". Inductive reasoning must be based on "all the available genuine evidence" (Goodman 1978, 126).

Goodman is happy to appropriate the idea of "making" for both facts and fictions, but he offers no consolation for those who would in other ways weaken that distinction. Indeed, he takes a remarkably restrictive view of imaginative fiction, identifying such fictions as literal falsehoods (1984, 124). At best, he allows literary fictions only metaphorical truth.

Although he is to be commended for keeping apart his metaphysical theory—the world is man-made—and his literary theory—fictional narratives are false—Goodman, I believe, has not made out his case on either side. We need not pursue the matter directly. For our purposes, certain general conclusions are already emerging. For example, epistemological fictions, or constructions, in their many forms from Locke to Goodman, provide no sharp line between what is made and what is real. Objects and truths themselves are viewed as products of human makings, even though the makings—Kantian synthesis, Russellian logical construction, Quinean positing—are of different kinds.

All this might seem congenial to the literary theorist. But our two schematic arguments, (A) and (B), do not automatically go through even for epistemological fictions. Makings there might be, but, as Goodman admits, we can still distinguish good (i.e., "right") and bad makings, in effect truth and falsity. They also occur at what Kant would call the transcendental, rather than the empirical, level. They do not occur at the level at which we distinguish between, say, a real person and a fictional character. In spite of superficial similarities, the creation of epistemological fictions is radically different from that of literary fictions. Premises about epistemological fictions will give little support to any poststructuralist scepticism about distinguishing imaginative from truth-stating discourse.

Before we return finally to literary fictions, I should offer some brief remarks on Richard Rorty's pragmatism, for Rorty purports to make a connection between what we say about truth and what we say about imaginative fiction. Rorty doesn't go as far as Goodman in speaking of making worlds, but he does believe that truth is "made" rather than "found". All this idea amounts to, though, is the reaffirmation of the long-established doctrine that truth is a property of sentences (i.e., linguistic entities) along with the further premise that "languages are made rather than found". Nearer to the heart of Rorty's position is the rejection of the correspondence theory of truth and, more generally, of what he calls the "picture picture" of language. He identifies the resistance to the idea of language as a "game" rather than a "picture" (of reality) with the anxiety, characteristic of the Western philosophical tradition, that we might lose the distinction between "responsible" and "irresponsible" discourse, "that need to distinguish sharply between science and poetry which makes us distinctively Western" (1982, 132). Rorty insists that this anxiety is unwarranted. We need constraints, certainly, on our claims to truth, but these need only be what he calls "conversational" constraints; there are "no wholesale constraints derived from the nature of the objects, or of the mind, or of language, but only those retail constraints provided by the remarks of our fellow-inquirers" (165).

However, it turns out for Rorty, as we might expect, that these "retail constraints" are all that the metaphysical realist might hope them to be, barring only the idea of a transcendent mind-independent world. It is not as if Rorty proposes a different kind of scientific research, different methods of experimentation or different standards of proof. Familiar practices remain intact. Nor does he propose, in the literary fictional case, that we somehow overlook the obvious differences between a work of fiction and a work of science or philosophy. For Rorty, the world of the realist is a world "well lost", but in effect all that is lost is Descartes's thought-experiment about massive illusion. Otherwise, the same familiar world remains. It is as much a question for Rorty as for the realist whether Alejandro Mayta really exists and what he is like. At the level at which these questions are raised, Rorty's view, like that of the realist, *leaves everything as it is*.

So what are the distinctions between fictional and nonfictional narratives that I have suggested are independent of ontological or epistemological theories about the real world? Rorty rejects the idea that there is a "problem" about fictional discourse on the ground that the perceived "problem" rests on the "picture picture" of language. As I see it, on the contrary, all the interesting problems remain, regardless of our view about correspondence theories of truth. We need to identify the special kind of "making" involved in fictional narratives, the purposes, the methods of assessment and indeed the relations that the narrative can bear with how things are in the world.

MAKE-BELIEVE FICTIONS

As a rough sketch as to how these questions might be answered, let me introduce the idea of a "make-believe" fiction, in contrast to both logical and epistemological fictions. There is an object and a description sense of make-believe fiction. A make-believe object is a fictional character. A make-believe description is, or is part of, what I will call a fictive utterance. Some fictive utterances make up fictional narratives. When I speak of a fictional narrative, it is make-believe fiction that I have in mind.

Just as narratives in themselves are indifferent to reference or truth, so fictive utterances have no semantic prerequisites. *Pace* Goodman, not all predications in fictive utterances are literally false. There is no reason why make-believe descriptions should not describe (truly) actual states of affairs. It is in virtue of other features, as we will see, that they are fictional. Likewise, not all proper names occurring in fictive utterances are names of make-believe objects. Fictive utterances could contain the names of real objects. Finally, not all make-believe fictions are literary. Literariness, as noted earlier, is an evaluative property while fictionality, in the make-believe sense, is simply a mode of utterance.

The defining feature of a make-believe fictive utterance, which includes fictional narrative, does not rest on a contrast between what is "made up" and what is "out there", nor does it presuppose a correspondence view of either reference or truth. Instead, it lies in a network of practice-based relations at the centre of which is a set of attitudes I will label the "fictive stance" (Lamarque and Olsen 1994, 43f). The fictive stance is not a property of sentences or utterances but rather an attitude taken towards them by participants in the "game" of fiction. The fictive stance is made possible only within a complex, loosely rule-governed practice which determines storytellers' intentions and readers' responses. We could conceive of a society with a language indistinguishable from ours, in vocabulary, syntax and semantics, but which lacked the practice of fictive utterance. We could even suppose that this society had textually identical narratives to ours. But without the conventions of fiction, we could not classify these narratives as fictional in the make-believe sense. We would have to suppose that they performed quite different pragmatic functions.

How is fictive utterance to be characterised? Many attempts to define fictionality in pragmatic terms appeal to either speech-acts or the idea of pretence.[7] Neither, I believe, is necessary. We do not need to postulate a special speech-act of fiction, nor do we need to suppose that writers of fiction necessarily pretend anything.

First of all, fictive utterance, as I define it, involves a disengagement from certain conventional commitments associated with communicative acts. For example, many standard inferences are blocked from a fictive utterance back to the speaker or writer, notably inferences about the speaker's or writer's beliefs. What looks like an assertion from the storyteller should not be assumed to be such; there is no automatic inference that the storyteller believes what is said to be true or that the names and descriptions refer to items in the real world. Readers also should be wary of attributing attitudes expressed in the narrative to the real author.[8] This feature underlies the postulation of a narrator or implied author separate from the real author. The characterisation of a narrative voice, or narrative attitude, although employing a psychological vocabulary, can proceed to a large extent autonomously from any real individual's psychological states.

Second, fictive utterance involves an invitation to a response of a particular kind—namely, the adoption of the fictive stance by an audience. This at its simplest is an invitation not so much to *believe* the propositions presented in a narrative as to *make-believe* that they are presented with standard commitments (e.g., being offered as worldly truths) while recognising that they are not. This is how the "game" of fiction is played. The audience, in taking up the fictive stance, engages the practice of fiction which dictates what kind of attitudes to the content are appropriate and inappropriate, involving evaluation, interpretation, reasoning, questioning. Note that, strictly speaking, it is not propositions (or sentences) that are fictional or make-believe—only the mode in which they are presented. The propositions themselves, independent of this context, might have determinate truth-values. The context of make-believe storytelling promotes various kinds of "distancing" (hence the familiar notions of disinterestedness, suspension of disbelief, etc.). Just as fictive utterance distances an audience from an author's beliefs, so, too, it encourages a certain focus of attention away from world-directed relations of reference and truth towards internal relations of sense and form.

We have seen that narrative can be identified (as narrative) purely in terms of form or structure. That does not mean, of course, that our interest in a narrative must be confined to its formal features. On the contrary, a characteristic of our interest in, for example, historical narrative is a concern with wider matters, not least regard for evidential support. However, with fictional narratives, in the make-believe sense, there is a close connection between the formal features of the narrative and the attitudes definitive of fiction.

To explain this, it is important to retain the distinction between fiction per se and literary fiction; the prescribed responses are not identical. Make-believe fiction per se, presented in the fictive mode, invites a reader to give primary attention to an imaginary world which, however similar to the real world, gains its distinctive character and interest through the manner of its presentation. Make-believe objects and make-believe events owe their very existence to their characterisation in the narrative sentences (this is the topic of chapter 8). Attention is directed, as it were, inwards to this characterisation rather than outwards to verification and worldly fact. The world of the narrative takes shape through the linguistic resources chosen not for the pragmatic end of asserting truths but for painting a picture that gives pleasure for its own sake. We might say that in this sense, the fictive stance involves the foregrounding of the formal features of narrative.

With fictional works of literature, the fictive stance is still operative but further kinds of engagement are encouraged. For example, through thematic interpretation attention is directed towards more universal features of the narrative content. Returning to *The Real Life of Alejandro Mayta*, we recall the narrator invoking "Mayta's world"; it is a "world", not an individual, which we are invited to consider. In Aristotle's terms, the universality of poetry, not the particularity of history, shapes our response to the narrative. To make sense of Mayta's world and the complex narration through which it is presented, we need certain universal thematic concepts: time, the fragmentation of history, memory, nostalgia. A literary focus gives prominence to such themes.

None of this proves, of course, that *Mayta* is either a literary work or a fictional one. Maybe a word-for-word identical text could be offered and read as an exclusively historical or biographical narrative.[9] (Whether it would match up to the criteria of evaluation demanded in other practices is another matter.) A great deal of contextual and institutional stage-setting would be required to make sense of this possibility. But that is just the point. It is not part of my argument that a narrative is *intrinsically* fictional or historical or philosophical. I offer only a pragmatic, externalist account of the differences. Intention, modes of utterance, practice-based conventions, invited response, criteria of judgement—in these lie the distinctiveness of the fictional. It is thus that make-believe fictions are radically different from logical and epistemological fictions. It is neither the semantic eliminability of names that explains their fictionality nor the ideas of logical construction or posit. Make-believe fictionality is not an inherent property of a narrative in any respect.

Nevertheless, I do believe that an author can signal the fictive mode through conventional, albeit defeasible, means. The narrative devices employed in *Mayta*—the complex time frame, the contrived symmetries in dialogue, the fragmented characterisation—draw attention to themselves in such a way as to encourage and reward both the fictive stance and the quest for universal themes (literariness).

No doubt we could read any narrative as fictional, in the make-believe sense. We could direct our attention to narrative form, adopt the appropriate distance from truth-telling or assertive commitments and reflect only on the characteristics of the world depicted, not on its reality. But nothing follows from this about the "fictionality" of all narratives. It merely shows that we as readers can always adopt the fictive stance. We are not required to do so, nor are we always invited to do so. Above all, there are no metaphysical implications in doing so. Questions about reference and truth-value will still remain open.

CONCLUSION

My theme has been the juxtaposition of narrative and fictionality. The presence of narrative structure and technique in history, philosophy and biography, as well as literary fiction, attests to the flexibility of the narrative form as a mode of representation. It is a commonplace that "telling stories" can help us make sense of the world. If we inject into this commonplace even the modest claims of classical empiricist epistemology, we can give at least minimal respectability to the more daring idea that our access to the world is always mediated by the stories we tell. The role of narrative in our cognitive processes is further enhanced by Kant's epistemology, which gives primacy to temporal and causal organisation in the very conception of an "objective world". The first glimmer of the mind- or even narrative-dependence of the world comes in Kant's Copernican revolution, which defends the "transcendental" subjectivity of both time and cause.

Once storytelling and mind-dependence become established in epistemology, it is a short step to far more radical conclusions—for example, that there is no difference in principle between modes of storytelling and that there are no special privileges accorded to any one kind of storyteller, historian, philosopher, scientist or novelist, with regard to the "representation of reality". Add to this an anti-realism that discards the correspondence theory of truth and we are well on the way towards "fictionalising" all stories or narrative, at least in the sense that what is fictional is what is "made up" or "invented".

The final destination of this line of thought, with its comforting egalitarianism, is the claim that there is nothing *more* fictional about the novelist's narratives than those of the historian, the philosopher or the scientist.

My aim has been to put a damper on this euphoric progression. I have sought to show that what we say about narrative must be kept apart from what we say about metaphysics. Questions of ontology and truth are strictly independent of the formal features of narrative in the sense that it is always open to ask of any narrative what its referential commitments are. I have also offered a preliminary examination of the idea of fictionality, identifying logical, epistemological and make-believe fictions. In none of these do we find support for a general "fictionalising" of narratives. The novelist and the historian might both be storytellers but nothing is gained by blurring their different ways of telling.

NOTES

1. Page references that follow are to Vargas Llosa (1986).
2. The term comes from Putnam: "[T]he assumption that no psychological state, properly so-called, presupposes the existence of any individual other than the subject to whom that state is ascribed" (1975, 220).
3. Note the slide towards anti-realism in the following, not uncharacteristic, passage from a book on literary structuralism: "A wholly objective perception of individual entities is therefore not possible: any observer is bound to *create* something of what he observes. Accordingly, the *relationship* between observer and observed achieves a kind of primacy. It becomes the only thing that *can* be observed. It becomes the stuff of reality itself. . . . In consequence, the true nature of things may be said to lie not in things themselves, but in the relationships which we construct . . . *between* them" (Hawkes 1975, 17; italics in the original).
4. For example, Norris (1985), particularly chapters 4 and 6.
5. For a defence of this view, see Rorty (1986), 3.
6. It is common to find independent support for this conclusion in Nietzsche's famous aphorism: "[T]ruths are illusions of which one has forgotten that they *are* illusions" (1997, 92).
7. Standard examples being Currie (1985) and Searle (1975).
8. No doubt *some* attitudes can be attributed directly to the author: see, for example, Lyas (1983).
9. The implications of such a thought-experiment are explored in Danto (1987), 16ff.

Chapter Three

On Not Expecting Too Much from Narrative

Everyone agrees, and rightly so, that narratives are prominent in human lives, not only in the obvious places like literature, history and biography but also in virtually all forms of reflective cognition, from the education of young children to the self-image of adults. But how much significance should be attached to this? Not much, I suggest. There is little intrinsic interest in narrative per se, and I suspect that many narratologists are blind to this because there *is* intrinsic interest in *some* narratives. For example, the great literary works—epic poems and novels—are of immense interest, and their narrative structures, plots and characters reward detailed study. But, arguably, it is not the fact that these works are *narratives* that gives them interest, but rather the fact that they are *literary* narratives. Once we see how little is involved in being a narrative—how minimal the conditions are for narrativity—we will see that the focus of interest nearly always shifts away from mere narrative itself.

A central reason behind the overrating of narrative is precisely the paradigmatic status given to literary (fictional) narratives, itself a consequence of the origins of narratology in structuralism and literary criticism. But this has had a markedly deleterious effect. It has encouraged certain myths about narrative which need to be confronted: for example, that all narratives are *au fond* fictional, that narratives create the objects or events they describe, that the self is a creation of narrative, that narratives are complete with beginnings, middles and ends (possess "closure"), that there is no structure of events independent of narrative, that even when narratives do depict an independent reality they inevitably distort that reality. If these theses were correct, then, in the light of the agreed ubiquity of narrative, the repercussions would indeed be momentous. Fictionality and invention would be at the heart of human thought processes; a radical epistemic anti-realism would pervade; history would be reduced to a *product* rather than a subject of narrative; structural analyses familiar to literary critics would become norms for history, philosophy, even science; and questions about narrative genres and the pragmatics of narration would overwhelm questions about truth. Of course, there are those who believe such repercussions do obtain and who promote just such a sweeping anti-realism.[1] But I hope to show that no such conclusions follow from premises about narrative itself.

DEFINING NARRATIVE

So what exactly is narrative? To narrate is to tell a story, but the minimal conditions for storytelling or for what counts as a story are indeed minimal. One condition is that a story must be told, it is not found.[2] More on that later. Another is that at least two events must be depicted in a narrative and there must be some more or less loose, albeit non-logical, relation between the events.[3] Crucially, there is a temporal dimension in narrative, not just in the sense that component sentences are tensed but also in that there must be a temporal relation between the events, even if just that of simultaneity. "The sun shone and the grass grew" is a narrative, but "Bill kicked the ball and the ball was kicked by Bill" is not because the latter does not involve two events temporally related, but rather a single event represented in logically equivalent sentences. Narratives can be identified from formal features alone of individual sentences or sentence strings and no implications about reference, truth, subject matter or discursive ends can be drawn from such formal identification.[4] Narrative per se is neutral on such matters, in the sense that narratives can be about real or imaginary entities; they can be true or false (or truth-valueless, depending on one's view of fiction); they can be about virtually any subject and can serve a multitude of ends, from entertaining or informing to philosophising. Very little of substance can be inferred from the premise that a piece of discourse is a narrative.

A further complication is that narrative has a three-way product-act-object ambiguity (see Wilson 2003, 392–93). The *product* of narrative (i.e., the story told) is sometimes referred to as a narrative, as when we speak of different versions of the same narrative. The *act* of narration (i.e., the telling of the story) can also be classified as narrative, as when we say that the narrative lasted over an hour. And sometimes the *text* of a story is called a narrative, as when we speak of reading a narrative. It is important in different contexts to specify which of these three is meant. But a common element should be stressed—namely, that of narration. There can be no narrative without narration, a point sometimes overlooked by those who see human life in terms of narratives untold or waiting to be told. Thus the product sense of "narrative" must be treated with care. The stories of which there are different versions can only be stories (i.e., narratives in this first sense) if they have already been told. It is not until the first Faust story has appeared that there can be different versions of it. The first Faust story might be a version of events in the world, but it is not yet a version of a story in the relevant sense of that term.

With this minimal characterisation of narrative at hand, let us look at some of the substantial claims made for narrative and see where, as it were, credit lies. I will pursue the enquiry through different aspects of narrative: structural features, reference and truth, and narrative practices (these three being roughly characterisable as the syntax, semantics and pragmatics of narrative), and then finish with some remarks about values and the explanatory powers of narrative with particular attention to claims about narrative and personal identity.

STRUCTURAL FEATURES

In the heyday of structuralism, it came to seem as if narrative structure was of more significance than any other aspect of narrative, including reference and truth. Observing structural similarities between narratives could be a more powerful reason for grouping the narratives together than factors to do with genre or subject matter. Thus did "myths" become a special interest of the structuralists (e.g., Lévi-Strauss 1972) and they seemed to crop up everywhere, from Homeric legends to the Christian story of Christ's resurrection, to children's folk tales, to stories of Empire (their rise and fall), to the plots of world literature. The question of status—myth or religion or folklore or history or fiction—was subsumed under a preoccupation with "grammar" or "transformations" or "codes". Again, it seemed as if a literary paradigm was at work.

Literary analysis of narrative, of a formalistic kind, does indeed dwell on structural features, in both poetry or novelistic fiction, noting symmetries, oppositions, parallels, repetitions, digressions and reversals. These are the stock-in-trade of the literary critic, perhaps also of the student of ancient myths. But they are not obligatory points of focus or styles of reading for all narrative. Not all historians are myth-makers. Historical narrative will, of course, have structure, but given the radically different aims of the scholarly historian and the dramatist or poet, the role of structure in each enterprise cannot be assumed to be the same. A recent comprehensive historical study of the Battle of Gettysburg (Trudeau 2002) is a simple, if arbitrarily chosen, case in point. There have been numerous accounts of Gettysburg, as well as novels and films, many no doubt forms of myth-making. Trudeau's study is both an attempt at objective scholarly analysis and a poignant and endlessly fascinating narrative, drawing on a massive array of contemporary documents and reports. A structural analysis of Trudeau's narrative, along the lines of either Lévi-Strauss's analyses of myths or a literary critic's analysis of a novel, would be possible but largely a diversion from the true focus of interest. Trudeau's aim is to tell a story, but his constraints are those of the historian. He structures his story in the service of explanation, interpretation and balanced perspective and adheres to a strict chronological time frame. His account might be contrasted with the fictionalised version of the same events in Michael Shaara's novel *The Killer Angels* (1974). To appreciate the novel, attention to its structure is all important: the clever use of narrative point of view, the juxtaposition of scenes from both armies, internalised monologues, parallel lives, reflective (invented) dialogue highlighting personal fears and desires, all lure the reader into a sympathetic imagining of the events from each side of the battle. But similar literary analysis is unlikely to reveal the success of the historian's painstaking attention to accuracy and detail. It seems reasonable to conclude that while narratives often do have complex structures amenable to subtle formal analysis, there is nothing about narrative per se that *demands* structural analysis or gives such analysis high priority.

Another feature of narrative structure that has caused controversy is the role of the narrator. Narratives must be narrated: that is how they come into being. They are human artefacts, not natural or even platonistic entities waiting to be discovered. And if they are narrated, they need an actual person, not merely a fictional character, to do the narrating, to tell the story. Events narrated might well be mind-independent but narratives cannot be. The latter must originate in human acts of some kind. Of course, there is considerable variation in the ways that narrators are identified. The basic identification is between narrator and author (the original teller of the story), but these can pull apart in different circumstances: when, for example, in the simplest scenario, it is not the author who narrates (i.e., tells) the story on a particular occasion but a third party (i.e., someone reading the story aloud or retelling it in other ways). A storyteller need not always be the story's originator. Another familiar possibility is first-person narration in which the narrator is a character in the story, as with Nick Carraway in *The Great Gatsby*. In such cases, the actual narrator—storyteller or story author—assumes the role of, or perhaps pretends to be, the fictional narrator. Even in third-person narratives, the narrator (or what might be called the narrative voice) can possess identifiable characteristics that are not those of the author. Again, the author is projecting this persona. Finally, it is common in literary reading to postulate an "implied author", not explicitly a character in the story or a third-person narrator as described or identical with the actual author, but a personality constructed by the reader from the tone and manner of the third-person narration. This implied author might be different in striking respects from the real author, from a fictional narrator, if there is one, or indeed from anyone narrating the story out loud. But only in the loosest sense is an implied author characterised as a narrator.

These are commonplaces of narrative analysis, but it would be incorrect to suppose that at the more subtle end (e.g., when an implied author is postulated) some profound truth about narrative itself is being revealed. It is not. Many narratives do not have—or do not need—an implied author. The latter plays a useful role in understanding certain kinds of narrative fiction, but that tells us more about a literary genre or style of literary reading than it does about narrative per se. When I explain to you in prosaic terms how I spent yesterday afternoon, I have presented a narrative but no interesting questions arise about the logical status of the narrator.

Finally, it is easy enough to recognise narrative devices right across the range of narratives: irony, suspense, anachrony (in which narrative order does not reflect the temporal order of events described), point of view, figuration, allusion, double entendre and so forth. The fact that similar rhetorical features are found in narratives of different kinds—philosophical, historical or literary—has led some to blur the boundaries or to suppose that the commonalities are more important than the differences. Once again, literary narratives are taken as a model, and because some historical, autobiographical or philosophical narratives exploit similar devices, it can be tempting to conclude that all narratives are *au fond* literary (or, in particular, fictional). The matter is further complicated by the fact that it is possible to read philosophical narratives—for example, Descartes's *Discourse on Method—from a literary point of view*. Doing so precisely entails giving prominence to structural or formal or rhetorical aspects. There is often insight and interest in such reading. But there is no legitimate inference from noting the literary devices of philosophy to the reduction of philosophy to literature. A literary focus on a philosophical narrative does not preclude or supersede or make redundant the focus of a philosopher on the text's arguments and conclusions.

REFERENCE AND TRUTH

Narrative itself presents no special problem for either reference or truth. The thought that problems do arise again stems from taking fictional narratives as the norm. In standard historical narrative, names denote and sentences have truth-values according to recognised criteria. Consider this passage from *Gettysburg*:

> Robert E Lee planned to cross the Potomac himself this morning [June 25, 1863]. Just before and just after he did so, he penned letters to Jefferson Davis.

> In the first (written "opposite Williamsport"), Lee worried that his thrust into the North might prove *too* successful. (Trudeau 2002, 71)

The names "Lee", "Potomac" and "Jefferson Davis" refer in a straightforward manner and the truth claims are well supported by contemporary official records, including copies of Lee's letters. Whatever philosophical problems there might be about reference and truth, it seems clear that no additional problems arise from the appearance of names and assertions in narratives of this kind. Even in fictional narratives, there is no reason in principle why names of real people or objects should not secure their normal denotation (Lamarque and Olsen 1994, ch. 5). Those literary structuralists who identify a "referential fallacy", so-called, in fictional or poetic narrative (Riffaterre 1973) are focusing less on a feature of narrative and more on contentious claims about literary interpretation. Of course, there are difficult and intriguing questions about the status of names of fictional characters and about the truth-valuation of sentences in works of fiction (Lamarque and Olsen 1994, pt. I; Lamarque 2003). But these issues are associated with fictionality rather than narrative, and it is important to insist that the two are distinct, as the case of historical narrative shows.

Unfortunately, questions about reference and truth in narrative cannot quite be left at that. Two familiar ideas need to be addressed—the first is that narrative, by its nature, *distorts* the events it purports to describe, whereas the second, a stronger claim, is that it *creates* those events at least in the sense that there are no plot-like structures of events independent of narrative. We should note straightaway that strong versions of the anti-realist claim conflict with the weaker distortion claim. An event can only be distorted by a narrative if it exists independent of that narrative.

What grounds are there for the distortion thesis? The motivating idea is that narratives are of necessity selective and perspectival. Narratives can never be comprehensive or totally transparent.[5] Even fact-based narratives like history or biography involve both selection and ordering of fact; some events are given prominence over others, causal relations and teleological progression are postulated and ends or closure imposed. Narrators perforce narrate from some point of view or another, however impartial they might intend to be, and narration inevitably involves interpretation and evaluation, if only in weighing some facts as more significant than others.

There is no denying the general truth of these claims, but it is important not to exaggerate the implications. The conclusion that historical narrative is a kind of fiction (White 1989, 27) and that the coherence that narrative gives to events is an imaginative invention is not warranted. It is wrong to conflate history and fiction on the grounds that historical writing is perspectival and selective. For one thing, as we have seen, reference by means of proper names or singular descriptions is not affected by the use of the names in historical narratives nor is the truth-valuation of individual assertions. The simple recounting of Lee's crossing of the Potomac quoted earlier itself embodies no especially distorting perspective on that simple event, although it is accompanied explicitly by a description of Lee's own perspective. Nor is it unduly distorting to assign historical significance to the event, within a broader pattern, even though many historically significant events are not recognised as such at the time. In this case, Lee and his army were well aware that the event was symbolically important albeit lacking knowledge of what the consequences would be.

Distortion is not an inevitable feature of descriptive narration, even though there is always that danger when meanings are assigned to intrinsically mundane occurrences. To suppose it is inevitable, even at a descriptive level, might seem to imply an ideal "transparent" narrative, mapping facts without any discrimination or weighting, which as an ideal is surely unwarranted and unreasonable.[6] Also, it is wrong to blame narrative itself for more general problems associated with imprecision in descriptive language. Description of any kind, whether or not in narrative discourse, is subject to ambiguity, vagueness, figuration, evaluative or emotive connotation, speaker bias, half-truth, implicature and, of course, plain falsehood. Language is always subject to distortions arising from such features, but they are not to be laid specifically at the door of narrative. Selectivity of fact is inevitable in historical narrative, but the extent to which distortion follows is a central factor in the evaluation of such narratives. Historians are rightly taken to task when lack of objectivity, neglect of detail and misleading emphasis are evident. Finally, distortion not only comes in degrees but also is subject to different assessments in different contexts. A novelist who deliberately distorts historical events for artistic ends is not subject to the same judgement as the historian whose distortions are due to ignorance, bias or deception.

What about the anti-realist claim that narrative creates the events it describes? Two paradigms underlie such anti-realism. The first is that of fictionality. If all narration is a kind of fiction and fiction par excellence is the creation of character and event, then it seems a short step to the conclusion that all narration involves creation. Perhaps the imaginary worlds of the artist are not different in kind from the worlds of the scientist or historian.[7] The second paradigm for narrative creation comes from history itself. Undoubtedly, what might be called "meta-events" are created by historians as part of narrative structuring. The Middle Ages, the Renaissance, the Industrial Revolution and the Cold War are artefacts of historical narrative.

However, no general anti-realism about events follows from either of these paradigms. Not all narratives are fictional—a claim I will return to in the next section—and not all events belong in the category of historical meta-events. Thus the event of Robert E Lee's writing to Jefferson Davis on 25 June 1863, as again in our earlier example, is not a creation of any historian.

Only some further metaphysical or epistemological theory could establish the ideality or constructivist nature of an event of that kind. No such theory follows from premises about narrative. It might be objected that no clear line exists between simple more or less freestanding events of the latter kind and those more global events which give shape to history. In particular, while no individual event has intrinsic significance, an event's place in the narrative of history might afford it the status of a "turning point" or the "beginning of the end" which only some broader perspective reveals. The point, however, although correct, goes no way towards establishing an inherent anti-realism in narrative. To assign *significance* to events or to place events within a structure that identifies beginnings and endings is not to create the very events themselves. The structures that historians impose on clusters of events, like the Middle Ages, are markers of significance not inventions of fact. Disagreements among historians about the assigning of significance are resolved, if at all, in quite different ways than disagreements over fact. As for other structures, such as causal sequences of events, there is no reason to think that these are creatures of narrative. Again, only some independent anti-realist theory of causation could establish that the event sequences do not exist prior to narrative (or other kinds of) description.

NARRATIVE PRACTICES

It has been a central contention in the argument so far, against over-inflating the importance of narrative, that there are radically different kinds of narratives and thus that it is a mistake to blur distinctions or take one kind of narrative—particularly fictional narrative—as the norm (see chapters 2 and 4 in particular). We have seen that all that narratives have in common are minimal formal conditions about the ordering of events in a story. So how are narratives to be distinguished? They can differ in many aspects—in aim, style, structure, subject matter, seriousness and reader response. I suggest that the most fruitful way of drawing the distinctions that matter is in terms of narrative practices. It might be thought that to preserve a distinction between, say, history and fiction, the most important factors are semantic ones: historical, in contrast to fictional, narratives being identifiable by truth and denotation. This is a mistake. Truth and reference are not distributed so neatly across narratives (Lamarque 1996, ch. 2; Lamarque and Olsen 1994, pt. I). Narrative practices are rule-governed, the rules or conventions encapsulating the point of a narrative and the intentions and expectations of the participants. Broadly speaking, and subject to important qualifications, fiction aims not at belief but at make-believe (Currie 1990; Lamarque and Olsen 1994); a fictional narrative is assessed for its imaginativeness, coherence, stylistic or literary properties and the pleasures of reading.[8] It is not assessed on the criteria of assertion, or argumentative validity, conformity to fact, or appeal to evidence.

Until we know what *kind* of narrative is involved, we do not know the appropriate mode of assessment. The point of biographical narrative, for example, is to convey its subject's life in a reasonably coherent form, but it must also in a sense justify its own existence, showing that this is a life of some interest, worthy of attention. A mere factually accurate day-by-day chronicle of a life will not succeed as a biography even though it gets everything right. Biography is deeply imbued with value-judgements: that the subject rewards attention and that these, rather than other events, are of significance and contribute to a sense of the unity of the life. Assessment of biography partly rests on the acceptance of its implicit value-judgements.

In nearly every case, a higher priority should be given to locating a narrative in a practice, thus determining its point and the conventions it follows, than to focusing either on its internal structure or on its referential or truth status. Until it is known what kind of narrative is involved, the relevance of its structures or semantic characteristics cannot be determined. When we know that a narrative is a work of fictional literature, we know that attention to its formal structure is especially appropriate and potentially rewarding while the literal truth of its component sentences is less important (see chapter 7). For a historical narrative, the opposite, broadly, is the case. Of course, within generic narrative practices, like history or literature, there are numerous subgenres with their own conventions. Novels can be picaresque, romantic comedies, satires, murder mysteries, science fiction, spy stories or coming of age narratives. We not only value such works according to the expectations their genres encourage but also know what to look for and how we are meant to respond.

NARRATIVE VALUE

No narrative has value simply in virtue of being a narrative. Narratives are not of intrinsic value or interest. Some narratives are boring, rambling, disorganised, lacking coherence and on a subject of little significance. Narratives have to earn the right to engage our interest. The fact that narratives are ubiquitous in human self-reflection does not imply that they all invite or merit close attention. There are no intrinsic narrative virtues in the sense that there is some particular feature such that any narrative whatsoever is better possessing rather than not possessing that feature (this excludes, of course, defining features of narrative). It might be thought that structural unity is a pretty basic virtue for narratives. Yet *Tristram Shandy*'s narrative is admired precisely for its lack of unity. What about fine rhetoric? Yet, as Hume (1963) aptly points out, too much eloquence of expression in recounting an actual tragedy (in contrast to the eloquence of tragic drama) can be distracting and inappropriate. The value of narratives rests entirely on criteria internal to narrative practices. What makes a historical narrative valuable is determined by factors governing the ends and expectations of history. What makes a work of literature valuable is defined by the norms of literary criticism (see chapters 7, 9 and 10). Going much further down the scale, there are humdrum conversational narratives, such that occur in pubs or over garden fences. These have value to those involved. No doubt some minimal coherence is required to make the narrative intelligible, but the primary value is that of the interest of the subject matter to the participants. Of course, some people are better storytellers than others, and there are rough and ready criteria for ranking neighbourhood raconteurs. Style, wit, suspense and orderliness are pro tanto virtues in conversational storytelling. We should not balk at identifying something approaching a practice here. As Alasdair MacIntyre notes, "[W]e allocate conversations to genres" with their own structures like "digressions and subplots" (1985, 211).

NARRATIVE IDENTITY AND LIFE NARRATIVES

A good test case for the interest of narrative as a theoretical tool is the now-familiar claim that human lives are embedded in and explicable through narrative—"life narratives"—and that the unity of the self "resides in the unity of a narrative" (MacIntyre 1985, 205). The psychologist Donald E Polkinghorne puts the view succinctly: "[W]e achieve our personal identities and self concept through the use of the narrative configuration, and make our existence into a whole by understanding it as an expression of a single unfolding and developing story" (Polkinghorne 1988, 150). My view again is that the appeal to narrative in this context promises more than it delivers.

So what is the thesis exactly? Alasdair MacIntyre, an early exponent, introduced the idea of narrative to counterbalance a tendency that he found in both analytical ethics and existentialism to view actions atomistically. MacIntyre argued, persuasively, that if we are to understand an agent's actions and intentions, we must locate them in a broad setting with both temporal and social extension. We should not treat actions as isolated unconnected events. It was only a short step to the notion that "narrative history . . . [is] the basic and essential genre for the characterisation of human actions" (1985, 208). However, this unexceptional step yields somewhat less than it might suggest. A narrative, as we have seen and as MacIntyre recognises, is the depiction of an ordered sequence of events, so representing actions in a causal and temporal sequence—seemingly the most straightforward, if not the only, way to do so—is, in this minimal sense, to represent them in a narrative.

The trouble is, MacIntyre warms to his theme and having introduced narrative in this innocent seeming fashion comes to read more and more into it and, like so many others in this alluring context, becomes seduced by the parallels with *fictional* narratives. First, he introduces genres. These need not be confined to the literary, but his examples—tragedy, saga and hagiography—suggest the higher reaches of literature and biography. Worse still, he asks not about genres of *narratives* but, in a crucial slip, what genres people's *lives* belong in (1985, 212–13). This merging of life and narrative is a mistake. A narrative, being a story, must be narrated, but a life need not be narrated. He talks about embedded narratives—stories within stories—alluding to a device, as he notes, common in fiction. Before long, he speaks of "each of us . . . [as] a main character in his own drama" and describes us not only as "actors" in our own narratives but also as "co-authors" (213). "The difference", he writes, "between imaginary characters and real ones is not in the narrative form of what they do; it is in the degree of their authorship of that form and of their own deeds" (215). The final step in this progression is to explain personal identity itself in terms of narrative. "Personal identity is just that identity presupposed by the unity of the character which the unity of a narrative requires". MacIntyre asks, "In what does the unity of an individual life consist?" And he replies, "[I]ts unity is the unity of a narrative embodied in a single life" (218). However, the idea that personal identity—the self—is somehow dependent on narrative is, as I will show, much more problematic than this easy progression of argument reveals.

Many have followed MacIntyre's lead, both philosophers and psychologists. David Novitz, for example, speaks of "life narratives" and insists that "narrative is integrally involved in our search for a coherent self-image" (1992, 92). Novitz nicely balances anti-realist and realist strands to his thesis. Like MacIntyre, he points up comparisons with literary narratives, happily accepting that "the views that we take of ourselves are constructs, and are invented rather than discovered" (99), and stressing the "fundamental similarities between the creation of works of art . . . and narrative identities" (104). But he also insists that "the facts in terms of which we assess a given life-narrative may be known independently of any specific history or story" and that life narratives "may be shown to be true or false" (101). Novitz in effect pulls back, surely rightly, from the thought that the narratives of our lives are fully fledged fictions.

What should we make of this widely held conception of personal identity as narrative-bound? Novitz's squeamishness about anti-realism seems to get to the heart of it. We have seen how it is illegitimate to conflate narrative with fiction. When we narrate stories about ourselves, we *might* be inventing fictions—people write novels with themselves as characters—but there is no necessity that we do so. We must ask about life narratives what *kind* of narratives they aspire to be. As noted earlier, only when we know that do we know how to assess them. The narrative theory would be exciting and challenging if it were true that we invent ourselves as novelists do fictional characters, defining our identity through our role in elaborately structured plots. Fictional characters *do* owe their identities to narratives at a deep level; what they are is what the narratives say they are (for more on the identity of fictional characters, see Lamarque 2010, ch. 9). But none of the basic premises in, say, MacIntyre's theory implies any such thing about real persons. The truth is more prosaic. We do tell stories about ourselves, but more often than not they are mundane, fragmented, inconsequential and for the most part blandly true rather than grandly inventive.

Psychologists have done an immense amount of experimental work on actual "life narratives", much of it of considerable, if at times prurient, interest.[9] Jerome Bruner, for example, has done detailed analyses of the "spontaneous autobiographies" of ordinary people. This is his overview of what he found:

> As stories of development, these "spontaneous autobiographies" were constituted of smaller stories . . . each of which achieved its significance by virtue of being part of a larger-scale "life." In this respect they shared a universal feature of all narratives. The larger overall narratives were told in easily recognisable genres—the tale of a victim, a *Bildungsroman*, antihero forms, *Wanderung* stories, black comedy, and so on. The storied events that they comprised made sense only in terms of the larger picture. At the center of each account dwelled a protagonist Self in process of construction: whether active agent, passive experiencer, or vehicle of some ill-defined destiny. And at critical junctures, "turning points" emerged, again culturally recognisable, produced almost invariably by an access of new consciousness aroused by victory or defeat, by betrayal of trust, and so on. It soon became apparent not only that life imitated art but that it did so by choosing art's genres and its other devices of storytelling as its modes of expression. (1994a, 120–21)

Bruner's account, of which this is just a snippet, is not without interest, especially in the notion that narrators not only recount but also justify their actions; yet it is hard to find any *deep* truths about the Self or about personal identity emerging. It is important to bear in mind that these ordinary narratives, although "spontaneous" in the sense that they were not prepared or polished for publication, were nonetheless self-conscious and reflective, in response to a request from a university professor. We should be wary to infer from the fact that they were so structured and wide-ranging that they thereby reflect an entirely natural and inevitable activity common to all humans seeking a unified Self. In addition, the use of conventional literary genres as structuring devices speaks less of inventiveness as of cliché and lack of imagination. The question, though, is whether Bruner's experiment or others like it establish any deep connection between personal identity and narrative.

What seriously undermines the narrative theory of personal identity is that only in the rarest of cases—full biographies or autobiographies—do individual narratives offer anything like a comprehensive or even moderately extensive coverage of whole lives. Few people ever attempt to tell the complete story of their lives. Even Bruner's subjects had to truncate their narratives, a fact that itself encouraged simplified patterns. Yet if the unity of a life somehow depends on the unity of a narrative, then most lives will turn out to have no unity because there is no such narrative. But that is a *reductio* because a life is always *someone's* life. The problem stems from the elicit conflating of narrative and life, as we saw earlier. Narratives are stories that only exist when they are told. Without narration there is no narrative. Yet where there is no narrative, it seems illegitimate to infer there is no subject of thought and action. Novitz is well aware of the lack of actual life narratives and somewhat obscurely comes to identify life narratives as "*dispositions* to select, relate, and think of the events of one's life" (1992, 94; italics added; see also Novitz 1987, 227). But a story can hardly be a disposition.

Perhaps two further conflations underlie the mistake of the narrative theory of the Self. The first is between personal identity and self-conception. Telling stories about ourselves might well aid, develop and clarify a *conception* of ourselves as persons of a certain kind or nature: ambitious, strong, shy, introverted or maybe mirroring lives we admire. How we conceive ourselves is to some extent a matter of decision—something we invent as much as discover. But conceiving or thinking of ourselves along certain lines is far from grounding our personal identity in the sense that concerns philosophers, that of identifying an enduring subject of experience across time. Arguably having a self-conception—thinking of oneself as ambitious or extroverted—already presupposes a self in the philosopher's sense.

The second conflation is that of narrative and drama. Drama does not necessarily involve narration, although there might be narrative elements in drama. People often dramatise their lives (or parts of them) in the sense of adopting a persona or playing a role. Such a notion figures integrally in Sartre's notion of "mauvaise foi". But there need be no narrative here, and the relation with personal identity is unclear. Standardly, the distinction between actor and role is secure even if in principle they might merge. Viewing our lives as a drama in which we are the central character might be the nearest we get to a "life narrative"; yet it need not involve narrative at all.

In truth, the most that gets narrated in most lives are life fragments, highly selected and salient incidents. But a narrative fragment, a clip of narration ordering isolated sequences of events, is an impoverished thing indeed and no basis for grand claims about personal identity. In fact, the very theory of narrative undercuts the aspiration of life-wide unity, given that narratives are characterised by their perspectival nature. For important sequences of events, most people have more than one narrative to tell. All of us return to the major events in our lives and recount them over and over in different narratives from different points of view. The whole idea of unity and coherence crumbles away. The more important the event, the more perspectives it invites, thus the more narratives we relate, often in conflict with each other. Novitz recognises the fragmentariness of life narratives and even their formulaic nature: "[F]or the most part our life-narratives are reduced to pat formulae in terms of which we habitually see ourselves". He even suggests that we might abridge our story into succinct summaries, like "I'm a loser" (1992, 93).

But he doesn't realise how damaging this is to his overall theory. Fragments of narrative, sometimes in conflict with each other, are no basis for an account of personal identity or the unity of a life. The impression given by the term "narrative" is of a complete, rounded story with a beginning, middle and end that helps make sense of complex events. The model is historical narrative or the complex narratives of fiction. But personal narratives virtually never attain completeness, closure or unity. Again, a misleading paradigm is invoked. The whole idea of a "life narrative" is far too literary and grandiose. When we run through a sequence of events in our minds, we are seldom constrained by high-minded literary ideals.[10] Even when we do resort to narration, that only means that we give a rough and ready order to our thoughts, although clichéd genres (the victim, the antihero, the loser) might provide rudimentary structure.

Suppose we grant the best case: the reflective person who takes trouble to articulate a narrative about himself encompassing major events in his life. Such a person, we might say, has a conception of himself as living a worthwhile and meaningful life with projects set and goals attained. How important is narrative in this most favourable case? Not very important. It is far from clear that narrative *produces* unity or personal identity. More plausibly, the narrative *presupposes* this unity. Our case envisages a person with a strong sense of self, which is precisely what one might suppose motivates the unified narrative. Those of us without any such self-assurance will hesitate to embark on a grand self-narrative, being too aware of the tensions, inconsistencies and multiple personalities in our lives.

But do we not inevitably assign significance to particular events over others in our lives? Do we not seek out connections between things we say and do which might not be obvious to an outsider? Indeed so. It is just such facts that give the narrative theorist a modicum of plausibility. But again, it amounts to very little. The model of the historian, or particularly the novelist, is inappropriate to capture these weightings and orderings, at least in the context of small-scale structures in people's lives. And in any case, the selections and emphases and omissions might just as well be products of self-deception as of impartial self-analysis. The final card of the narrative theorist is to stress the explanatory value of narratives. This was where MacIntyre began. A narrative can explain why someone acted as he did; it can explain people's values; it can forge connections; it can weigh priorities. But once again, the thought that narrative can have explanatory value, while true, is not especially profound. Narratives can spell out causal sequences and can marshal reasons for actions. This could indeed help explain the events and actions. But the value here lies not in what narrative itself can offer but in the truth of the claims about causes and reasons. If the truth isn't there—perhaps because of self-deception or distortion—then no valid explanation will be forthcoming. Narratives have the right *form* for explanation—this happened because of something else happening—but the form is not enough to secure an actual explanation in particular cases.

CONCLUSION

My intention has not been to dismiss narrative altogether as of interest to philosophers. At most, it has been to put into perspective the enthusiasm for narrative that has been evident among philosophers, literary theorists, psychologists and anthropologists for at least fifty years. Literary narrative is one of the great art forms and rewards careful study; narrative has its place in philosophical writing and is at the very core of history. Nor should we deny the role of narrative in so many aspects of ordinary life. But the very ubiquity of narrative should be the clue to understanding its broad and flexible nature. The minimal conditions for narrative are easily met and turn out to be no more than a formal feature of discourse universally realised. The mistake is to treat some particular modes of narrative, notably novelistic narrative, as archetypal. Narrative is not identical with fiction, and to classify a discourse as narrative has no implications for reference, truth-valuation or any other kinds of value. A narrative must earn the right to be an object of attention; most narratives are ephemeral, insignificant and, in the long term, without interest or value. If we start from that perspective, then we will appreciate all the more the narratives that do reward attention. Those might well be the life narratives of individuals as well as the great novels and the canonical tomes of history. But the former, to match up to the latter, must prove their worth.

NOTES

1. Examples would include Hayden White: "[A]s for the notion of a 'true' *story*, this is virtually a contradiction in terms. *All* stories are fiction" (1989, 27). Or Roy Schafer, a psychoanalyst: "[R]eality is always mediated by narration. Far from being innocently encountered and discovered, it is created in a regulated fashion" (1981, 45). Or Joseph Rouse: "[W]e live within ongoing stories as a condition of being able to tell them" (1990, 188). Or C G Prado: "[N]arratives . . . are not representations at all . . . they themselves constitute what the world is for someone at a given point" (1984, 119). Or Stephen Crites: "[T]he self is a kind of aesthetic construct, recollected in and with the life of experience in narrative fashion" (1986, 162).

2. Even an apparent anti-realist about narrative accepts this condition: "Stories are told or written, not found" (White 1989, 27).

3. Noël Carroll (2001, 126) offers a precise specification of what he takes the required connection to be, although arguably these are stronger conditions than needed for basic narratives:

> (1) the discourse represents at least two events and/or states of affairs (2) in a globally forward-looking manner (3) concerning the career of at least one unified subject (4) where the temporal relations between the events and/or states of affairs are perspicuously ordered, and (5) where the earlier events in the sequence are at least causally necessary conditions for the causation of later events and/or states of affairs (or are contributions thereto).

4. Even in marginal or controversial cases, there is usually agreement whether something is a narrative. Consider the so-called six-word novel attributed to Ernest Hemingway: "For sale: baby shoes, never worn". The compression eliminates core features such as sentence sequences and tensed verbs. But these are implicit, and most people would probably accept that this counts as (an attenuated) narrative.

5. Note that to read for transparency, as discussed in chapter 1, is only to allow for the possibility of alternative access to the same narrative content: in other words, the content is read as not tied so closely to the mode of its presentation (i.e., as not so fine-grained) that the structure of events characterised could only be identified in this way under this perspective.

6. Noël Carroll makes a similar point in speaking of the "inapplicability of the copy ideal of an empiricist view of correspondence truth" (2001, 145).

7. Goodman's irrealist view of "worldmaking" encourages just such a conflation, notably in his insistence on the "fabrication of facts": "Of course, we must distinguish falsehood and fiction from truth and fact. But we cannot, I am sure, do it on the grounds that fiction is fabricated and fact found" (1978, 91).

8. No doubt other kinds of narrative (e.g., history, biography and neighbourhood gossip) are assessed partially on similar criteria, but their conventional aims are not confined to enhancing make-believe over belief.

9. Lieblich and Josselson (1997) cast intriguing light on narratives from unexpected sources: "Israeli ritual bath attendants", "Older Southeast Asian refugee women" and so forth.

10. The imaginative sequences described by simulation theory for predicting or making sense of behaviour are seldom "literary" and as likely to be strings of images as self-conscious narration (see Davies and Stone 1995).

Chapter Four

On the Distance between Literary Narratives and Real-Life Narratives

It is a truth universally acknowledged that great works of literature have an impact on people's lives. Well-known literary characters—Oedipus, Hamlet, Faust, Don Quixote—acquire iconic or mythic status, and their stories, in more or less detail, are revered and recalled often in contexts far beyond the strictly literary. At the level of national literatures, familiar characters and plots are assimilated into a wider cultural consciousness and help define national stereotypes and norms of behaviour. In the English-speaking world, Shakespeare's plays or the novels of Jane Austen, the Brontë sisters, Dickens and Trollope provide imaginative material that reverberates in people's lives every bit as much as do the great historical figures like Julius Caesar, Elizabeth I, Horatio Nelson or Winston Churchill. What is striking is how often fictional characters from the literary tradition—like the well-loved Elizabeth Bennet, Jane Eyre, Oliver Twist, Pip, Tess of the d'Urbervilles—enter readers' lives at a highly personal level. They become, as Martha Nussbaum puts it, our "friends" (1990, 44), and for many readers the lives of these characters become closely entwined with their own. Happy and unhappy incidents in the fictional worlds are held up against similar incidents in the real lives of readers, and such readers take inspiration from the courage, ingenuity or good fortune of their fictional heroines and heroes. Nowhere is it more true that life imitates art.

Works in the canonical literary tradition—more so than merely popular fiction, whose influence is lost over time—are thought to be especially valuable for holding up a mirror to life. Their characters appear richer, more rounded and more finely developed than in lesser productions, their plots better structured and their writing more elevated and elevating. Such works also exemplify the fundamental genres of narrative that are supposed to help structure ordinary lives: from the broad genres of the tragic, comic, epic or romantic to narrower genres of the anti-hero, the picaresque, the noir or the coming of age. It seems natural for people who are telling stories about themselves to take as a model the very works that define the literary tradition, that is, define what stories at their best are like. All this might seem both obvious and innocuous.

But the underlying picture, I maintain, is a serious distortion of what makes literary narratives distinctive and valuable. Closer inspection reveals that the role of fictional characters in literature does not closely mirror the role of real people living real lives. Nor do real-life narratives bear a close relation to literary narratives. It is not just that ordinary lives tend to be more humdrum, less dramatic or less structured. To see literary characters as our friends, as ordinary people like ourselves, their lives as essentially like our lives, is to set aside nearly everything that makes great literature what it is. In effect, it is to ignore all essentially literary qualities and reduce literature to character and plot at the same level of banality as found in the stories we tell of ourselves.[1]

The first inkling that this is the case can be found in the poverty of general knowledge of the great iconic characters. Most people who have heard of Oedipus, Hamlet, Faust or Don Quixote, as in my earlier list, know little more about them than the most rudimentary facts: Oedipus unknowingly killed his father, Hamlet hesitated in avenging his father's murder, Faust made a pact with the devil and Don Quixote tilted at windmills. Such impoverished knowledge should not be mocked, for it provides a core means of identifying iconic characters and serves to locate them in cultural mythology. But it is plain that characters of this kind, as they enter the cultural mainstream, are bare abstractions. Their literary origins are irrelevant and often not known. It makes no difference, for example, which version, if any, of the Faust story underlies this usage. It is the same with the lesser characters mentioned, like Elizabeth Bennet and Oliver Twist; to the extent that they are loved and emulated, they are again mere abstractions far removed from literary detail. A summary of their lives would do just as well as the original novels in capturing what is appealing about them. (The popularity of film versions confirms the point.)

To reduce literary works to abstracted characters and summarised plots is precisely to lose everything that makes them literary in the first place. When literary characters become our friends and offer models for our behaviour, they lose their literary bearings; they cease to be literary. If this is right—and I will offer further arguments for it—then it seems that real-life narratives are far removed from literature per se. The thought that there is something special about the narratives of the canonical works in guiding our lives comes to seem less plausible. The more we try to restore the distinctively literary features of such narratives, the more remote they become from real life.

Indeed, a stronger point can be made. To the extent that literary features are brought to bear on real-life narratives, they have a distorting and pernicious effect on the self-understanding that such narratives are supposed to yield.

LITERATURE AND FICTION

The case that literary works are remote from the narratives of real life rests on the peculiar features of such works. It might be thought that the case cannot get going without a preliminary definition of literature. And that, it might seem, is where the argument gets bogged down right from the start. In fact, I will not attempt to define literature but will rest my argument as far as possible on fairly uncontroversial observations drawn from literary criticism and the ontology and epistemology of fiction.

The first point to make is that "literature" and "fiction" name separate concepts, with different meanings and different extensions (Lamarque and Olsen 1994, ch. 11). Fiction is a species of language use (applied to names, sentences and discourses) and is neutral as to value. Literature, even in the narrowest sense applied to imaginative and creative writing, is a kind of discourse, essentially valued, which affords and invites a distinctive kind of appreciation. Not all literary works are fiction, nor all fictional works literature. It would be wrong to suppose that literary works are merely a subset of fictional works marking off those, for example, that are especially well written or especially admired for other reasons. A work of fiction could reach the highest standards as fiction—say, within a popular genre—without even aspiring to the aims of literature. One condition on literature, which does not apply to fiction per se, is the aspiration to a kind of moral seriousness; a literary work in some way or other must have more to say, of general interest, beyond the particularities of its plot. Literary works are more than examples of good storytelling or fine writing.

Examining the role of character in literary works, we see a principal example of the richer connections between content and mode of presentation. There are two ways in which fictional characters enter the consciousness of readers. One is through the imagination. In what I have called the internal perspective (Lamarque 1996, 12ff, ch. 8)—that is, a perspective internal to a fictional world—characters are imagined to be real humans, speaking, acting and interacting just as ordinary people do. Of course, one must be careful about generalising across genres, for realism is not always a literary aim. But even works that transport us into non-realistic or extra-human realms invite imaginings. The second way is through attention to linguistic modes of presentation; this is a perspective external to fictional worlds, rooted in the real world of artifice, style and narrative technique. As well as imagining characters, readers can become aware of the descriptive means by which the characters are presented. Broadly speaking, it is a characteristic of literary works that they invite attention to their own literary artifice,[2] while genre fiction of a non-literary kind encourages more transparent access to its imagined content.

CHARACTER IDENTITY PRINCIPLE

There is an ontological point about characters near at hand. Their identity conditions are bound up with their modes of presentation. Let us call this the character identity principle:

> *In literary works, character identity is indissolubly linked to character description.*

Part of what this means—the familiar part—is that characters come into being only through being described. They have their origins in narratives. This is a necessary truth, though the scope of the necessity is debatable. It is a matter of contention whether, for example, Emma Bovary might have been created by some author other than Flaubert and even in some other novel than *Madame Bovary* (Lamarque 2010, ch. 9). Note that an Emma Bovary that cuts loose, as it were, from Flaubert can be given only coarse-grained identity conditions of the kind that allow the character of Faust a trans-work identity across its exemplifications in Christopher Marlowe, Johann Wolfgang von Goethe and Thomas Mann. But fictional characters cannot come into being independent of narrative altogether.

Another part of what the character identity principle means is that the manner of character description determines the very nature of the character described. This applies to fine-grained identity conditions, according to which we might say that the Marlowe, Goethe and Mann versions of Faust depict different characters. Characters under these fine-grained conditions are in a special sense perspectival entities.[3] This implies not just that the precise nature of the characters rests on the precision of their identifying descriptions but also, for example, that the descriptions embody points of view on them both physical and evaluative. Take an example from Dickens's *Our Mutual Friend*. When Dickens first introduces the despicable Veneerings, he does so with a well-known flourish both comic and contemptuous:

> Mr and Mrs Veneering were bran-new [*sic*] people in a bran-new house in a bran-new quarter of London. Everything about the Veneerings was spick-and-span new. All their furniture was new, all their friends were new, all their servants were new, their plate was new, their carriage was new, their harness was new, their horses were new, their pictures were new, they themselves were new. . . . [A]ll things were in a state of high varnish and polish. And what was

> observable in the furniture was observable in the Veneerings—the surface smelt a little too much of the workshop and was a trifle sticky. (1964, 20)

The superficiality, the worship of possessions and ostentatious wealth, the shallowness connoted in the very name "Veneering"—these are all intrinsic qualities of the characters themselves. Dickens's judgement of the Veneerings, which he invites us to share (indeed, which we must share if we are to grasp the role of the characters in the novel), is part of the very identity of the characters. It is not as if there is some other perspective on the Veneerings under which they subsist as decent, honest, kindly, altruistic folk who have somehow been falsely captured by the mocking tone of the narrator. The mocking tone, as it were, makes them the characters they are.

If characters are perspectival in this way, then the character identity principle reveals a further important fact about characters which points to something fundamental about literary appreciation. The character descriptions, indissolubly tied to character identity, are seen to have a dual function: a characterising function and a connective or thematic function. The characterising function is simply to provide us with information about the characters: we take it to be true of the Veneerings that everything they own is new. This guides our internal imaginative perspective on them so that when we picture the Veneerings, we picture them as surrounded by brand-new objects shiningly clean. But the mocking tone that informs the description has a wider function in the novel as a whole. It serves to locate the Veneerings in the social scheme of things, to situate them among a cluster of characters, like the Lammles and the Podsnaps, who see no value beyond monetary value. It also sets up a thematic contrast with characters like John Harmon, Eugene Wrayburn and Lizzie Hexam who reject these false values and the social attitudes they engender. The Veneerings are not just people in a world but also elements in an artistic design.

OPACITY PRINCIPLE

In addition to the character identity principle, we should take note of another, related, principle which I will call opacity. According to the opacity principle:

> *In literary works, not only are characters and incidents presented to us but attention is conventionally drawn to the modes of presentation themselves.*

This principle is well known to literary critics and informs critical practice; it will be explored in detail in chapter 8. The principle acknowledges the fact that linguistic resources are not merely contingent elements in literary artifice—rejecting the thought that somehow the very same content might have been presented in other ways—and also what Roman Jakobson called the "palpability of signs" and other structuralists called "foregrounding" (Erlich 1965, 183).

It is a peculiarity of literature, in contrast to fiction per se, that attention is drawn to the connective and thematic functions of character descriptions. Rather than being merely transparent vehicles for prompting imaginings, the descriptions provide a more opaque kind of perspective for observing and making sense of a fictional world. Although, of course, imaginings are prompted by literary works and we are able to picture the goings-on as if they were real events, we find in the literary case that there is a nice interplay between what we imagine and what we notice of the literary artifice that prompts the imagining. At the same time that we picture the Veneerings, we notice the modes in which they are presented to us, particularly the attitudes we are invited to take and the significance of those attitudes in the wider canvas of the novel.

PRINCIPLE OF FUNCTIONALITY

Another familiar principle of literary criticism also encourages the thought that there is more to literary description, be it of character or incident, than the conveying of fictional facts. This concerns the curious role of descriptive detail. We have already seen in the character identity and opacity principles how detail determines identity. But detail also is assigned significance. What operates is a principle of functionality, as follows:

> *It is always reasonable to ask of any detail in a literary work what literary or aesthetic function that detail is performing.*

This principle applies across all the arts. As Roger Scruton has written, "Art provides a medium transparent to human intention, a medium for which the question, Why? can be asked of every observable feature, even if it may sometimes prove impossible to answer" (1983, 117). Take the brief but poignant scene near the beginning of *Tess of the d'Urbervilles* in which Tess's father's horse Prince is killed in an accident on the road. Tess had fallen asleep when driving her carriage and the mail-cart had rammed into her, piercing the horse's heart. This is how the critic Dorothy Van Ghent describes the passage:

> With this accident are concatenated in fatal union Tess's going to "claim kin" of the d'Urbervilles and all the other links in her tragedy down to the murder of Alec. The symbolism of the detail is naïve and forthright to the point of temerity: the accident occurs in darkness and Tess has fallen asleep—just as the whole system of mischances and cross-purposes in the novel is a function

> of psychic and cosmic blindness; she "has put her hand upon the hole"—and the gesture is as absurdly ineffectual as all her effort will be; the only result is that she becomes splashed with blood—as she will be at the end; the shaft pierces Prince's breast "like a sword"—Alec is stabbed in the heart with a knife; with the arousal and twittering of the birds we are aware of the oblivious manifold of nature stretching infinite and detached beyond the isolated human figure; the iridescence of the coagulating blood is, in its incongruity with the dark human trouble, a note of the same indifferent cosmic chemistry that has brought about the accident; and the smallness of the hole in Prince's chest, that looked "scarcely large enough to have let out all that had animated him," is the minor remark of that irony by which Tess's great cruel trial appears as a vanishing incidental in the blind waste of time and space and biological repetition.

Significantly, Van Ghent completes the paragraph by observing the otherwise naturalness of the scene and its description:

> Nevertheless, there is nothing in this event that has not the natural "grain" of concrete fact; and what it signifies—of the complicity of doom with the most random occurrence, of the cross-purposing of purpose in a multiple world, of cosmic indifference and of moral desolation—is a local truth of a particular experience and irrefutable as the experience itself. (1979, 429–30)

We are reminded again of the internal and external perspectives. Imaginatively and sympathetically, the scene of the accident is pictured to be just what it seems, a terrible accident. From the external critical perspective, it serves a narrative function as well, anticipating, with awful foreboding, all the main events to come and assigning weight and significance to them.

Symbolism is a common literary device. The mud and fog at the beginning of *Bleak House*, as every trained reader immediately recognises (Dickens himself rather heavy-handedly spells out the connection with the High Court of Chancery), are more than just passing descriptive detail. Here is how the critic J Hillis Miller interprets the symbolism:

> The mud and fog of the opening paragraph of the novel are not, we can now see, the primeval stuff out of which all highly developed forms evolve. They are the symptoms of a general return to the primal slime, a return to chaos which is going on everywhere in the novel and is already nearing its final end when the novel begins.
>
> The human condition of the characters of *Bleak House* is, then, to be thrown into a world which is neither fresh and new nor already highly organised, but is a world which has already gone bad. (1977, 951–52)

The functionality principle, though, does not relate exclusively to literary symbolism, at least in the narrow sense of the term. Having symbolic significance is only one kind of function—indeed, one kind of significance. Drawing connections across a work is another function of literary detail. The opening scene of *Macbeth*, with the contradictions and confusions of the witches ("Fair is foul and foul is fair"), connects with multiple elements throughout the play, developing what L C Knights has called "the themes of the reversal of values and of unnatural disorder" (1964, 29).

An interesting third function of narrative detail is identified by Roland Barthes in what he calls the "reality effect". Barthes is intrigued by the way that realist novelists, like Flaubert or Balzac, pile up apparently random descriptive detail. In a somewhat laboured manner, he describes it as follows:

> The truth of this illusion is this: eliminated from the realist speech act as a signified of denotation, the "real" returns to it as a signified of connotation; for just when these details are reputed to *denote* the real directly, all that they do—without saying so—is *signify* it; Flaubert's barometer, Michelet's little door finally say nothing but this: *we are the real*; it is the category of "the real" . . . which is then signified; in other words, the very absence of the signified, to the advantage of the referent alone, becomes the very signifier of realism. (1986, 148)

The idea, more plainly put, is that the accumulation of seemingly trivial detail in a literary narrative serves to *signify* (or connote) reality while failing to denote it. This provides a striking contrast between the use of trivial detail in nonfictional narratives. Where the details actually *do* describe the real, where there is no "absence of the signifier" or no "referential illusion", there can be no "reality effect". What Barthes sees as definitive of literary realism is, curiously, missing—and impossible—in the case in which facts alone are described. The piling up of detail might have the same impact in the two cases—enriching the atmosphere—but they operate, if Barthes is right, under almost exactly opposite narrative constraints.

TELEOLOGY PRINCIPLE

A fourth principle concerns the kinds of explanation available to incident and action in a literary work. In the real world of fact and action, explanation is causal or rational. To explain why something happened, we offer causes or an agent's reasons. To the extent that we imagine, from the internal point of view, the events in a literary work, these are the explanations we reach for. What caused Tess's accident? The answer, within the fictional world, is that she fell asleep and was run into by the mail-cart. Why did Tess kill Alec d'Urberville? The answer, as one critic writes, is that it was "an act of desperate assertion which places Tess in the line of folk heroines who kill because they can no longer bear outrage" (Howe 1979, 451). But there is a literary mode of explanation quite different from the causal and the rational.

As the critic just cited goes on to say of the killing, "[I]t signifies an end to Tess's journey"; it is "traditional, part of the accepted heritage that has come down to us through popular and literary channels". In other words, the killing has a conventional function in the structure of the plot. It happens, we might say, because it has to happen in a story of this kind. That explanation is of a radically different kind from an explanation in terms of agents' reasons.[4]

A principle operates here that I will call the teleology principle, as follows:

> *In literary works, the explanation of why an episode occurs as it does and where it does often centres on the contribution the episode makes to the completed artistic structure.*

Thus, in the reverse order of normal causal explanation, we might explain a prior event in terms of a later event. Oedipus's fateful remark early on in Sophocles's play that those who have brought disaster on Thebes will suffer a terrible fate acquires its literary significance and purpose from the revelations at the end of the play. In a different example, consider how the word "explains" is used by this critic, speaking of the character Frank Churchill in Jane Austen's *Emma*:

> *Frank is important because he explains Emma herself.* He embodies the vital difference between the artistic principles governing Emma—foolish conduct resulting from faulty judgement, but from motives fundamentally irreproachable, invariably honest and as frank as possible—and his own downright wrong actions causing deliberate and consistent deceit, which produce some of the same effects as Emma's own. (Craik 1972, 445; italics added)

Again, just like the Veneerings in the earlier example, Frank Churchill is not just a person in an imaginary world; he is also an element in a structured plot. His actions and failings gain their significance in contrast to superficially similar failings in Emma herself—tactlessness and lack of self-awareness—though the implied judgements are different. It is characteristic of literary criticism to explain the artistic role of such elements: the explanation is a kind of teleology. Another critic notes the role played by the married pairs at the end of the novel:

> The young generation poses a challenge to the moral order of Highbury, and the book ends when the challenge is fought off, when the young are married and have been assimilated by the mature generation. The story, of course, is first and foremost Emma's story, but she is flanked by important characters. Frank Churchill and Jane Fairfax, Mr Elton and Augusta Hawkins, Harriet Smith and Robert Martin, all these couples form important variations on the theme of assimilation. (Olsen 1977, 13)

THEMATIC PRINCIPLE

The reference to variations on a theme brings me to my final, again familiar, principle, in literary appreciation. The principle concerns literary themes, perhaps the most important factor in characterising the literary realm. Themes are conceptions that bind works together, encapsulating a work's significance and what I call its moral seriousness. They can be identified under different kinds of description, including stand-alone predicates like "love" or "despair", noun phrases like "the conflict between private and social duty" or whole sentences like "human life is governed by forces beyond an individual's control". The presence of sentential characterisations of themes raises questions about literary truth, but that is not at issue here (see chapter 7). Themes can be of more or less universal interest. Sometimes they are merely local: "the radicalisation of British universities in the 1960s". Sometimes they are of more timeless human concern: "intimations of mortality". Themes can be stated directly in a work itself, as in Gloucester's agonised cry in *King Lear*: "As flies to wanton boys are we to the gods; / They kill us for their sport". Or they might be elicited in an interpretation by a critic. In an essay on "private vision and social order" in Charlotte Brontë's *Jane Eyre*, a critic writes:

> There can be no doubt . . . that the reduction of the world to the terms of a single vision, no matter how moral its content or how sanctified its motives, is attended by the most dreadful violence. The power of the "I" of this novel is secret, undisclosable, absolute. . . . The violence with which it simplifies the differences labelled "inferior," "poorer," "richer," "better," or "higher," the killing and maiming and blinding which are the consequences of its dialectic, tell us as clearly as fiction can that even fantasy must subdue a real world. Jane Eyre's vision masters her world, but the price of her mastery is absolute isolation. When she knows her world completely she is out of it by the most rigorous necessity. I know no other work that so effectively demonstrates the demon of the absolute. (Craig 1971, 478)

This critic starts his thematic exploration of private visions in *Jane Eyre* from the premise that "no heroine dreams more often or more successfully than the heroine of this strange romance" (Craig 1971, 472). That premise, in turn, is supported by direct reference to passages in which dreams and visions are described.

Thus we can formulate a thematic principle:

> *Appreciation of literary works as literary works is an appreciation of how their subject acquires significance and unity under thematic interpretation.*

A theme in a literary work is an organising principle that brings unity and significance to the work's subject. The subject is in effect the material that a reader is invited to imagine. It is a characteristic of literary works that they invite thematic interpretation. A reader looks for internal connectedness through overarching themes. A good literary work is one that both shows a consonance of subject and theme and provides an illuminating development of themes of broad human interest.

REAL-LIFE NARRATIVES

Such is my all-too-brief exploration of some salient features of literary works and their content. In this final section, we can return to our original question concerning the relation of real-life narratives to literary narratives. I have deliberately quoted frequently in the foregoing discussion from literary critics going about their business. What is notable from these familiar kinds of comments conventionally associated with literary narratives is how utterly inappropriate most of them would be if applied to real-life narratives.

What do I mean by real-life narratives? At the most formal extreme would be biographies or autobiographies of real people. These can look most like literary narratives and, of course, in the broad sense of "literature"—belles-lettres or fine writing—they can be classed as literary. They exhibit the same kind of completeness and "closure" of certain kinds of novels, they often yield broad themes and can be given genre classifications like tragedy or romance. It seems clear, though, that they still differ in significant ways from literary fictional narratives. I will return to them as we proceed. Other real-life narratives are much less formally constructed. Yet these more casual narratives are thought to epitomise those real-life narratives that draw inspiration from the literary realm. These are narratives or narrative fragments that, on familiar accounts, supposedly help structure our lives and ground a coherent sense of ourselves. They might be snatches of memory or summaries of significant events or tales of self-justification.

But as I suggested at the beginning, I don't think that these narratives either owe much to literature or are similar to literature (or at least literature *taken as literature*). We might well abstract characters and incidents from the great works and hold them up as mirrors to our lives. Indeed, it is common to turn the names of iconic characters into general terms: someone can be a Faust or an Oedipus. To be a Faust is merely to be someone who, metaphorically, sells his soul or makes a pact with the devil. But these abstracted and etiolated entities have little to do with the original literary narratives from which they are derived. Just how remote are the humdrum narratives of real life from potential literary antecedents can be shown from the inapplicability of our five principles. I will briefly comment on each.

The character identity principle, which links character identity to character description, immediately shows the gulf between fiction and reality. No real person derives his identity from how he is described, nor is a real person perspectival in the sense outlined earlier. No doubt there is a privileged first-person perspective possessed by each individual. But this determines special epistemic access, not a special kind of being; it is epistemological not ontological. Mr and Mrs Veneering, in contrast, come into being *under a description.* The narrator's perspective on them, including the negative value judgement, is not just one among possible perspectives; rather, it is definitive in determining the kind of characters they are. If nothing else, this is a simple consequence of the fact that fictional characters are created. It is absurd to suppose that a real person exists "under a description". Of course, people take on roles, so we can say that under the description "mayor of Middletown", Smith is the official representative of the city, but no one would suppose that Smith's very identity as a person rests on that description. It can only be a contingent fact that Smith became mayor. Narratives about people can be true or false, accurate or inaccurate, but there is no limit to the number of possible narratives about any one person. Truth and accuracy are constrained by factors independent of narrative. One of the more obscurantist aspects of narrative theory is the suggestion that even real-life narratives serve an identity-defining function exactly comparable to that applied to fictional characters. The fashionable idea that personal identity resides in the narratives we tell about ourselves—with the implication that without the narratives we would somehow lack identity—is shown to be an absurdity, in its extreme form, when we bring to mind the literary case in which strong perspectival identity really does obtain.

The opacity principle, in which attention to literary works is conventionally directed to modes of presentation as much as to the material presented, again distances real-life narratives from literary ones. Simple narratives concerning real life will normally aim for high degrees of transparency of transmission, offering up facts, as it were, "unvarnished", even if the storytellers are not entirely indifferent to narratives modes. With biographies and autobiographies, it will not be uncommon for readers to attend, and be invited to attend, to the narrative vehicle. This, though, is largely dictated by broader literary concerns with fine writing and stylistic effect. Like all fact-stating discourses, biographies aim to transmit information and are primarily constrained by "getting it right". What this means is that there are natural limits to the opacity desirable or possible in such discourses. Too much opacity—or strictly too much focus on opacity in reading—will frustrate pragmatic discursive purposes. Therein lies the crucial difference. In literary works, opacity is an asset—it is sought, and it enriches character identity—while in referential discourses opacity is a weakness, to be minimised, and merely clouds personal characterisation.

Functionality in literature—the idea that detail bears a functional role—has an analogue in real-life narratives but should not be confused with it. The analogue is a principle of selectivity which operates in all narrative. Of detail in all narrative, it can be asked: Why was that detail selected? Immediately, a difference between fictional and nonfictional narrative is apparent. In nonfictional narrative, detail is *selected* from preexisting facts; in fictional narrative, detail is *created*. Among principles of selection are relevance, significance and interest. Among principles of creation are artistic purpose and thematic connectedness. We saw that one artistic purpose might be Barthes's "reality effect". The fact that detail can be said to acquire "significance" in each case should not conceal the difference between significance conceived as interest and significance conceived as bearing meaning.

In the literary case, but not the real-life case, detail is significant for conveying meaning. When Tess is first introduced in Hardy's novel, as a young girl in a May Day parade, she, like all the other girls, is wearing white, but unlike the others Tess has a red ribbon in her hair. No further reference is made to this ribbon. But in the literary context, according to the functionality principle, it is legitimate to ask what function that tiny detail is performing. Here is one suggestion: If the white dresses connote virginity and innocence, the redness of the ribbon has other connotations heralding events to come; it is the colour of blood, it connotes sensuousness and sin, in the seventeenth century the scarlet letter A was pinned to adulterers (a connection with Hawthorne's novel *The Scarlet Letter*, from 1850) and so forth. If this were a real-life narrative, what matters primarily is that the detail be accurate. It might be selected in a narrative to suggest the connotations mentioned, but the fact itself could bear no such intrinsic meaning.

One serious danger in modelling real-life narratives on literary ones is that a kind of mysticism is encouraged which assigns meanings to facts in the world. A misplaced functionality might encourage this but also, and worse, a misplaced teleology. The teleology principle in literature seeks explanations of literary events in their contribution to artistic structure. When real-life narratives take on the appearance of artistic structures—and again biographies and autobiographies sometimes aspire to this—they can easily foster the illusion of seeing lives themselves as works of art. Narratives are dangerous and distorting when they appear to offer false explanations: "that first meeting was no coincidence, it was meant to happen", "the seeds of a tragic life were there from the beginning" and so on. Narratives find patterns in people's lives and give structure. There is nothing wrong with that. But the literary model, in which patterns are deliberately created and can determine (and thus explain) fictional content, is entirely inappropriate for narratives of real lives. Explanations for nonfictional events must stay in the realm of causes and reasons. Nothing in the real world happens because some structured design determines that it must happen.

Finally, the literary critical search for unifying themes can also find analogues in real-life narratives. After all, biographies can exhibit familiar themes of unrequited love, corrupting power or unrestrained ambition. But the central point that has been at the heart of all our deliberations on the literary principles applies here, too—namely, that literary works are finely wrought artistic structures affording a special kind of internal connectedness. The consonance of subject and theme, which I described earlier as a literary value, is an end in itself in a way that cannot be applicable to narratives that have the further purposes of describing and explaining the lives of real individuals. To think otherwise is to aestheticise, if not fictionalise, real lives. To study someone's life, or one's own, primarily to see how factual detail coheres under some overarching theme is to direct attention away from the underlying explanations of that person's actions. Maybe some biographies or autobiographies aspire to the status of novels and explore literary themes in a comparable manner. But the very eccentricity of this—and the dangers it brings in accuracy and truth-telling—shows that this is not a model that captures the essence of the real-life narrative.

We have come a long way. I hope to have shown by identifying familiar principles of literary narratives how different they are from the narratives we tell about ourselves. If we take, as it is commonly supposed we do take, the great literary works to be models for our self-directed narratives, we are prone to two serious mistakes. The first is the more serious because it is potentially dangerous: to suppose that our own life narratives are mini-works of literature, complying with the principles of literary appreciation. It is not the hubris of this that matters but the false image of ourselves as kinds of fictional characters whose identity rests on narrative description and whose actions are explicable in functional, teleological or thematic ways. The second mistake moves in the opposite direction: to suppose that literary works are simply stories about people like you and me, a species of real-life narratives. Under this tendency, we think of fictional characters as our "friends" and we sometimes model ourselves on them. But literary characters, as our principles show, are quite different from us, both ontologically and epistemically. They move in a world of artifice and structure, and their actions and very identity are subject to principles that, again, have no application to the world the rest of us inhabit. In being swept up in narrative fever, we must beware of running radically different kinds of narratives together.

NOTES

1. To use the terminology of "opacity" and "transparency", introduced in chapter 1, what is happening is that transparent readings are supplanting opaque readings. What this means is that character and plot become detached from their fine-grained specification in the original works and loose summaries become substitutable for the works themselves; this is a sign of transparency because the content of the works is taken to be accessible to multiple ways and only loosely tied to the descriptive modes of presentation which initially served to constitute the content. It was argued in chapter 1 that it is a feature of a "literary" reading of a work that the

work is read opaquely with special attention directed to the fine-grained delineation of character and incident.

2. Again, this is the kind of "opaque" reading characterised in detail in chapter 8.

3. See chapter 8.

4. J David Velleman has characterised another species of explanation, beyond the purely causal, in narrative based on narrative's "power to initiate and resolve an emotional cadence in the audience" (2003, 18). Although this kind of explanation is different from the one here alluded to, in terms of genre conventions, nevertheless it might seem that there is some relation. Genre conventions (e.g., in tragedy) might be thought of as practice-based realisations of more basic psychological responses involving emotional resolutions in stories.

Chapter Five

Fiction and the Nonfiction Novel

The border between fiction and nonfiction is full of intriguing curiosities, but the narrative theorist must tread with care. It would be a mistake to conclude too hastily that because of shifting ground and difficult cases the distinction itself is a mere illusion. Publishers and bookshop managers on the whole have a robust sense of a fiction/nonfiction divide if only for the pragmatic reason that they have to parade their offerings in catalogues and on bookshelves. Nor should we dismiss this circumstance as merely superficial, for how a book is marketed determines to a considerable extent how it is read.

But did American readers of Thomas Keneally's *Schindler's Ark* (1982) read it differently from British readers? Perhaps. In America, it was published as nonfiction (entitled *Schindler's List*), and in Britain as fiction; indeed, in Britain it won the Booker Prize for fiction. On the other hand, Stephen Spielberg's film version of the book would surely, on both sides of the Atlantic, count as fiction—albeit based on a true story—rather than documentary. A stranger case is that of the autobiography of Forrest Carter, *The Education of Little Tree*, published in 1976, telling the story of the author's upbringing by Cherokee Indian grandparents. The book rose high in the *New York Times* nonfiction list, selling hundreds of thousands of copies by the early 1990s to a readership moved by its insider's account of a simple life in tune with nature. In 1991, however, the true author was exposed as Asa Carter—segregationist, ex–Ku Klux Klan member, Southern racist—who had written speeches for Governor George Wallace, and with only minimal connections to the Cherokees. The book became the first in the history of the *New York Times* list to be moved from the nonfiction to the fiction grid.

Other examples from the borderlands come flooding to mind, so it is worth trying to bring some order to the proceedings and sketch at least a rough-and-ready classification of types. I make no claim to exhaustiveness in the classification, or watertightness, for I am interested not in taxonomy for its own sake but in philosophical reflection on a concept (that of fiction). Indeed, the leakiness of the categories around the edges and the inevitable uncertainties in some cases about what item belongs in what category should, if anything, sharpen up our intuitions about the underlying distinctions. The types identified seem to call for different kinds of explanation, and that will be a useful point of departure for the philosophical discussion. Although each case raises questions about the nature of fiction and its relation to nonfiction, it should not be assumed that there is necessarily doubt about whether particular examples are fiction. In many cases, there is no doubt at all. The idea is to identify fictions that, for whatever reason, look like nonfictions and nonfictions that, for whatever reason, look like fictions.

A PROVISIONAL TYPOLOGY

Type A: Paradigmatic Fictional Novels

These are paradigmatic works of fiction that by all appearances look like works of nonfiction. They are important because they go back to the origins of the novel in English, and there is now a strong body of theory, both historical and literary critical, accounting for precisely why they should appear as they do.[1] Typical examples would be Daniel Defoe's *Robinson Crusoe* and *Moll Flanders* and Samuel Richardson's *Pamela* and *Clarissa*. It might confuse matters to include Henry Fielding's *Tom Jones* because Fielding is far too self-conscious a storyteller to sustain the impression that what is being narrated is pure fact. Defoe, in contrast, famously goes out of his way to develop the conceit that what he presents is a true "history", and Richardson's use of the epistolary form enhances the impression of nonfiction. The realist novel, in a tradition that runs through Smollett, Balzac, Dickens, Trollope, Conan Doyle, up to, say, Evelyn Waugh and Kingsley Amis, has always been marked by the appearance of factual reportage.[2] However, the status of these novels as fiction has rarely been questioned, nor would many readers be misled on this score. The characters and incident are, for the most part, entirely imaginary or, in cases like *Robinson Crusoe*, based loosely on actual events. We shall see, though, that the devices of the realist novel of type A have been adopted in other contexts in which the fiction/nonfiction distinction is far from clear-cut.

Type B: Historical Fiction

These are cases of historical fictions based in a much more systematic way on fact and for the most part involving real historical personages. The genre is older than the novel and could be traced back to classical Greek tragedy.

Aristotle claimed that "the finest tragedies are always on the story of some few houses, on that of Alemeon, Oedipus, Orestes, Meleager, Thyestes, Telephus, or any others that may have been involved, as either agents or sufferers, in some deed of horror" (*Poetics*, 1453[a], 7, trans. Bywater). He clearly took these families to be real and the stories true, even though he admitted, and made much of, the necessary artifice in the structure of the plots. If it seems too tendentious at this point to include Greek drama in the category of historical fiction, on the grounds that the Greeks didn't possess a sufficiently well-developed conception of fiction, then we can readily find our paradigms elsewhere. The modern genre of the historical novel probably began with Walter Scott's *Waverley* (1814), but the genre's diversity would be illustrated by including Leo Tolstoy's *War and Peace*, Georgette Heyer's Regency romances, Gore Vidal's *Burr*, and Alexander Solzhenitsyn's *August 1914*. To differentiate type A and type B cases, we need a distinction between a novel's being substantially *about* a real person or historical event and a novel's being more incidentally *based on* some actual person or event.[3] The distinction I have in mind is that between, on the one hand, the relation between *War and Peace* and Napoleon's invasion of Russia or *August 1914* and Russia's role in the First World War and, on the other, that between *Robinson Crusoe* and Alexander Selkirk or the Sherlock Holmes stories and Dr Joseph Bell. In the former cases, an adequate understanding and appreciation of the novels demands recognition of, and reflection on, the historical setting, while in the latter case a literary assessment does not rest, in any essential way, on the works' relations to their original inspiration. Few, if any, novels are not based in some way on actual people and events, but that does not make them *ipso facto* instances of type B.

Type C: Moral or Philosophical Fictions

Here we have cases of fictions with a central concern for "truth" but not necessarily involving the historical dimension of type B. It is in virtue of their overriding concern with a moral, philosophical or political vision that this nonfictional aspect of such works can seem to dominate the fictional aspect. Simple cases might be Jesus Christ's parables, Aesop's fables, *Everyman* (the fifteenth-century morality play) or John Bunyan's *Pilgrim's Progress*; more complex cases might be Rousseau's *Émile*, Voltaire's *Candide* or Samuel Johnson's *Rasselas*. There are fictional characters in these works and for the most part made-up stories, but the focus of interest seems to be more on the ideas conveyed, the moral or philosophical principles implied, than features of plot or character development. Works of type C are fictions that are most likely to be discussed or cited outside a narrowly literary context. Admittedly, type C is problematic in many respects, partly because there are those who assume a core value in all literary works to be the presentation of truths, partly because the presentation of truths is a sliding scale. Most fictions can be said to imply some attitude towards the real world, and interest in fiction is often centred on perceived connections with ordinary life. Soap operas, romances, satires, science fiction, detective stories, spy thrillers and ballads are often judged for their trueness to life and the light they shed on reassuringly familiar aspects of the world. On a more solemn level, philosophers have sought philosophical insight from literary works, even if those works are not ostensibly in the business of conveying a message. Martha Nussbaum (1990) looks to the novels of Henry James to supplement moral philosophy, and Stanley Cavell (1987) sees in Shakespearean tragedy a contribution to debates on scepticism. However, it would not be helpful to extend type C too broadly. In paradigm cases, the primary aim is to use fiction for an essentially nonfictional purpose, making the former subordinate to the latter, although without forfeiting the status of fiction. There is a sense in which *Émile* is recognisably a philosophical fiction in a way that *The Golden Bowl* is not, and Aesop's fables are moral tales in a way that P G Wodehouse stories are not. However, we might want to include in type C: satires such as *Gulliver's Travels*, poems such as T S Eliot's "The Love Song of J. Alfred Prufrock" and novels like Flaubert's *L'Éducation sentimentale*.

Type D: Nonfiction in a Fictional Frame

We now move to ostensibly nonfictional works which nevertheless have a strong element of fiction. It is interesting how close these cases can come to type C yet without simply collapsing into that type. Obvious examples would be philosophical dialogues, like Plato's *Republic* or the *Symposium* or Hume's *Dialogues on Natural Religion* or Berkeley's *Three Dialogues Between Hylas and Philonous*. The idea that these are direct reports of actual conversations is no more credible than that *Moll Flanders* is an autobiography. The protagonists are fictional characters, or at least, in Plato's case, fictionalised versions of real people, and it can be safely assumed the conversations never took place as reported. Yet it would be eccentric to classify these philosophical dialogues as works of fiction—it is not something that publishers or bookshop managers would do. What makes them close to type C is that the fictional frame is subordinate to the philosophical content, but it nevertheless seems *more* subordinate than in the paradigm type C cases, in which fictionality is something more than an incidental device. It is *possible* to take a literary interest in the philosophical dialogues, although this intuitively seems less of a *requirement* than taking such an interest in *Pilgrim's Progress* or *Candide*. Philosophers present their ideas in all manners of ways, by no means restricted to expository prose and analytic argument. The philosopher Daniel Dennett (1978) has a well-known essay, exploring ideas of personal identity, entirely in the form of a fictional story. And most of the essays in *The Mind's I: Fantasies and Reflections on Self and Soul*, edited by Douglas Hofstadter and Daniel Dennett, are fictions of one sort or another even though the purpose of the volume is clearly philosophical. In philosophy, the use of the "thought experiment" is commonplace—the prince and the cobbler (Locke 1979, bk. II, ch. xxvii), fission and fusion in personal identity (Parfit 1984), brains in a vat (Putnam 1981, ch. 1), the Chinese room (Searle 1980), the trolley problem (Thomson 1976), Jim and the Indians (Smart and Williams 1973, 98–99) and many more. These are all species of fiction, invented for philosophical ends. The status of other philosophical works, such as Nietzsche's *Thus Spake Zarathustra*, Jostein Gaarder's *Sophie's World* and Robert Pirsig's *Zen and the Art of Motorcycle Maintenance*, is not so clear, and these works genuinely hover between types C and D, in the sense that they could be viewed either as philosophical works with a fictional frame or as fictional works with a philosophical theme.

Type E: Paradigmatic Nonfiction Narratives

It would be helpful at this point to introduce a contrastive category made up of those works which actually *are* what the works in type A (or even type B) purport to be—namely, memoirs, autobiographies, histories, collections of letters, published diaries, reminiscences, travelogues and eye-witness accounts. What they have in common is that they are narratives, stories told from a first- or third-person perspective, about events that actually took place and are asserted by the author to have taken place. Just as cases of type A are paradigmatic of the fictional, so type E cases are paradigmatic of the nonfictional. What makes the matter intriguing in this investigation is that types A and E can often be indistinguishable from each other in *appearance*—in terms of their formal or rhetorical qualities or their qualities as *narratives*. Yet it is also important to observe that readers seldom mistake these two types, no doubt, again, due to guidance from publishers and booksellers. When they do, as in the case of *The Education of Little Tree*, there is a sense of disorientation, not to mention outrage and moral indignation. Those who fled New York upon hearing Orson Welles's radio broadcast of *The War of the Worlds* probably looked back on the episode with a degree of embarrassment. Type E can range from relatively straightforward historical narratives, exemplified by Arthur Bryant or David Starkey, through biographies like Elizabeth Longford's *Wellington*, the diaries of Scott of the Antarctic or Antony Beevor's *Stalingrad*, to more complex works like de Quincey's *Confessions of an English Opium-Eater*, George Orwell's *Homage to Catalonia* or D H Lawrence's *Etruscan Places*. In other words, they might be more, or less, self-consciously *literary*, in a sense that we will return to later, but their status as nonfiction is reasonably secure.

Type F: The Nonfiction Novel and New Journalism

Finally, we come to cases central to our enquiry, which perhaps seem most puzzling for the fiction/nonfiction distinction, and for which the term "faction" has been coined. It is only by locating this class in the context of types A to E that we can get a clearer conception of its status. It is not entirely certain who coined the term "faction", but it was Truman Capote who introduced the expression "nonfiction novel" to describe his *In Cold Blood: A True Account of a Multiple Murder and Its Consequences* (1966), and it seems likely that "faction" gained currency shortly after that and in the light of it. It might help to subdivide type F into those cases most naturally falling under the heading "nonfiction novel" and those cases—usually shorter, occasional pieces appearing in newspapers or magazines—for which the term "New Journalism", made popular by Tom Wolfe (1973), is more readily applicable. Admittedly, Wolfe himself would want to include the nonfiction novel under New Journalism, and it might be that this distinction rests on little more than narrative length and is akin to a distinction between novel and short story. Nothing of theoretical importance hangs on dividing things up this way. However, the term "novel" does not apply across the board, and the very idea of a "nonfiction novel" has a provocative and paradoxical ring which inevitably catches the attention of the theorist of fiction, more than does "New Journalism".

Nonfiction novels, in the mode of *In Cold Blood*, would include the following: Norman Mailer's *The Executioner's Song*, on a theme similar to Capote's, and *Armies of the Night*, about an anti-war demonstration in 1968 (subtitled "The Novel as History; History as the Novel"); Tom Wolfe's own *The Electric Kool-Aid Acid Test*, about the psychedelic movement, *Radical Chic & Mau-Mauing the Flak Catchers*, about black-white confrontations, and *The Right Stuff*, about training American astronauts; Joe McGinnis's *The Selling of the President*, about Nixon's 1968 campaign; and Gay Talese's *Honor Thy Father*, about the Mafia. Perhaps Keneally's *Schindler's Ark* belongs in type F and also Simon Schama's *Dead Certainties*. Less clear candidates, by no means ruled out, would be Ernest Hemingway's *Death in the Afternoon*, George Orwell's *Down and Out in Paris and London*, James Fox's *White Mischief* and the anonymously published *Primary Colors*, although the authors of these works, except for the latter, would be unlikely to describe them as "novels".

New Journalism, in the form of shorter pieces written for newspapers and magazines, is characterised by vivid, usually first-person, descriptions of specific events or encounters written and published shortly afterwards. The style now has become mainstream, and it is common to find articles in popular news magazines, for example, starting a serious news report with a personalised vignette, of this kind: "Joe Smith, in a quiet street in the Bronx, first heard the shooting as he sipped his morning coffee. . . ." This is a watered-down version of a style pioneered in the early 1960s in US publications like *Esquire* or *New York*, written by journalists such as Gay Talese, Jimmy Breslin and, of course, Tom Wolfe himself. The anthology *The New Journalism* contains a piece by the English journalist Nicholas Tomalin from the British *Sunday Times* entitled "The General Goes Zapping Charlie Cong", in which Tomalin gives a horrifically vivid account—complete with laconic and violent dialogue—of a sortie he flew in the Vietnam War with a US General, aiming to clear some Vietcong from a road in the jungle. It begins, "After a light lunch last Wednesday, General James F. Hollingsworth, of Big Red One, took off in his personal helicopter and killed more Vietnamese than all the troops he commanded". Wolfe describes the piece as having "the most astonishing impact in England, creating for English readers the emotional reality of the war" (1973, 197).

THE DISTINCTION BETWEEN FICTION AND NONFICTION

Does the existence of "faction" or the "nonfiction novel" cast doubt on the distinction between fiction and nonfiction? I think in the end it does not, but it does force the theorist of fiction to look hard at the basis of that distinction and to ponder where in the spectrum of narrative prose such writing properly belongs. Rather than start the enquiry with a definition of fiction, it would be more illuminating to let a definition, or at least a conception, of fiction emerge from consideration of the different aspects brought to the surface by reflection on the complex relations between types A to F.

A good starting point would be the expression "nonfiction novel". A simple observation might be that "nonfiction" designates the content, while "novel" designates the form or style or techniques employed. Setting aside for the time being the idea of nonfictional content, what can be said about the techniques which justify the term "novel"? Helpfully, Tom Wolfe spells it out for us, listing four devices learnt from realist fiction:

1. The first is "scene by scene construction, telling the story by moving from scene to scene and resorting as little as possible to sheer historical narrative".
2. The second is the recording of dialogue, which "establishes and defines character more quickly and effectively than any other single device" (1973, 31).
3. The third involves the first-person point of view, "presenting every scene to the reader through the eyes of a particular character, giving the reader the feeling of being inside the character's mind and experiencing the emotional reality of the scene as he experiences it".

4. The fourth is "the recording of everyday gestures, habits, manners, customs, styles of furniture, clothing, decoration, styles of traveling, eating, keeping house, modes of behaving toward children, servants, superiors, inferiors, peers, plus the various looks, glances, poses, styles of walking and other symbolic details that might exist within a scene". (32)

It is striking, if not surprising, how closely these devices echo the descriptions given by Ian Watt in characterising the emergence of the realist novel in the early eighteenth century. Watt identifies as typical features: the rejection of traditional plots, the "individualization of . . . characters and detailed presentation of their environment", a "causal connexion operating through time" and "attention to the description of milieu . . . [and] solidity of setting" (1957, ch. 1). The close relation between New Journalist writing and, as it were, old-fashioned literary realism is not surprising and is directly acknowledged by Wolfe. Indeed, Wolfe accounts for the rise and appeal of New Journalism in terms of a reaction away from modernist, anti-realist developments in the novel, or what he calls "mythic" fiction—exemplified by the work of Samuel Beckett, Harold Pinter, Franz Kafka, Hermann Hesse, Jorge Luis Borges—in which "characters have no background, no personal history, are identified with no social class . . . and act out their fates in a locale that has no place name" (1973, 41).

On closer inspection, however, the relation between New Journalism (i.e., type F writing) and classical literary realism (i.e., type A) is highly problematic, *for the aims of each are almost exactly opposite*. The novelistic style of type A, epitomised by Defoe and Richardson, was motivated by a self-conscious imitation of type E writing (i.e., straightforward histories, autobiographies, epistolary correspondence, memoirs). The aim was to disguise the obviously fictional elements, the justification being that anything too overtly fictional would not be taken sufficiently seriously by its readership. Thus did Richardson write to Bishop Warburton expressing his reluctance to use the preface written by the bishop for *Clarissa* (a preface that called attention to the work's fictional nature):

> Will you, good Sir, allow me to mention, that I could wish that the *Air* of Genuineness had been kept up, tho' I want not the Letters to be *thought* genuine; only so far kept up, I mean, as that they should not prefatically be owned *not* to be genuine: and this for fear of weakening their Influence where any of them are aimed to be exemplary; as well as to avoid hurting that kind of Historical Faith which Fiction itself is generally read with, tho' we know it to be Fiction.[4]

The one thing that the early realists did not want was for their works to look like works of fiction; the appearance of being something other than fiction was the principal motivation behind their chosen techniques.

In contrast, the avowed motivation of the nonfiction novel, type F, is precisely to try to imitate type A—in other words, to have all the appearance of being fiction. This presumably is the point (or one point) of using the term "novel". Furthermore, and ironically, given the pains that the early realists took to hide the fictionality of their works so that they might be taken seriously, the thought motivating the nonfiction novelists was that they would be taken *more* seriously and have more of an impact if they could make their writing seem like novels or short stories. So, in a nutshell, while type A authors tried to imitate type E authors, type F authors tried to imitate type A authors, precisely to *avoid* being like type E.

There are further twists still. We might expect the New Journalists to choose the term "novel" because of qualities peculiar to fictional narrative. They clearly saw themselves as using distinctively "novelistic" techniques. However, the techniques listed by Wolfe, as mentioned previously, are not peculiar to novels. Just such techniques can be found in any vivid narration, from the pub raconteur to the travel writer to the lively autobiographer to the impassioned letter writer. Indeed, it is for that reason that the techniques were adopted by the early realists who after all were seeking to imitate just such modes of narration—and to get away from more stylised, traditional literary forms. If we are looking for novelistic techniques that are truly *sui generis*, we should look not to the realists, who try to disguise their fictions, but to those writers who draw attention to their writing *as fiction*. And the obvious models to turn to would be the very novelists apparently scorned by Tom Wolfe and his comrades—that is, the modernists, the avant-garde, the stream-of-consciousness writers, the *non-realists*. If we want to find narration that could *only* be novelistic, without even the pretence of being anything else, we should not turn to Defoe, Richardson or P G Wodehouse but to Beckett, James Joyce, Alain Robbe-Grillet, Christine Brooke-Rose or Italo Calvino. The prose of the latter group is studiedly novelistic, constantly foregrounding its own experimental and *sui generis* devices. Notice that the techniques of type F writing also help to draw attention to its own peculiarity, but the peculiarity in this case rests on a contrast with norms of journalistic reporting. The very same techniques in the realist novel do not serve to draw attention to themselves; indeed, they have the opposite effect, disguising fictionality, blending in with familiar forms of narration.

There is, then, to say the least, something tendentious about using the term "novel" in the expression "nonfiction novel" on the basis of formal techniques alone. The term is meant to highlight formal similarities with realist fiction, and yet realist fiction in its classical manifestation strives to hide its novelistic qualities and adopt the appearance of something that is not fictional and not novelistic. It would be entirely misleading, therefore, to claim that type F writing is imitating *sui generis* features of the *novel* as such, when what it is really doing is imitating *sui generis* features of one particular style of *narration* (one might simply call it *vivid* narration), which might or might not be fictional.

Once again, it is important not to confuse or run together *fiction* and *narrative*. Narrative is storytelling, but there is no reason to suppose that all stories are fictional; indeed, they are clearly not. Storytelling is an integral part of much type E writing. No doubt there are characteristic techniques associated with different modes of narration. There are styles and conventional norms for writing letters, keeping a diary, describing a historical chain of events or composing a stream-of-consciousness novel. The techniques identified by Wolfe for the New Journalism and by Watt for the early realist novel are no doubt characteristic of these respective modes of narration, and there are likely to be similarities between the cases. But not much of theoretical interest can be inferred from this. Calling a work a "nonfiction novel" only has paradoxical resonance because "novel" standardly implies "fiction". But nothing said so far goes any way towards establishing that type F is, after all, a species of *fiction*. All that is established is that type F is a species of *narrative* similar in some respects to the narratives of the realist novel. If, on the other hand, "nonfiction novel" just means "nonfiction narrative", then theoretical interest diminishes, given the non-identity of narrative and fiction. It would remain only to demarcate different kinds of nonfiction narratives.

Pressing home the point, it is worth emphasising a tenet now familiar among theorists of fiction (Searle 1979; Currie 1990; Lamarque 1996), namely this: *there are no formal techniques of rhetoric, style, syntax, sentence construction, or composition, which are necessary or sufficient for writing to count as fictional.* The very fact that writing as different, formally, as that of the early realist novels and that of the *nouveau roman* can be classified as fiction seems to confirm that no set of techniques is necessary. And the fact that the techniques identified by Wolfe and Watt—the former (avowedly, if ambivalently) associated with nonfiction, the latter with fiction—indicate that those techniques are not sufficient to determine fictionality. As for other, more markedly "literary" techniques, like those of the *nouveau roman*, it seems clear that even these in principle could be appropriated for nonfictional aims, showing that they, too, could not be sufficient for fiction.

We cannot quite leave the subject of narrative techniques or literary devices. Suppose that defenders of type F writing were to weaken their claim from insisting that they *are* writing novels (or short stories) to the claim that what they are writing is very *like* novels (or short stories). That weakened claim might seem pretty anodyne and certainly does nothing to disturb the fiction/nonfiction distinction, particularly when the likeness rests only on formal techniques. But we should ponder for a moment just how like (fictional) novels—of the classical realist kind—type F writing actually is. Yes, they broadly share the surface features outlined by Wolfe (in [1] to [4] mentioned previously). But a further question is whether the *function* of these devices is the same or similar in the two cases. We will see later how important the idea of function is when trying to characterise special features of the literary. At first, it might seem that the function is similar, and Wolfe identifies one shared function explicitly when he writes that the devices give the realist novel "its unique power, variously known as its 'immediacy', its 'concrete reality', its 'emotional involvement', its 'gripping' or 'absorbing' quality" (1973, 31).

But, looking more closely, some disanalogies appear. Take the case of Wolfe's device (4) of the "nonfiction novel", which involves the piling up of minute details. He compares this with the technique used by Balzac to help the reader get "inside" his characters. The descriptions of furnishings, room decoration, colour schemes, clothing, gestures and "looks, glances, poses, styles of walking" and so forth (see [4] mentioned previously) increase the richness of the atmosphere and the precision with which a reader can locate the characters in the social nexus. All that is obviously right and presumably is a motivation also for similar details in the nonfiction novel. But something else is going on, too, in the realist novel—what Roland Barthes has called the "reality effect" (see chapter 4). Barthes is noting an aesthetic goal behind the piling on of *fictional* detail, involving a "referential illusion". The accumulation of minor detail gives the "effect" of reality. But in the nonfiction case, it is not the *effect*—the appearance—of reality that is sought but the reality itself.

It should be emphasised, though, that detail in the realist novel has aesthetic functions beyond just that of the "reality effect". Details can be used to connect, to symbolise, to develop character, to add coherence, to advance a theme. Sometimes, deeper connections are needed to tie together apparently disordered or uninteresting series of events. Here is a critic's comment on Daniel Defoe's *Moll Flanders*:

> This fundamental irony, produced by the reader's continuous and simultaneous awareness of the two sides of Moll's nature, transforms what would otherwise be a dreary and tedious chronicle of petty deceptions and crimes, unadorned by sensuousness or vividness of description, into a clearly focused and coherent story. Obviously *Moll Flanders* can lay no claim to being tightly constructed, and certainly a great part of its characteristic quality would be destroyed by any effort to contain its substance within the rigidities of a dramatic plot. Nevertheless, the novel does have a more or less clearly defined center in the competing concerns of the two Molls, producing a continuous abrasion that gives to the novel both edge and form. (Donovan 1973, 404)

What the passage shows is how natural it is to move from concerns about fiction to more distinctively *literary* concerns—irony, sensuousness, coherence. We should not assume that such concerns have no bearing on the "nonfiction novel" just because we have diffused any ambivalence about the *fictional* nature of its characteristic techniques. Indeed, it would be reasonable to investigate its literary aspirations, for that, of course, would be another, rather different, way of justifying the term "novel".

NONFICTIONAL CONTENT

Before turning to literary qualities, though, we should return to the other part of the expression "nonfiction novel"—namely, "nonfiction". If "novel" alludes to a work's formal techniques, as it was suggested, then "nonfiction" applies to its content. So what is it about content that makes it "nonfictional"? The answer, it might seem, is straightforward. Content is *nonfictional* if it is factual, based on or answerable to the facts, about real events or making claims to truth, while content is *fictional* if it essentially involves what is imaginary, made up or invented, as with the plots and characters of typical type A works. But the association of fiction with what is *imaginary* or *invented* and nonfiction with what is *factual*, *real* or *truth-seeking* is far from straightforward, as has been pointed out in earlier chapters.[5]

Rather than rehearsing familiar arguments, it is worth reflecting again on some of our other types of writing. For example, type B, historical fiction, immediately raises doubts about defining fiction in contrast to fact and reality. Type B fiction uses fact and real events as its basic subject matter; these are works that are *about* real people and events. Authors of type B fiction typically go to great pains to research their subject, to make historical and period detail as accurate as possible and to adhere strictly to known facts. In this, they are just like type F authors. Is there no difference, then, between type B and type F? Perhaps there must be *some* invented detail to qualify for fiction status, to distinguish type B from type E. Normally, of course, that will be the case. But does it need to be?

Kendall Walton thinks not. He says he can find no reason "why there couldn't be a genre of historical novel in which authors are allowed no liberties with the facts and in which they are understood to be asserting as fact whatever they write" (1990, 79). For Walton, to be fictional is to be a "prop in a game of make-believe"; performing the function of being such a prop, regardless of whether this is intended, is sufficient for fictional status. He concludes from this that at least some examples of type F writing—he instances Norman Mailer's *The Executioner's Song*—are indeed *fiction*, in spite of any stated intention, because they have the "function of prescribing imaginings" (80).

The trouble with Walton's account is that it is going to have counterintuitive consequences for many type E and even type D cases. Plenty of historical works, memoirs, travel books and correspondence serve the function of prescribing imaginings, even if their principal aim is elsewhere. In Walton's view, "Any work with the function of serving as a prop in a game of make-believe, however minor or peripheral or instrumental this function might be, qualifies as 'fiction'" (1990, 72). He is resigned, therefore, to include, by implication, all type D cases: that is, all philosophical works which contain an element of fiction, explicitly offering Berkeley's *Three Dialogues Between Hylas and Philonous* as an example of a work of fiction.

This is too blunt an approach, even though Walton is right to distance fiction from too close an association with fact, reality and truth (or their opposites). If possible, it seems desirable to retain some distinction between types A, B, D and E in terms of fictionality. Type B, historical fiction, is a difficult case in trying to explain content, fictional or otherwise. Can we allow, as Walton does, that a work can remain fictional even though it deviates not at all from fact and is constrained throughout by historical accuracy? I think we can—just—but we must insist on quite stringent conditions relating to the *purpose*, *aims* and *commitments* of such writing, if we are not simply to relocate it into type E. It is not enough to say, as Walton does, that the test of "prescribing imaginings" (or having that "function") will mark the desired distinction, particularly when intention is removed. Any history or biography of any eloquence will invite, or be seen to invite, imaginings on the part of its readers, but that cannot be enough to qualify it as fiction. Nor is Walton right to allow that writers of historical fiction could be "asserting as fact whatever they write". Someone who asserts a historical fact is not, and cannot be, at the same time speaking, or writing, in a fictive mode. The aims are incompatible.

To assert is to stand in a certain relation both with the matter asserted and with those persons to whom the assertion is made. As Searle has reminded us, someone making an assertion "commits himself to the truth of the expressed proposition"; he "must be in a position to provide evidence or reasons for the truth of the expressed proposition"; the proposition "must not be obviously true to both the speaker and the hearer in the context of utterance"; and he "commits himself to a belief in the truth of the . . . proposition" (1979, 62). Yet to speak fictively is precisely to release oneself from such commitments and to pursue a quite different communicative aim—namely, to get the respondent to *make-believe* that what is heard is an assertion even while knowing that it is not. The very *practices* of assertive discourse and fictive discourse are different; the conventions and expectations are different; the appropriate modes of response and evaluation are different. It seems entirely implausible to try, as Walton does, to remove intention altogether from a definition of fiction (Levinson 1996, 296; Lamarque and Olsen 1994,

47–49). The response *aimed for* by an author or *invited* from a reader must play a role in determining the status of a piece of writing.

What is needed is a notion of "fictive utterance", which incorporates the intentions of the fiction-writer and establishes constraints on norms of response. Several philosophers have attempted this, even though there is still some disagreement around the edges (e.g., Stock 2011a). What might be called the orthodox view is nicely summarised by Noël Carroll: "[A] fictive intention . . . is the intention of the author . . . of a structure of sense-bearing signs that the audience imagine the content of the story in question on the basis of their recognition that this is what the sender intends them to do" (1997, 181). What is instructive about Carroll's definition is that it allows him to develop a theory of *nonfiction* film—his example is film, but it can carry over to written narrative—which he calls "the film of presumptive assertion". Here is how he defines that notion:

> *x* is a film of presumptive assertion if and only if the film-maker *s* presents *x* to an audience *a* with the intention (1) that *a* recognizes that *x* is intended by *s* to mean that *p* (some propositional content), (2) that *a* recognizes that *s* intends them [*a*] to entertain *p* as an asserted thought (or as a set of asserted thoughts), (3) that *a* entertains *p* as asserted thought, and (4) that 2 is a reason for 3. (1997, 188)

Some such account seems to be along the right lines. Note how far it diverges from Walton's, both in contrasting assertion with fiction and in giving prominence to intention. What an analysis of this kind suggests is that fictional content is subordinate to fictive mode (or fictive utterance). Thus might it be, in our hypothetical case, that the content of a historical novel is entirely true to the facts—and thus is in some sense nonfictional—while the mode of utterance by which it is presented is fictive or non-assertive. In such a case, we can still retain the work in type B as a historical *fiction*. The mode of utterance, along with the normative constraints on response, is what differentiates type B from type E. Historical writing of type B submits to the discipline of history; at its most serious, it demands rigour of proof, argument, citation of sources, defence against alternative hypotheses, engagement with ongoing debate, falsifiability in the face of counter-evidence, an explanatory framework and all the restrictions imposed by the assertive mode (the points are well made in Evans 2000). But historical fiction, even under the normal constraints of accuracy and verisimilitude, falls under different conventions. The historical novel is allowed to deviate, within certain bounds, from known fact; invented detail, unsupported hypothesis, imaginative embellishment, made-up dialogue, compression of time, even the introduction of entirely fictitious characters and other devices are well established in the genre and are justified to the extent that they enhance the overall literary effect and help to draw in the reader. The very expression "poetic licence" is instructive, for a novelist possesses a *licence*—approved by the genre norms—to loosen the grip of historical assertion and the expectation it invites.

There is another sense in which content is subordinate to mode of utterance. In the assertive mode, of type E, what is true in a historical account is determined by how things are in the world. The fictive mode, on the other hand, can make things true in a fictional world merely by stipulating them. What might be called fictive states of affairs are brought into being by fictive utterance and how they are is determined by how they are said to be. When Tolstoy describes some detail about Napoleon in *War and Peace* ("Napoleon took a lozenge, put it in his mouth and glanced at his watch" [Bk. 3, pt. 2, ch. 29]), this state of affairs becomes true within the world of the novel, independently of facts in the real world. Not all content in historical fiction has its truth determined in this way, but the truth-generating potential of fictive utterance has no counterpart in assertive utterance (except in the peculiar case of performatives).

CONSTRAINTS ON THE NONFICTION NOVELIST

We have now reached a curious position with regard to the nonfiction novel. When the emphasis was on the formal techniques, shared with the realist novel, we appeared to be pointing towards the *fictional* aspect of "faction". But closer inspection revealed that the presence of these techniques indicated only a species of narrative, in itself neutral on the fiction/nonfiction issue. The novel-like devices were not sufficient to establish the status of a novel. Turning to the content, with its grounding in fact, we seemed to have sure ground for identifying a contrasting *nonfictional* aspect of "faction", poised nicely in tension with the preceding fictional aspect. Yet what our recent investigation has shown is that the fact-based content is itself neutral on the fiction/nonfiction question and that there is nothing in the content itself which allies type F more with type E than with type B.

The nonfiction novel, then, has not yet revealed itself to be either determinately fictional or determinately nonfictional. But the terms of the debate have shifted, for we look now not to formal narrative techniques or to factual content as decisive marks of the works' status but to the mode of utterance to which the works conform. In a word, we look to the authors themselves, to the commitments they take on, the responsibility they assume for what they write and the norms of evaluation they engage. Do they avail themselves of the "licence" of the novelist, retreating from the commitments of assertion, allowing themselves the freedom to invent and embellish (a freedom that can be exercised to different degrees)? Or do they submit to the tougher regimen of the historian or (serious) journalist, committed to factual accuracy and answerable to the norms of empirical proof and argument? Nothing in the formal style of the writing forces them into one or the other stance. If they opt for the former, they become novelists and are open to appraisal along conventional lines for type B writing. It might well be that there are constraints on accuracy—getting the facts right—for type B genres, but these constraints fall well short of those for the professional historian and the focus for the readership is different. If they opt to be judged as historians or responsible journalists recording the facts and seeking to be reliable sources of information, then much of what might be admired by readers of historical fiction—Tom Wolfe's four devices listed earlier—can come to seem a distraction, even an irritation; invention and embellishment cease to be pleasing accompaniments to a core of fact but become a potentially fatal flaw compromising the probity of the reporter.

The "nonfiction novelist" cannot have it both ways: cannot claim the high ground of the serious reporter or historian and also the imaginativeness and inventiveness of the novelist. There is a moral dimension here as well as a theoretical tension between practices. It is morally irresponsible—a kind of dishonesty—to demand, on the one hand, the status of the historian, the integrity of a writer whose work answers to the highest standards of evidence, while, on the other hand, dismissing or excusing deviations from strict accuracy on the grounds of literary "licence".

It would be wrong, of course, to brand all New Journalists as morally irresponsible. Many do not adopt the double standard described. They incline one way or the other on the stance they take to their material, to the commitments they incur, to the kind of response they seek from their readers, to the mode of assessment they invite. Readers, too, soon acquire a sense of what is going on. Readers, for example, of Hunter S Thompson's *The Hell's Angels* (1966), an account of the author's own experiences with the Hell's Angels, offering a graphic description of their milieu, would no doubt expect matters of substance to be accurate but, being swept up with the story and characters, would hardly demand—or care about—strict evidence for every incident or conversation related. Thompson recounts a conversation with one of the group on just this topic:

> "What are you doin' now?" Barger asked. "Are you writin' something else?"
>
> "Yeah," I said. "A book."
>
> He shrugged. "Well we don't ask for nothing but the truth. Like I say, there's not much good you can write about us, but I don't see where that gives people the right to just make up stuff . . . all this bullshit, hell, ain't the truth bad enough for em?" (1973, 348)

The truth that the Hell's Angel member asked for—one assumes—was less the truth of minute detail and more the truth of an overall impression. And that is the truth aspiration of the historical novel. The basic facts must be right, licenced deviations aside, but as important is "truth *to* the facts". Historical fiction is judged for the extent to which it captures a world, a milieu, a way of life, a period. The *feel* or atmosphere must be right. This is a species of verisimilitude and is an important narrative constraint on genres of realist or historical fiction. The movie *The Patriot* (Roland Emmerich 2000) received a bad press in Britain for its distortion of fact and milieu in the depiction of the American War of Independence, with the British portrayed as almost uniformly evil and wantonly cruel and the Americans as almost uniformly patriotic and racially united. The film—admittedly a fictional representation—was judged (by British critics) artistically flawed for this simplistic and sentimental treatment of the historical events.

LITERARY ASPIRATIONS

New Journalism often aspires to another kind of truth, also more associated with literature than history or reporting. This is the broader truth or "vision" that offers a moral comment on human nature, a generalisation beyond the specific case. Consider the following passage from Joan Didion's *Slouching Towards Bethlehem*, about a wife's murder of her husband in San Bernardino County, California:

> Unhappy marriages so resemble one another that we do not need to know too much about the course of this one. There may or may not have been trouble on Guam, where Cork and Lucille Miller lived while he finished his Army duty. There may or may not have been problems in the small Oregon town where he first set up private practice. . . .
>
> It might have been anyone's bad summer, anyone's siege of heat and nerves and migraine and money worries, but this one began particularly early and particularly badly. . . . By July 8, the conventional tensions of love and money had reached the conventional impasse in the new house on the acre lot at 8488 Bella Vista, and Lucille Miller filed for divorce. Within a month, however, the Millers seemed reconciled. . . . It seemed that the marriage had reached the traditional truce, the point at which so many resign themselves to cutting both their losses and their hopes. (1973, 307–8)

The first sentence echoes (and reverses) the opening of *Anna Karenina*. The next two sentences are factually uninformative but convey a sense of world-weariness, of inevitability. The word "conventional" is repeated, the idea picked up again in "traditional"; the resignation reported in the last sentence is a resignation in a type, not just an individual. This is a story about a particular case but also about suburban life and suburban dreams, human weakness and desire. The factual details are important and are conveyed with authority, quoting police tapes, eye-witness accounts and court reports, but it is more than a straightforward report of a murder (just as is *In Cold Blood*). It reveals the literary aspiration of the New Journalism. But some care is needed to characterise this aspiration.

What does it mean to invite a *literary* response? What is it for a reader to adopt a *literary* point of view or offer a *literary* judgement? The introduction of "literature" and literary values does not imply a reintroduction of *fiction*. It is possible to judge a work for its literary values regardless of whether it is deemed to be fictional. Of course, the conception of literature remains a matter of controversy, and there are broader or more specific uses of the term, but there is not fundamental disagreement about the nature of literary qualities (Lamarque 2001). What must be avoided is too formalistic an account of the literary. Certainly, there are literary "devices", some of which we have looked at, and literature is associated with "fine writing". But the great works of literature are not just those that are well written or well constructed. They also engage imaginatively with themes of general human interest; they have a "moral seriousness" which makes them worthy of renewed attention and reflection. Works of literary fiction not only tell a story but also elevate the reader's mind beyond the particulars of the subject matter to what might be called "perennial" concerns.[6] The point is familiar from the well-known passage in the *Poetics* (1451b) in which Aristotle locates poetry between philosophy and history, contrasting the universality of poetry with the particularity of history. A work's literary qualities reside in how effectively the linguistic means—the devices, the overall design, the development of character and incident—are consonant with these higher literary ends (see chapters 7 and 9).

There seems little doubt that many works of type F aspire to literary status and invite attention from the literary point of view. They have a story to tell but more than a story to tell. They are constrained to get the story right, but they aim to illuminate aspects of human life deeper than the particularities of the story they relate. It is in this that they emulate the great novels—not by imitating their style but by imitating their aspiration.

However, this literary aspiration does not sit entirely comfortably with the aims of journalism or history. If we take imaginative works of literature—notably, but not exclusively, realist literary fiction—as paradigmatic of the literary, then we notice the special ways that literary form can promote literary vision. The most obvious is that of symbolism, in which a character, or a place, or an incident comes to stand for something more than its own material existence and is woven into a pattern which invites description in the "universal" terms identified by Aristotle. Here is a typical example from a critical analysis of Emily Brontë's *Wuthering Heights*:

> [W]hat we might call the skeleton of *Wuthering Heights* [is] in the opposition between the Heights and the Grange. The antithesis is repeated in terms of locality as well as of the people respectively identified with that locality, so

> that the whole action could be noted down in outline as a series of clashes between opposites. This is why it is so tempting to read the novel as a storm-calm allegory. . . . The schematic structure of *Wuthering Heights* gives Emily Brontë the means to explore human material about which she has ambivalent feelings, while at the same time holding it in firm control. Again the sets of opposites do not add up to a simple contrast; they intertwine into a complex pattern. To begin with, as the windy Heights on the moors are contrasted with the Grange, sheltered in the leafy valley, so the Earnshaws are contrasted with the Lintons. Interior decoration is made symbolical here, as the farm house with its stone floor,
>
>> [R]anks of immense pewter dishes . . . towering row after row, in a vast oak dresser . . . the chairs, high-backed, primitive structures, painted green: one or two heavy black ones lurking in the shade,
>
> is opposed to the description of the Grange in which poetry is made out of early-Victorian tastes . . . The Earnshaws have dark eyes and complexion, the Lintons are fair and blue-eyed. The Earnshaws ride to church in winter, the Lintons roll up in the "family carriage, smothered in cloaks and furs". With Catherine's attraction to that soft and bright world of the Grange, there develops the opposition of Heathcliff and Edgar . . . As Heathcliff goes out and Edgar comes in, the contrast, Nelly thinks, resembled
>
>> what you see in exchanging a bleak, hilly coal country, for a beautiful fertile valley.
>
> And the first crisis in the book is pivoted on Catherine's analysis of the two kinds of love she has for Edgar and Heathcliff, respectively:
>
>> "My love for Linton is like the foliage in the woods: Time will change it, I'm well aware, as winter changes the trees—my love for Heathcliff resembles the eternal rocks beneath—a source of little visible delight but necessary. Nelly, I *am* Heathcliff!"
>
> The geographical opposition between Heights and Grange has here developed into natural imagery which defines character opposition. (Ewbank 1972, 325–26)

A literary reading of this kind is one that explores the functionality of detail. Literary detail performs a function different, characteristically, from that of journalistic detail. The latter is there to substantiate, to fill in the picture, to lay out the facts; the former might also be doing those things but always invites an additional kind of attention—that of interconnectedness. Barthes might be right about the "reality effect" of some detail, but the function of literary detail to symbolise, connect and point beyond itself (as the example illustrates) is also absolutely central, albeit a commonplace of literary reading. Yet it is here that the danger arises for the nonfiction novel.

The attempt to invest detail with symbolic or thematic force is at odds (at least potentially so) with the attempt to provide an objective and accurate account of facts. The conflicting constraints on the selection of detail in the two cases reinforce the tension between a literary aspiration and a journalistic one. Characters or lives in imaginative literature can be portrayed as emblematic because they are the products, by and large, of the imagination and are created with literary ends in mind. But the individuals described in the non-fiction novel are not creations and their actions have no intrinsic meaning other than that inherent in the intentions and purposes of the individuals themselves. Any other meaning is an external imposition and the quest for meaning and universality can so easily distort mundane sequences in every-day life. (This idea is developed in chapter 4.)

Curiously, there is a mirror image of this danger in the literary novel itself. Arguably, Charles Dickens's *Hard Times*, a type A work with a potential claim to type C, explores its chosen theme—the heartlessness of "utilitarian economics and Commissioners of Fact"—with such single-minded attention to exposing general ills that the particularities of character and incident suffer. It is generally agreed, for example, that the treatment of Stephen Blackpool, a "mixture of sentimentality and melodrama" (Craig 1969, 28), is a literary weakness in the novel. His role as representative worker and martyr overwhelms any more refined interest in the development of the character.

Again, New Journalism need not succumb to a similar failing, even though the danger is there. Joan Didion's moral tale about the murderous relation of Lucille and Cork Miller, as cited earlier, seeks to draw out general features of what she calls the "golden dream", but hers is a relatively straightforward narrative, recounting the events with precision, as well as painting a picture of a certain kind of life. There is no temptation to call her work "fiction" or to suppose that it blurs the distinction between fact and fiction. It has a literary aspiration of a modest kind, but that does not detract from its essentially journalistic aim. Nevertheless, there is a sliding scale that we should notice. The more emphasis there is in journalistic writing on literary aims, on symbolism, thematic unity and literary form, the more attention tends to be drawn away from the specifics of the particular case. Something rather different happens in the case of literary fiction—at least the paradigmatic type A cases—as here the particularity of character and incident is not compromised by but positively enhances the wider frame of theme and significance. How do we account for the difference? It returns us to the opacity discussed in chapter 1. In works of fiction, the characters are *constituted* by the modes of their presentation; they acquire not just their identity but also their contextual significance from the literary forms that bring them into being. This is a feature of fictional characters that sets them apart from actual real-world people (as argued in chapter 4). Readers of literary fiction attend to fine-grained delineation of character in the service of aesthetic ends—

symbolic resonance, internal coherence, connectedness, functionality, thematic development—and in a manner that would be inappropriate when real lives are being explored and explained. If the New Journalists adopt a similar perspective towards their subjects, giving focus to higher themes, there is a danger that it might seem to matter less whether the fine-grained details are accurately recorded.

This is where, once again, the issue of moral responsibility arises. If authors of the nonfiction novel want to compete with authors of imaginative literature, using their devices and sharing their aspirations, then they need to signal carefully whether they seek to be judged as historical novelists or as serious journalists. To fudge that distinction is essentially to deceive their readers. There is no possibility of having it both ways: claiming, as we noted earlier, the high ground of the recorder of fact while at the same time allowing leeway on the facts in the name of poetic licence and literary insight.

CONCLUSION

We have come a long way from initial puzzlement over borderline cases between fiction and nonfiction. First, it looked as if questions about form—the use of novelistic "devices"—would be crucial to how we classified works of "faction". Doesn't *looking like* novels make them into novels? Perhaps such was the view of those who promoted the label "nonfiction novel". But we found that formal features cannot mark the distinction between nonfiction and fiction. Nor, secondly, do questions about content. A largely factual content can appear in works of fiction, without muddying the distinction. Historical fiction is fiction for all that. With the shift away from both form and content, what emerged was the importance of the complex of attitudes taken by both writers and readers and the mutually agreed norms constraining act and judgement. The assertive mode of the serious historian contrasts with the fictive mode of the novelist, and this cuts across issues of technique and factual content. Of course, it is not always clear what attitude a writer is adopting towards his written material and hence what are the appropriate norms of response and evaluation. It is not always clear what game is being played and thus what rules are in force. This is especially problematic where new forms of writing—guided by new practices—come into effect. But where authors deliberately conceal their intentions, apparently inviting response under one set of norms (e.g., serious reporting) while hiding behind the privileges of another (e.g., literary licence), then, as we saw, the question of moral responsibility inevitably comes up. A writer who exploits a reader's trust invites only censure—and mistrust.

Further complications arise when the literary dimension is introduced. A work can be judged as literary and can reward literary attention without necessarily being classified as fiction. But when the literary stance is adopted—fine writing and literary structure promoting wider human themes that give meaning to the particularities of character and plot—a reader's interest is likely to be drawn away from the details of "mere" factual reporting. This can—although it need not—be another occasion for authorial dishonesty: distorting the facts to fit an overall "vision", while purporting to record those facts accurately and dispassionately.

The existence of "faction" or the nonfiction novel does not disturb the theoretical distinction between fiction and nonfiction; it certainly does not cause us to abandon that distinction or water it down. But having been shown to contain elements from all our categories from type A to type E, "faction" is an intriguing phenomenon, forcing us to reflect harder on what is involved in belonging to those, sometimes fluid, categories and not letting us forget the multiply varied aims of writers and writing.

NOTES

1. Still the best modern account is probably that in Watt (1957).
2. There are, of course, many distinctions to be made among the ends and achievements of literary realism, between realism, naturalism, social or psychological realism and so forth, and also between French and English exponents. But these distinctions are not important in this classification.
3. For a detailed working out of this distinction, notably on how to define "about" in literary cases, see Lamarque and Olsen (1994), ch. 5.
4. Quoted in Nelson (1973), 111–12. Also cited in Lamarque and Olsen (1994), 269.
5. The associations have been undermined in different ways in at least the following: Currie (1990); Walton (1990); and Lamarque and Olsen (1994).
6. The role of "perennial themes" in literature is discussed in Lamarque and Olsen (1994), ch. 16.

Chapter Six

Wittgenstein, Literature and the Idea of a Practice

It is a commonplace of literary theory that literature is embedded in social practices that both define what literature is and help explain the values it embodies. This idea took a distinctive turn in analytic philosophy in the mid-twentieth century when a conception of a rule-governed practice, derived largely from Wittgenstein, moved into the mainstream of ethics and aesthetics. The first notable application of this conception came in John Rawls's paper "Two Concepts of Rules" (1955),[1] in which he defined "practice" as a "technical term meaning any form of activity specified by a system of rules which defines offices, roles, moves, penalties, defenses, and so on, and which gives the activity its structure" (3n1). This idea has played a prominent part in analytical literary aesthetics over the past forty years or so, although little explicit acknowledgement has been given to Wittgenstein. This chapter seeks to recover the Wittgensteinian ancestry, not through tracing historical influence but by looking at intellectual connections with the aim of consolidating and defending a conception that is of the utmost importance in aesthetics.

I shall lay out briefly what I take to be the central claims made for the idea of a rule-governed practice within literary aesthetics, then I shall make the connection—both convergences and divergences—with the use Wittgenstein makes of this notion, and finally I shall offer a defence against certain standard criticisms, drawing on insights from Wittgenstein's own treatment.

THE ROLE OF "PRACTICE" IN LITERARY AESTHETICS

First of all, there are two fundamentally different ways of conceiving the practice or "institution" within which literature is embedded.[2] They are not in competition and both are equally valid. One way is to characterise the practice (or practices) in sociopolitical terms. This is an empirical enquiry into the multitude of social interactions underlying what might be called the book industry: the activities of writing, reading, distributing and evaluating books of certain kinds. This might involve analyses of the class, age, gender and ethnicity of writers and the ownership of publishing houses and their policies and profits, as well as the patterns of readership of different kinds of books and sales, marketing, reviewing and so forth. In contrast, the analytical concept of a practice is more austere and differently focused. It takes the analogy of a game—notably Wittgenstein's own favourite example, that of chess—as paradigmatic and seeks to uncover the deeper constitutive rules in the practice that make possible certain basic activities such as the creation, appreciation, evaluation and interpretation of literary works and conventional relations between authors, works and readers.[3] It is not an empirical enquiry, but perhaps more like a transcendental enquiry examining what must be the case if it is possible for literature to count as an art form.

A second point is that this idea of a practice provides an activity-based as opposed to an object-based analysis of literature. Object-based analyses are atomistic in taking the individual work as primary, the creation of an individual writer, under consideration by an individual reader. Such an analysis seeks in each work certain features that might qualify the work as "literary", both intended by the author and recognised by the reader; it then argues by induction to a concept of literature founded on the set of all such common qualities. An activity-based approach, in contrast, looks not for common qualities—at least not common intrinsic qualities—across individual instances of authors, works and readers but rather at roles: author-roles, work-roles and reader-roles, subject to rules but realisable in different forms. Again, the chess analogy helps. All that is constitutive of the bishop in chess is its possible moves in a game, not facts about its physical appearance or strategies used by individual players. Likewise, on this conception, there is no restriction on what forms (e.g., genres) literary works might take and, in characterising the practice, no information is needed about individual authors or readers.

If we combine this point with the first, then we can derive the following: that participants in the rule-governed practice of literature are defined not by social or political criteria—class, gender, age, reader preferences and so forth—but by conformity to the roles in the practice.[4] Although it might be of sociological or literary historical interest to discover what kinds of people in what societies at what periods of history occupy the author and reader roles, and what specific kinds of works (sonnets, romances, realist novels) occupy work-roles, information of that kind is not needed in the characterisation of the roles themselves.

So to a third point: ontological implications arise. Without the established practice with its constitutive rules, there would be no literary works as such. Rawls makes the point generally:

> In the case of actions specified by practices it is logically impossible to perform them outside the stage-setting provided by those practices, for unless there is the practice, and unless the requisite proprieties are fulfilled, whatever one does, whatever movements one makes, will fail to count as a form of action which the practice specifies. What one does will be described in some other way. (1955, 25)

The games analogy again makes this clear, as there could be no such things as a pawn or castling on the queen's side without the rules of the game. An object physically indistinguishable from a conventional-looking pawn found on a prehistoric site could not be a *pawn* because the game had not been invented. As Rawls notes, we would need another description for it. In the literary case, the distinction between text and work draws on the same idea. A mere text or string of sentences cannot count as a literary work independent of the practice which defines the work-role and assigns texts to that role in particular instances. This point is important, as it implies that a literary work cannot simply be a sentence-string that somehow possesses literariness intrinsically.

A fourth point concerns internal and external perspectives on the practice. Within the practice, as determined by its own conventions, the existence of literary works is given. There might be disputes in marginal cases about what counts as literature, or especially what is valued as literature, but such disputes can only be settled by appeal to criteria internal to the practice. To ask from an external point of view whether there is such a thing as literature is to ask about the practice itself: whether it is still sustained, whether it ought to be abandoned or radically modified. Rawls marks the distinction is this way:

> [O]n the practice conception [of rules], if one holds an office defined by a practice then questions regarding one's actions in this office are settled by reference to the rules which define the practice. If one seeks to question these rules, then one's office undergoes a fundamental change: one then assumes the office of one empowered to change and criticize the rules, or the office of a reformer, and so on. (1955, 28)

The distinction bears certain affinities to that drawn by Rudolf Carnap (1956) between internal and external questions of existence. According to Carnap, once a "framework" of entities has been established, then the question of whether an entity exists can be answered within the framework by either logical or empirical methods according to the nature of the framework. But to ask an external question about the existence of the entities is to question the desirability of the framework itself: this is a "pseudo-question" for Carnap because it calls for a decision rather than a discovery. External questions about literature might challenge not only the existence of literary works but also their value. Questions about artistic value must, of course, be handled with care, but the practice conception of literature enforces a distinction between those criteria of value rooted in the practice itself and criteria brought to bear on the practice from outside. The idea of internal criteria of value is well illustrated once more by the chess example. Within a game of chess, the queen is more valuable than a pawn (excepting special situations in which a pawn might advance the game more effectively than the queen). But a chess queen has no value—no chess value—external to the game. The value of the material of which it is made—gold, ivory—is not a chess value. Literary value rests on broadly agreed criteria internal to the practice. The fact that some literary works can be used for non-literary purposes, for example, to fulfill social or political ends, is not itself evidence that these ends belong among the internal criteria for literary value.

A fifth and final consideration in the practice conception is that of initiation into the practice. Just as chess is a game that has to be learned and demands a high level of skill to be performed well, so reading literature is not a merely "natural" aptitude but also involves training. It, too, can be done better or worse. It should not be supposed, though, that initiation into the practice can only come about through the formal articulation of rules. Practitioners can learn by example.

THE ROOTS OF THE IDEA IN WITTGENSTEIN

All five of the factors identified in this conception of literature have their roots in Wittgenstein, both in his notion of a practice and in his more narrowly conceived notion of a language-game.[5]

First of all, it seems clear that the interest Wittgenstein has in characterising practices and language-games is not an interest in their sociopolitical makeup or in the kinds of people who engage in them. When he exemplifies the "multiplicity" of language-games in *PI* §23, which intriguingly includes "making up a story; and reading it" and "play-acting", he has no inclination for his purposes to delve into the sociology of these activities. And when he invents artificial language-games to illustrate, say, naming or giving an order, he is not concerned with delineating the types of people taking part. His interest is analytical. Although he crucially shifts attention from language as a picture of reality to language as social interaction between participants, he is concerned only with the *roles* of speaker and hearer, not with the realisation of those roles in sociopolitical terms. He is not interested in sociolinguistics.

Second, Wittgenstein's emphasis on practices as *activities* is beyond doubt. One motivation here is to weaken the idea that meaning and understanding must involve inner mental states or processes: "Thinking is an activity, like calculating. No one would call calculating, or playing chess, a state" (*PG* 172). "There is always the danger", he writes, "of wanting to find an expression's meaning by contemplating the expression itself, and the frame of mind in which one uses it, instead of always thinking of the practice" (*OC* §601). "The grammar of the word 'knows' is evidently closely related to that of 'can', 'is able to'. But also closely related to that of 'understands'. ('Mastery' of a technique.)" (*PI* §150). To think of literature in terms of activities associated with author-roles and reader-roles, rather than objects, removes the pressure to search for essential common features shared by all literary works and also pressure to explain these roles in terms of the psychological states of authors and readers. This is what the chess analogy helps reinforce: "Just as a move in chess doesn't consist simply in moving a piece in such-and-such a way on the board—nor yet in one's thoughts and feelings as one makes the move: but in the circumstances that we call 'playing a game of chess', 'solving a chess problem', and so on" (*PI* §33). Anti-essentialism is already evident in Wittgenstein's treatment of empirical concepts, and anti-psychologism in his treatment of meaning.

The games analogy, so important for Wittgenstein in connection with language use, must be treated with caution in the literary application. Although Wittgenstein uses the chess example extensively, he is at pains to point out that not all games have as strict a set of rules as chess: "There is a game consisting simply of everyone's throwing a ball as high as he can; and there is the game little children play of throwing a ball in any direction and then retrieving it. Or again someone throws a ball high into the air for the fun of it and catches it again without any element of competition" (*PG* 68). In fact, what Wittgenstein wants most from the games analogy is the basic idea of an activity with a broadly conceived "point". "A game", he reminds us, "does not just have rules, it has a point" (*RFM*, appendix 1 §20). This does not imply that rules are inessential—only that they might range widely from the precise and explicitly stated kind in chess to the much looser kind associated with minimal normative conditions marking success or failure, as in the game of throwing the ball high in the air and catching it. Presumably, the "point" of the latter game is to catch the ball, thereby affording a standard of success in the game. We must return to rules later as there are many misunderstandings about their role in practices.

Third, the idea that a word gets its meaning through its role in a language-game is fundamental to Wittgenstein's later conception of meaning. Without having a role in a language-game, a word has no meaning: "Naming is so far not a move in the language-game—any more than putting a piece in its place on the board is a move in chess. We may say: *nothing* has so far been done, when a thing has been named. It has not even *got* a name except in the language-game" (*PI* §49). "Theology . . . fumbles around with words, because it wants to say something and doesn't know how to express it. The *practice* gives words their meaning" (*RC* §317). Similarly, we cannot talk about literature until there is a language-game or practice in place which serves to ground the concept of literature. It is a short step to saying that there could be no such thing as a literary work (as distinct from a mere linguistic text) without the practice in place that makes talk of literature possible.

A further point, however, should be stressed, perhaps in tension with at least naive versions of the use theory, namely that the practice conception is concerned with *concepts*, not mere lexical items. There are those who object to this conception on the grounds that the *word* "literature" to cover works such as novels, drama and poetry is of relatively modern coinage, and thus that it is merely anachronistic to speak of literature prior to the eighteenth century (Stecker 2004, 67). But to show that there is no relevant *concept* of literature in earlier periods, it is not sufficient to point to lexicography. The practice of literature is not dependent on particular usage in this narrow sense, and to establish that the concept of literature is modern would require showing that there has been a radical break between our modern practice of engaging with literary works and earlier practices, involving judgements, evaluations and interests, encompassing poetry and drama. The evidence suggests there has been no such break.

Fourth, Wittgenstein has much to say in *On Certainty* about the difference between questions raised within a practice and questions that seem to challenge the practice itself. The latter can often seem illegitimate. Many of his examples involve teachers and pupils:

> The pupil will not let anything be explained to him, for he continually interrupts with doubts, for instance as to the existence of things, the meaning of words, etc. . . . Or imagine that the boy questioned the truth of history (and everything that connects up with it)—and even whether the earth had existed at all a hundred years before. . . . [T]his pupil has not learned how to ask questions. He has not learned *the* game that we are trying to teach him. . . . This doubt isn't one of the doubts in our game. (*OC* §310–§317)

There has to be a bedrock of agreement within a practice for the practice to have any kind of stability, even if individual propositions taken as secure within the practice can become open to questioning when others are held fast. A parallel might be with the literary canon. Within the institution of literature, there must be a set of works broadly accepted as canonical even if the justification for particular works in that set can, in the right circumstances, be questioned. But giving a reason for canonical status is not itself possible, except within the agreed criteria of the practice. "A *reason*", Wittgenstein writes, "can only be given *within* a game. The links of the chain of reasons come to an end, at the boundary of the game" (*PG* 97).

Two ideas from Wittgenstein are especially important in this context: that of agreement and that of making mistakes. For Wittgenstein, not any false belief can count as a mistake: mistakes need grounds. "Can we say: a *mistake* doesn't only have a cause, it also has a ground? I.e., roughly: when someone makes a mistake, this can be fitted into what he knows aright" (*OC* §74). He goes on:

> Would this be correct: If I merely believed wrongly that there is a table here in front of me, this might still be a mistake; but if I believe wrongly that I have seen this table, or one like it, every day for several months past, and have regularly used it, that isn't a mistake. (*OC* §75)

> In order to make a mistake, a man must already judge in conformity with mankind. (*OC* §156)

What can count as a mistake is determined within a practice. Certain kinds of radical doubts occur not internal but external to a practice. Like Carnap's pseudo-questions, they might be ungrounded.

Similarly, we should not expect the same demands of truth and proof in every practice. Participants within different practices (e.g., those of history and religion) might have different expectations:

> Queer as it sounds: The historical accounts in the Gospels might, historically speaking, be demonstrably false, and yet belief would lose nothing by this: *not*, however, because it concerns "universal truths of reason"! Rather, because historical proof (the historical proof-game) is irrelevant to belief. This message (the Gospels) is seized on by men believingly (i.e. lovingly). *That* is the certainty characterising this particular "acceptance-as-true", not something *else*.
>
> A believer's relation to these narratives is *neither* a relation to historical truth (probability), *nor yet* that to a theory consisting of "truths of reason". (*CV* 32e)

Practices, Wittgenstein holds, are grounded in agreement: "If language is to be a means of communication there must be agreement not only in definitions but also . . . in judgments" (*PI* §242). There is a connection with rules: "The word 'agreement' and the word 'rule' are *related* to one another, they are cousins. If I teach anyone the use of the one word, he learns the use of the other with it" (*PI* §224). Yet Wittgenstein sometimes suggests that agreement can be more basic than rules: "We do not learn the practice of making empirical judgments by learning rules: we are taught *judgments* and their connexion to other judgments. A *totality* of judgments is made plausible to us" (*OC* §140). Again, we will return to rules later.

The final connection with literary practice is the notion of being initiated into a practice, linguistic or otherwise. Wittgenstein's key thought is that one has to learn how to *act*, not just, for example, how to define terms. Part of learning is being able to ask certain kinds of questions.

> But is it wrong to say: "A child that has mastered a language-game must *know* certain things"?
>
> If instead of that one said "must be *able to do* certain things", that would be a pleonasm, yet this is just what I want to counter the first sentence with.—But: "a child acquires a knowledge of natural history". That presupposes that it can ask what such and such a plant is called. (*OC* §534)

Likewise, a definition or ostensive definition will not be sufficient for understanding without seeing the point of what is being taught, fitting it into a pattern of actions.

> I am explaining chess to someone; and I begin by pointing to a chessman and saying: "This is the king; it can move like this, . . . and so on."—In this case we shall say: the words "This is the king" (or "This is called the 'king'") are a definition only if the learner already "knows what a piece in a game is". That is, if he has already played other games, or has watched other people playing "and understood"—*and similar things.* Further, only under these conditions will he be able to ask relevantly in the course of learning the game: "What do you call this?"—that is, this piece in a game. (*PI* §31)

PROBLEMS WITH THE PRACTICE CONCEPTION OF LITERATURE AND LESSONS FROM WITTGENSTEIN

The idea that literature is best explained as a rule-governed practice or institution involving interactions between authors, works and readers has been subjected to criticism. The most persistent criticism concerns the analogy with games and the idea of rules governing the practice (e.g., Blackburn 2010, 87). Most other criticisms reflect this central worry to some extent. For example, it is thought too restrictive to suppose there is any single practice governing the production and reception of literary works (Eagleton 2012, 51); the underlying assumption is that there are, in fact, multiple practices, not least grounded in radically different critical "approaches". It is thought, too, that deep disagreements between critics about the value of individual works and their interpretation count against any uniform practice. Additionally, what are taken, by defenders of the practice conception, to be constitutive rules are often challenged as not universally applicable (Gaut 2005, 124–26). Finally, there is a criticism that Rawls himself raises more generally about the practice conception of rules—namely, that it leads to a kind of conservatism in which one is stuck with the practices one has. Rawls, though, I suggest, is right to dismiss this:

> There is no inference whatsoever to be drawn with respect to whether or not one should accept the practices of one's society. One can be as radical as one likes but in the case of actions specified by practices the objects of one's radicalism must be the social practices and people's acceptance of them. (1955, 32)

I shall focus on the objection about rules and the games analogy because I believe that once we get those notions clear, responses to the other objections will follow straightforwardly. The objection is quite simply that the chess analogy is inapplicable because it presupposes a precision and explicitness of rules that just does not obtain in the production and reception of literature. A standard response is to concede the point that such rules as there are in the literary institution are unlike chess rules in important respects (Olsen 2005, 21).[6] It is accepted that practitioners are often unable to state the rules and the practice is not learnt (except perhaps at the margins) by internalising explicit rules. It is also emphasised that such rules—or conventions[7]—as there are in the literary sphere are in the nature of constitutive rules in the sense offered by John Searle, concerning what counts as what in such and such circumstances (1969, ch. 2; 1995, 43f). They are not regulative rules concerning specific techniques of reading but apply at a much more general level. They characterise the kind of focus of attention required when a work is read as literature: for example, an attention to form, to thematic as well as subject content, to inner connectedness, to distinctive kinds of value (Olsen 1978; Lamarque 2009b, ch. 4). Such constitutive rules leave open the possibility of a wide range of applications or "approaches". The point is only that unless there are some constraints on what can count as reading from a literary point of view or taking a literary interest in a work, there could be no such thing as literature.

But the lesson from Wittgenstein is salutary. Maybe the emphasis on *rules*—as encouraged by Rawls—is misleading. Wittgenstein asks us to dig deeper to understand what it is for a practice to be governed by rules. Rules, he tells us, relate to agreement ("[t]he phenomena of agreement and of acting according to a rule hang together" [*RFM* 344]), and agreement within a practice takes different forms. There is agreement in action, in definitions and in judgements. Agreement in action might be founded on cognitive abilities and behavioural dispositions that are more fundamental than rule-governed practices themselves. "It is our *acting*, which lies at the bottom of the language-game" (*OC* §204); "the phenomenon of language is based on regularity, on agreement in action" (*RFM* 342). Agreement in definitions is the acceptance of shared concepts, while agreement in judgements is agreement in the application of concepts. These latter kinds of agreement help explain what it is to conform to a rule and all three seem integral to engaging in a practice (at least a practice using language). To follow a rule, Wittgenstein tells us, need not involve first interpreting the rule: "[T]here is a way of grasping a rule which is *not* an *interpretation*, but which is exhibited in what we call 'obeying a rule' and 'going against it' in actual cases" (*PI* §201). "I cannot describe how (in general) to employ rules, except by *teaching* you, *training* you to employ rules" (*Z* §318). "Not only rules", he writes, "but also examples are needed for establishing a practice. Our rules leave loop-holes open, and the practice has to speak for itself" (*OC* §139). Even with the chess example, the rules seem subsidiary to playing the game: "One can . . . imagine someone's having learnt the game without ever learning or formulating rules. He might have learnt quite simple board-games first, by watching, and have progressed to more and more complicated ones" (*PI* §31).

These remarks, following on from the earlier reminders of just how varied games and their rules can be, suggest that there is more to a practice than being constituted by rules and that it is more illuminating to think of conforming to a practice as engaging in activities of a certain kind, underlain by agreements, than merely to emphasise the rule-bound nature of practices. Thomas Morawetz anticipates the direction of this line of thought:

> Rather than invoking games with their constitutive rules to explain the possibility of practices and rule-governed ways of proceeding, we need to invoke practices in order to understand the possibility of having games. . . . [Indeed] games [can be seen as] specialized and simplified cases of practices and can be learned and practiced only by those who already have a context of shared activity in practices. (1978, 56)

Might it be that the idea of agreement at the heart of a practice—agreement of all the kinds mentioned—is doing more explanatory work than an appeal to rules on the model of games? Nor is this suggestion undermined in the literary case by reference to the sometimes radical *disagreements* among critics over interpretation or evaluation, for to the extent that such disagreements are grounded, thus subject to debate, within the practice of criticism, they must already presuppose fundamental *agreement* about what count as constraints on debates of that kind (about literary meaning and value).

It would be a mistake, however, to throw out talk about rules or the games analogy altogether to illuminate the practice of literature. Take rules first. Those who engage with literature or adopt the "literary point of view" on a text recognise that there are limits on what counts as a *correct* or relevant or appropriate way of proceeding. Such agreement amounts to a shared recognition of norms, of right and wrong, of standards to follow. It is possible to be *mistaken* in what counts as a relevant mode of response to literature read as literature. Where there are accepted norms, there seem to be implicit rules.

Thus, talking about agreement helps to explain, not to eliminate, rule-following.

Wittgenstein suggests that what is interesting about a rule is not the rule itself but its application: "The rule which has been taught and is subsequently applied interests us only so far as it is involved in the application. A rule, so far as it interests us, does not act at a distance" (*BBB* 14). That last phrase recalls the suggestion from Gordon Baker and Peter Hacker that there is an "internal" relation between a rule and acts of following it: "This rule would not be the rule that it is, nor would this act be the act that it is, if this act were not in accord with this rule. Because the relation is internal, no intermediary can be interposed between its two terms to effect a connection" (Baker and Hacker 1995, 91). They go on:

> The apparent logical gulf between a rule and its "extension" arises from the mistaken assumption that understanding a rule is at least partly independent of how it is projected on to actions. But however it is formulated or explained, a rule is understood only if it is correctly projected. To be ignorant or mistaken about what acts are in accord with it is to be ignorant or mistaken about what the rule is. (97)

If this is right, then it suggests that we need not be overly concerned about the apparent lack of explicitly formulated rules in the practice of literature. The rules, such as they are, are made apparent in the activities that ground the practice, and the agreements endorsed by practitioners. Shared assumptions by practitioners "regulate" their "activities" in responding to, talking about, evaluating, interpreting and "appreciating" literary works.[8] These are assumptions about the *point* of literature, about what kinds of things merit attention in literature, what features of works are of literary interest, what works are canonical and so forth. Whether a reader's response is in conformity to the "rules" of the practice is shown not by looking up the response in a rule book but by its endorsement, or otherwise, by qualified practitioners. This is why agreement in action can seem more fundamental than following a rule, even though the two are not strictly separable.[9]

If the appeal to rules requires finessing in this way, so, too, does the analogy with games. One reason for caution with the analogy relates to the objection raised earlier that there is not a single practice related to literature but multiple practices in complex interrelations. A response to the objection might be to recognise an overarching practice of literature (encompassing the very idea of literary appreciation in all its applications) that subsumes subsidiary but independently characterisable practices, like, for example, the practice of fiction-making. While it is plausible to think of practices embedded in other practices, only in rather special circumstances can one speak of games embedded in games.

But, again, we should not abandon the games analogy altogether. There are two features of the analogy, at least, that should be retained. The first is the ontological point that chess pieces, like the king or rook, have no existence independent of the game of chess. So it is that literary works, as distinct from strings of sentences, also cannot exist without the practice that recognises and constitutes them as such. The second point relates to value. Chess value is constituted within the practice of the game and attains a level of objectivity in that context. Likewise, literary works are valued as such in the terms of the practice that makes them possible. Internal disagreements over value might arise, but they can be adjudicated only relative to normative expectations shared by practitioners. To try to judge them outside that context is not to judge them as literature but perhaps only as sentence-strings fulfilling other functions.

So finally, and briefly, what does constitute the practice of literature if not narrowly conceived game-like rules? No doubt it is not enough to cite "activities" without saying exactly what these are. They are the activities of the production and reception of works by those initiated in the practice, grounded in general interests and expectations. Here, for example, is C S Lewis talking about a couple of lines from John Gower's fourteenth-century poem *Confessio Amantis*:

> Venus promises the lover that he will find peace
>
> Noght al per chance as ye it wolden,
> Bot so as ye be reson scholden.
>
> —lines which describe, perhaps unconsciously, the very nature of life's discipline in this, as in a thousand other matters, and which might even express the promise kept by Venus to successful lovers. This is the deepest note in Gower; but though it is heard distinctly only at the end, its influence is over the whole poem. For when once he has hit upon the theme "Love cured by Age", he has no more need for the clumsy device of a separate palinode: the whole story becomes a palinode, and yet remains a love story—a pathetic, yet not dismaying, picture of Passion at war with Time, while more than half aware that Reason sides with Time against it. It is this latter, this half-awareness, that saves the *Confessio Amantis* from the spiritual shallowness of a mere lament over the vanished pleasures of youth. It also explains certain places in the poem which are commonly misunderstood. Critics smile when Genius, priest of Venus, denounces Venus herself as one of the false deities; and if we insist on the original significance of Genius (the god of reproduction) there may be some absurdity. But it is not quite the kind of absurdity that we are tempted to suppose. Gower has not blundered into it by an oversight. He knows very well what he is doing, and goes out of his way to underline what we consider the inconsistency. Genius himself is well aware of it. (1969, 218–19)

The practice, we might say, makes commentaries of this kind possible; it also makes them intelligible and worthwhile. Lewis is exhibiting a literary interest in the poem; he is assigning significance to its parts and drawing out general value judgements about the whole. He is also engaging in a debate with other readers, those who think it merely "absurd" or inconsistent for Genius to denounce Venus. He gives attention to certain formal structures of the poem (whether it involves a palinode), and he characterises its genre (a love story of a specific kind, not merely a "lament over the vanished pleasures of youth"), identifies a theme ("a pathetic, yet not dismaying, picture of Passion at war with Time, while more than half aware that Reason sides with Time against it") and proffers a value judgement ("save[d] . . . from . . . spiritual shallowness") supported by reasons.

In all such ways, Lewis is proceeding in his "actions" under a core of assumptions shared with fellow critics about what is valued in literature, what literature is and what kinds of judgements, both interpretative and evaluative, count as literary judgements. The practice allows plenty of room for other readers to challenge the particular judgements that Lewis makes, to point to other features of the poem that strike them as more salient or interesting, to arrive at different summary evaluations. Is Lewis following *rules*? Certainly his comments *count as* adopting a literary point of view; they comply with the *norms* of critical practice and they manifest criteria of relevance *agreed* by fellow practitioners. The analogy with the rules of chess adds nothing more than this. In contrast, those readers (of, say, novels) who concern themselves only, for example, with how fictional characters resonate in their own lives, or how gripping or emotional or amusing incidents are without any further regard to how these effects are brought about or to what end, are not taking a literary stance to the texts they read. There is nothing wrong with reading in this way, but it is not reading from a literary point of view, which makes different, more stringent, demands. The practice does not lay down sharp lines on the many different modes of appreciating literature as such, but there must be limits to what can count as a literary interest.

CONCLUSION

We have seen that all the features underlying the use of the notion of a practice in current literary aesthetics are already anticipated in Wittgenstein's later philosophy. This ancestry is not sufficiently acknowledged, nor is it of merely historical interest. The connection with Rawls and his "two concepts of rules" is more familiar; yet, as I have shown, the emphasis on rules is not the most helpful aspect of the relevant idea of a practice, nor is the primacy given to the games analogy. Wittgenstein offered us the games analogy but warned us to treat it with care; he gave us the idea of a practice which grounds activities but was alive to the divergences among practices; he encouraged us to think not of definitions or essential qualities in addressing a concept but of social interactions around which the point of the concept is revealed. When thinking of literature, we forget such things at our peril.

NOTES

1. Rawls mentions Wittgenstein only once in this paper, significantly with regard to borderline cases: "One expects border-line cases with any concept, and they are especially likely in connection with such involved concepts as those of a practice, institution, game, rule, and so on. Wittgenstein has shown how fluid these notions are" (1955, 29).

2. For a clear account of the distinction, see Olsen (2005).

3. Stein Haugom Olsen, one of the principal proponents of the analytical conception of a practice, writes:

> Literature is obviously a social practice in the minimal sense that it involves a group of people among whom literary works are produced and read. The present suggestion is that it is a social practice in a stricter sense; i.e. a practice whose *existence depends* both on a background of concepts and conventions which create the possibility of identifying literary works and provide a framework for appreciation, and on people actually applying these concepts and conventions in their approach to literary works. If literature is such an institution then aesthetic judgement must be understood as defined by the practice and apart from the practice aesthetic judgements are impossible. And a literary work must then be seen as being offered to an audience by an author with the intention that it should be understood with reference to a shared background of concepts and conventions which must be employed to determine its aesthetic features. And a reader must be conceived of as a person who approaches the work with a set of expectations defined in terms of these concepts and conventions. Somebody who did not share this *institutional background* would not be able to identify aesthetic features in it because he did not know the concepts and conventions which define these features. (Olsen 1987, 11; italics in original)

4. The point here is that the criteria for what counts as an *author* of a literary work, a *reader* reading from a literary point of view and a *literary work* itself are not specified in social terms. There are no restrictions, other than knowledge of the rules, on who might participate in the practice. Of course, there might be specific genres of literature—for example, children's literature or women's literature—aimed at particular kinds of readers, but that is not essential to the practice of literature itself.

5. In what follows, works by Ludwig Wittgenstein will be cited from the editions listed in the bibliography, with the abbreviations in parentheses.

6. Thomas Morawetz (1973) has argued in general that not all practices have rules anything like the rules of games.

7. "Convention" is the term favoured by Stein Haugom Olsen. He has a useful discussion of the different meanings of the term in literary studies (see Olsen 2000).

8. John Searle writes of dispositions in this context: "[H]e doesn't need to know the rules of the institution and to follow them in order to conform to the rules; rather he is just disposed to behave in a certain way, but he has acquired these unconscious dispositions and capacities in a way that is sensitive to the rule structure of the institution" (1995, 144). But Searle still persists with the games analogy.

9. For a conception of a "practice aspect of rule-following", see Johannessen (1988). Johannessen writes, "Practices might thus be said to have a logical grammar that is at least partially expressed by *inherited* ways of doing things"; he adds, "[T]he practice-aspect of rule-

following cannot be taught on the basis of rules. It has to be picked up by examples and by training" (366).

Chapter Seven

Literature and Truth

How do the great works of literature—novels, poems, drama—connect to truth? There is no disagreement that there is some connection. As we proceed, a multiplicity of connections will emerge. Yet the topic is controversial. One problem with the truth debate about literature is pinning down substantial points of contention and identifying precise claims and counterclaims. Can works of fiction convey truth? Can readers learn from works of fiction? Undoubtedly so. Examples are readily at hand. Readers of Trollope can learn about rural deans in nineteenth-century England. (Whether Trollope always gets it right is another matter.) Is it the aim of literature to convey truth? In some cases—so-called didactic literature—the answer is obviously "yes", even if there is not a clear "yes" in every case. Do we value literary works that convey truth? To the extent that truth is better than falsehood and learning better than ignorance, conveying truth is valuable and works that convey truth have value in that regard. But does truth contribute to *literary* value?

Not until here does an issue of genuine controversy arise. Other issues flow from it. If we value literature for its truth, is that because there is a special kind of truth involved? Do works of literature make any distinctive contribution to truth, in a way that enhances their value? The proper focus for the truth debate must rest with the question of value rather than the question of fact, and not so much with the value of truth, which is not controversial, but rather with the value of literature, which is.

NO EASY ANSWERS

Is truth a criterion of literary value? Is truth part of what makes great literature "great"? The questions might seem straightforward, but as we examine claims and counterclaims in the debate it becomes apparent that a range of different opinions can underlie positive and negative responses. It is not reasonable, in so intractable a debate, to expect an *obvious* "yes" or *obvious* "no" to our key questions, although there are some pressures in that direction.

Against an Obvious "Yes"

Two considerations, at least, might initially suggest an obvious "yes". The first is the vagueness or generality of the idea of "literature". There is a generic sense of "literature" which encompasses the great works of philosophy, history and biography. Are not David Hume's *Treatise on Human Nature* and Thomas Macaulay's *History of England* works of literature? Yet surely they aspire to truth and should be judged at least partially on that criterion? Thus philosophical acumen and historical accuracy seem to be obvious and recognisable criteria for the value of some works of literature. It might be tempting to forestall this response by delimiting the relevant class to *fictional* works of literature. But that is not helpful. For one thing, it threatens to exclude a literary paradigm, lyric poetry, which is not straightforwardly classifiable as fictional, and also the boundary between fiction and nonfiction is itself a matter of contention. Certainly our primary interest will be in poems, novels and dramas of a recognisable kind, but it would hopelessly beg the question to characterise such works, in contrast to the broader species, by postulating a line between works that aspire to truth and those that do not. A better move is to take a relaxed view of the extension of "literature" and focus instead on the idea of distinctively *literary* values or judging a work *from a literary perspective*. There might not be agreement on exactly what this entails, but it is at least not obvious that it must involve truth-assessment even in those instances in which the assertive mode is paramount. Arguably, what gives Hume's *Treatise* literary value, in a strict sense, is not its philosophical insight but the way it is written.

Further pressure to grant an obvious "yes" to our key questions comes from the time-honoured tradition, dating at least from Aristotle, that recognises an instructive as well as pleasure-yielding function for poetry. Its early manifestation in *Ars Poetica* by the Roman poet Horace in the dichotomy between "utile" (usefulness) and "dulce" (sweetness) is echoed over and over, as when Dr Johnson writes that "the end of poetry is to instruct by pleasing" (Johnson 1969, lines 280–82). The idiom of "truth" is never far behind; indeed, Johnson himself uses it in an often-quoted formula: "Poetry is the art of uniting pleasure with truth". Johnson goes on to say, "Epic poetry undertakes to teach the most important truths by the most pleasing precepts" (1905, 208). This weight of tradition might make it seem futile to resist the obvious "yes". However, it is far from obvious that the "instructive" element of poetry, Horace's "utile", *demands* an explanation in terms of truth, or even that when the truth idiom is used, as by Johnson, the notion of truth is anything like that familiar to philosophers. What Horace, and probably Johnson, too, seems to have had in mind was something more like the *seriousness* of poetry. Poetry, they thought, surely rightly, could offer more than just a passing or sensuous pleasure, often inviting serious reflection, opening the mind to new possibilities or stretching the imagination. At an early stage of the argument, it should not be assumed that the seriousness of poetry must automatically be associated with truth.

Against an Obvious "No"

On the other side of the debate, it is equally important to resist an obvious "no" to our questions. Those inclined to a swift "no" might stress the fictiveness of imaginative literature. It is not, and could not be, *truth*, they say, that gives literature its value but rather inventiveness, imagination, clever plots or engaging characters. Fiction, surely, is the very opposite of truth! Truth is the province of science or history, poetry resides in creativity and make-believe. Literature lifts us beyond the mundane world of fact and verification. But again this is too swift. Fiction and truth are much more closely intertwined, as Shakespeare recognised in observing that "the truest poetry is the most feigning" (*As You Like It*, 3, iii, 16). Fiction is an apt vehicle for teaching truths, as in parables, or moral tales told to children, or philosophers' thought-experiments, even police profiles. Additionally, works of fiction are usually set in the real world, often referring to real places, events or famous people and drawing on familiar facts about how humans behave, what clothes they wear, the sorts of things they say. It is no wonder that readers can learn from novels out of this background: about history, geography, etiquette, customs, modes of speech. Whether all this is a source of *literary* value is yet to be determined, but it cannot be ruled out without argument.

Another tendency towards an obvious "no" comes from those who either deny the existence of truth altogether or downplay its significance. Truth cannot be a value of literature if it is of no value itself. Radical scepticism of this kind, associated with the further reaches of poststructuralism, is sometimes attributed to Friedrich Nietzsche, who famously wrote, "[T]ruths are illusions of which one has forgotten that they *are* illusions" and truth is only "a mobile army of metaphors, metonyms, and anthropomorphisms" (1997, 92). Even when not strictly denying the existence of truth, poststructuralists sometimes see language as *self-reflexive*, pointing not outwards at the world (truth) but inwards at itself, an idea nicely captured in Roland Barthes's essay title "To Write: An Intransitive Verb". For Barthes, "*writing* can no longer designate an operation of recording, notation, representation, 'depiction' . . . rather, it designates . . . a performative . . . in which the enunciation has no other content . . . than the act by which it is uttered" (1977, 145–46). Paul de Man applies a similar thought to literature: "It is . . . not *a priori* certain that literature is a reliable source of information about anything but its own language" (1986, 11). But scepticism about truth is no less controversial than issues about literature's value, so it cannot provide any easy solution on its own.

THE CLASSICAL BACKGROUND

It is common in the truth debate to pit Aristotle against Plato as the first systematic proponents of the pro-truth and anti-truth lines of argument. Indeed, their positions have served to lay down the parameters for subsequent debate. However, they did not disagree at all points; both accepted, for example, that poetry (a generic term for what we now call imaginative literature) is a kind of "imitation" (*mimesis*) but also, notably for our purposes, that truth (especially moral truth) is in fact a criterion for judging poetry. They differ in that Plato thought that poetry must always fall short on this criterion, by the very fact of relying on *mimesis*, whereas Aristotle felt that poetry could make an important and distinctive contribution, precisely through *mimesis*.

Plato's Challenge

Plato put an entirely negative gloss on "imitation"—more like "mimicry"—and saw poets as mere tricksters who pretend to have knowledge they do not possess, using the charms of poetry to seduce a gullible audience into thinking they speak with real authority. As a purveyor of truth, poetry comes at the lowest level of cognition. Poets rely on inspiration (a kind of madness) rather than reason, they "imitate" appearance rather than reality, they are mostly ignorant of what they speak, they put pleasure before truth and they stir up emotion which must always cloud judgement. However, Plato offers one last chance to poets, or those who "champion poetry because they like it", to make a case that "there's more to poetry than mere pleasure—that it also has a beneficial effect on society and on human life in general"; "we won't listen in a hostile frame of mind", he says, "because we'll be the winners if poetry turns out to be beneficial as well as enjoyable" (1998, 362). So began two deeply entrenched lines of thought: that poetry is deceptive and potentially dangerous and that poetry's legitimacy can only be defended in terms of its "usefulness".

Aristotle's Response

Aristotle mounted one of the first "defences", conceding the terms of Plato's assault and in effect arguing for poetry's usefulness, especially in living up to the criterion of truth. Aristotle presented a more positive account of *mimesis*, allowing for different objects of "imitation": "as they were or are, or as they are said or thought to be or to have been, or as they ought to be" (*Poetics*, 1460[b], 10–11, trans. Bywater). Poetry can aspire to truth by describing not mere facts but "a kind of thing that might be". This, he argued, made poetry "more philosophic and of graver import than history, since its statements are of the nature rather of universals, whereas those of history are singulars". He goes on to say, "By a universal statement I mean one as to what such or such a kind of man will probably or necessarily say or do" (*Poetics*, 1451[b], 2–10, trans. Bywater). Aristotle also gave a more positive account of poetic form and diction, not, as with Plato, seeing these as devices of charm and trickery but finding for them an integral role in the presentation of a plausible plot out of which the universal truths can develop.

So it is that Aristotle, like Plato, initiated a stream of thought about poetry that resonated down the centuries. The positive idea of *mimesis* became the established "classical" conception of poetry, re-emerging most notably in the eighteenth century, again with Dr Johnson, who remarks that "[n]othing can please many, and please long, but just representations of general nature" (1969, line 1). The "universal" statements which Aristotle associated with poetry became the touchstone of both neoclassical theory and certain strands of Romanticism. There is a striking similarity between Dr Johnson's thought, in his novel *Rasselas*, that "[t]he business of a poet . . . is to examine, not the individual, but the species; to remark general properties and large appearances" (1985, 61) and that of Wordsworth: "Its [poetry's] object is truth, not individual and local, but general and operative" (2006, 526).

CONCEPTIONS OF POETIC TRUTH

The idea that poetry affords a species of general or universal truth needs to be pursued more carefully, not least because any precise claim to that effect is hard to pin down. However, it is by no means the only conception of truth in this debate.

Acceptability and "Ringing True"

The critic I A Richards in *Principles of Literary Criticism* (1924) identified two other senses of "truth" relevant to criticism: "acceptability" and "sincerity". Richards explains acceptability as equivalent to "internal necessity" or "rightness". So "the falsity of happy endings to *Lear* or *Don Quixote*, is their failure to be acceptable to those who have fully responded to the rest of the work" (1967, 212). The idea might connect with that of "ringing true". A work fails to "ring true" if it seems unconvincing, exaggerated, implausible or contrived.

Sincerity, Authenticity and Clarity

Truth as sincerity is different again. The operative idea is truthfulness or honesty, its opposite sentimentality or affectation. A work is "true" in this sense if it does not attempt to deceive or flatter or charm or soften the edges, if it confronts unpalatable facts with an unblinking eye, be they about the author's own hidden secrets or about worldly affairs. The idea of "authenticity" is related, as is the idea of "clarity" or seeing things clearly, without illusion. This latter notion is prominent in Iris Murdoch's philosophical writing:

> Truth is not a simple or easy concept. Critical terminology imputes falsehood to an artist by using terms such as fantastic, sentimental, self-indulgent, banal, grotesque, tendentious, unclarified, wilfully obscure and so on. The positive aspect of the avoidance of these faults is a kind of transcendence: the ability to see other non-self things clearly and to criticise and celebrate them freely and justly. (1993, 86)

> "Truth" is something we recognize in good art when we are led to a juster, clearer, more detailed, more refined understanding. Good art "explains" truth itself, by *manifesting* deep conceptual connections. Truth is clarification, justice, compassion. (321)

Iris Murdoch's conception of artistic truth is of special interest both intrinsically and because as a novelist herself she presumably saw as one aspiration in her own fiction the pursuit of a kind of truth found, she argues, in all great literature:

> [W]hat we learn from contemplating the characters of Shakespeare or Tolstoy . . . is something about the real quality of human nature, when it is envisaged, in the artist's just and compassionate vision, with a clarity which does not belong to the selfcentred rush of ordinary life. . . . [T]he greatest art . . . shows us the world . . . with a clarity which startles and delights us simply because we are not used to looking at the real world at all. (1970, 65)

Truth here becomes clear vision.

True to, Verisimilitude

There are other notions to take into account as well. One is that of being "true to": true to life, true to oneself, true to human nature. To be true to life, a fiction must offer recognisable characters and situations, must avoid implausibility in plot structure (a point emphasised by Aristotle) and must conform to norms of action and motivation. The idea is similar to that of "ringing true". It also connects to "verisimilitude", a conception of truth implying resemblance to fact or "realistic" description. There are further conceptions still. Cecil Day Lewis speaks of "poetic truth [as] . . . unverifiable . . . but operative" (1947, ch. 1), William Wimsatt (1954) of the "concrete universal", Morris Weitz (1955) of "depth meaning" and Colin Falck of "ontological truth" (1989, 74).

Beauty and Truth

A perhaps over-literal reading of Keats's line "Beauty is truth, truth beauty" (from his "Ode on a Grecian Urn") might suggest yet another notion: that beauty is sufficient for truth, that nothing could be beautiful and false. Although it would be contentious to attribute that conception to Keats from the evidence of the poem alone, it is often pointed out that he comes near to it in more prosaic moments, as in his assertion "What the Imagination seizes as Beauty must be Truth" (2009, 36). It is not just truth that is hard to tie down here but also beauty itself. Perhaps the underlying idea is not that different from the truth Iris Murdoch sees in an artist's "just and compassionate vision". What is beautifully expressed under the clarity of such a vision cannot but be true.

Departing from the Scientific Paradigm: Propositional Truth

What is notable about all these conceptions is that they depart from a simple paradigm of truth familiar to science, history and philosophy, nicely encapsulated in Aristotle's dictum: "[T]o say of what is that it is, and of what is not that it is not, is true". This paradigm is propositional truth. Defenders of poetic truth rarely seem satisfied with it. If literature is to be valued for its truth, so the thought seems to be, then it cannot be ordinary empirical or conceptual truth. But this puts pro-truth theorists in an uncomfortable position. They might well make a case for truth as a literary value if they define a *sui generis* notion of truth that suits the literary application. The trouble is that if this is not the standard kind of truth with a time-honoured connection to knowledge, then literature can seem a poor relation in the battle for ideas. If literary truth is too remote from philosophical (or scientific) truth, then literature cannot seem to compete for the high-ground of truth to which human cognition aspires.

There is no doubt that many of the "poetic" conceptions of truth just outlined do indeed connect with literary value. A good case could be made that a kind of sincerity, authenticity or clarity in literary writing is a mark of value in the literary sphere. Additionally, if attention is given to plot structure, characterisation or general subject matter, then plausibility, verisimilitude and "acceptability" are (exceptional cases aside) likely to be valued over their opposites. With a little help from examples, and a bit more precision and filling out, it does seem that under some at least of these conceptions a substantial "yes" can be given to our initial question of whether truth is a criterion of literary value. If truth means acceptability or sincerity, then truth, arguably, is a value of literature. But this can seem a hollow victory for the pro-truth camp. After all, no one supposes for a moment that sincerity (or beauty or "ringing true") is a mark of truth in the discourses of philosophy, history or science. Can poems or novels or dramas really not hold their own in that company?

PROPOSITIONAL TRUTH AND LITERATURE

When Aristotle, Dr Johnson and Wordsworth spoke of "universal" or "general" truth, it is not hard to see how their suggestion might be recast in terms of propositional truth. Some propositional truths are universal in nature, and arguably it is just such that are at the heart of philosophy and science. Perhaps, after all, literature can make a claim to truth at roughly the level (that of "universal truth") sought in these other discourses.

Where there is language, propositions cannot be far away, and it is not hard to find propositions, of a kind eligible for truth-valuation, in poetry or works of fiction. First, we must identify such propositions, and then enquire into their status and the relevance of their truth-assessment.

Distinctions Concerning Content

Some preliminary distinctions are helpful. One is between *explicit* propositional content, in the form of indicative sentences within works, and *derived* propositional content, the result of a reader's reconstruction of explicit content through inference and "filling in". Another distinction is between subject-level content and thematic-level content. The distinctions cut across each other. Subject-level content can be both explicit and derived, as can thematic-level content. What is meant by subject-level content are the characters, events, episodes and experiences presented in a work, from an emotional predicament in a short lyric to a complex narrative in a novel. Such content is often, but not necessarily, fictional, in the sense of being made-up. Derived subject content is that supplementary content filled in, imaginatively or inferentially, by a reader. Thematic-level content, in contrast, is rarely fictional and involves generalisations, sometimes explicitly given, sometimes derived by readers, on the work's subject.

Explicit Thematic Reflections

Writers often offer their own thematic reflections. Here is Wordsworth reflecting on human mortality:

> While we, the brave, the mighty, and the wise,
> We Men, who in our morn of youth defied
> The elements, must vanish;—be it so!
> ("Valedictory Sonnet to the River Duddon")

And what more impassioned and chilling statement of the fear of death could there be than Claudio's speech in *Measure for Measure*?

> Ay, but to die, and go we know not where;
> To lie in cold obstruction and to rot;
> This sensible warm motion to become
> A kneaded clod; and the delighted spirit
> To bathe in fiery floods, or to reside
> In thrilling region of thick-ribbed ice;
> To be imprison'd in the viewless winds,
> And blown with restless violence round about
> The pendent world. . . .
> —'tis too horrible.
> The weariest and most loathed worldly life
> That age, ache, penury, and imprisonment,
> Can lay on nature, is a paradise
> To what we fear of death.
> (Shakespeare, *Measure for Measure*, 3, i, 119–33)

Sometimes fictional characters almost incidentally set out a universal proposition, as when Macbeth describes sleep, the very sleep that he fears he has "murdered":

> the innocent sleep,
> Sleep that knits up the ravell'd sleave of care,
> The death of each day's life, sore labour's bath,
> Balm of hurt minds, great nature's second course,
> Chief nourisher in life's feast.
> (Shakespeare, *Macbeth*, 2, ii, 33–37)

Explicit generalisations in literature of this kind are the stuff of the quotation industry. We must return to these later.

Derived Thematic Reflections

Not all thematic reflections, though, are explicit. Some are constructed, or derived, by readers. Here is a critic summarising a theme in Dostoevsky's *Crime and Punishment*:

> [T]he criminal must, and wants to, accept retribution for the act that expresses the metaphysical self-determination of his free will. It is unjust to deny to the criminal that responsibility that raises him above the beasts, and also to deny

> him the punishment that purifies him and gives him new being. (Ivanov 1975, 584)

Here is an even more pithy statement about Tolstoy's *War and Peace*:

> [S]implicity [is] the supreme beauty of man; goodness and truth, the supreme aims for which man should live and work. (Edmonds 1979, xii)

Such generalisations are common at the thematic level. Here we have plausible candidates for propositional truth of a kind recognisable in philosophy and the social sciences. The question is what bearing their truth (if they are true) has on the literary value of the works from which they arise. Again, this will be pursued shortly.

Propositional Truth at Subject Level

Propositional truth at subject level should not be left out of the equation. Most novels have some grounding in the real world against which fictional events take place. Sometimes, explicit factual description characterises this background, as when the narrator in Malcolm Bradbury's novel *To the Hermitage* offers travelogue-like descriptions of Stockholm and St Petersburg: "To one end of the square outside lies the busy Nevsky Prospekt, filled with its rushing traffic and its whirring trolley buses; to the other is a grand classical façade, the front of the Pushkin Drama Theatre; everything in this city is named after one writer or another" (2000, 386).

Factual Mistakes in Works of Fiction

But what happens when mistakes creep into this factual background? This is surprisingly common. In the proofs of *Barnaby Rudge*, Dickens had to change a passage in which a man was hanged "for passing bad one pound notes" after it was pointed out that there were no one pound notes during the historical period when the novel was set (this and the following examples come from Ricks 1966). George Eliot, in *Middlemarch*, described Lydgate "with bright dilated eyes" from taking opium; when she learned that pupils *contract* from opium, she changed the passage, in a later edition, to "with a strange light in his eyes". Not all mistakes get corrected, though. In William Golding's *Lord of the Flies*, Piggy's glasses are used to light a fire. The scene is pivotal in the book. But Piggy is nearsighted and the concave lenses in his glasses could never focus the sun's rays as required. However, making him farsighted would have changed the dynamics of the plot, for that would not so obviously have been a disadvantage to him (the case is discussed in Rowe 1997, 334).

Are these clear cases of truth affecting literary value? The issue of falsehood—at the subject level—in literature is complicated. Authors will sometimes deliberately distort fact for literary ends. Even scrupulously researched historical novels involve fabrication when invented dialogue is attributed to historical characters. No one would suppose this is an artistic flaw, although the *kind* and *manner* of things said might be deemed inappropriate or anachronistic. A crucial consideration is genre. In some genres—historical fiction, science fiction of certain kinds, even political satire—departures from fact based on mistakes can seriously affect the overall achievement. Perhaps the best way to treat these cases is as breaches in genre conventions, rather than as general failures of literary truth. Factual accuracy is a convention of the genres mentioned. Just as it is a breach of convention in classical tragedy to depict the tragic hero as wicked or dishonourable, so it is a breach of convention to get the background facts wrong in certain kinds of fiction. Unintentional falsehood with no literary purpose then becomes a recognisable kind of literary failure.

Truth and Vacuity at the Thematic Level

Returning to our thematic generalisations, how important is truth in this context? When critics, such as Dr Johnson, praise literature for its truth, it is "universal" rather than straightforward factual truth that they have in mind. But universal propositions like those illustrated present problems of their own. It is not so much the risk of falsehood but the risk of vacuity that besets them. That man must "vanish" (i.e., die), that death is "horrible", that sleep is a "balm of hurt minds", that criminals should accept punishment, that "goodness and truth" are "supreme aims" seem true but curiously empty. Defenders of literary truth can find it difficult to articulate substantial truths from the works they admire, and it is perhaps for this reason that non-propositional conceptions of truth are preferred. Jerome Stolnitz pokes fun at the search for an artistic truth derivable from Jane Austen's *Pride and Prejudice*. Could it be, he asks, the "distressingly impoverished" thought that "[s]tubborn pride and ignorant prejudice keep attractive people apart" (2003, 338–39)?

But the triviality argument only goes so far. There is nothing trivial about the reflections on crime and punishment in Dostoevsky's novel and some of the complexity is manifest in the discussions of critics. The critical observation, for example, that "[m]an must suffer . . . because man, his intellect a delusion and its power demonic, trapped by his instinctive brutality and the conspiracy of his victims, does not will his destiny" is complex and, taken as a universal truth, far from uncontroversial (Beebe 1975, 596).

Cognitive Triviality and Expressive Triviality

In the normal run of cases, though, it might be helpful to distinguish cognitive triviality from expressive triviality. Shakespeare's description of sleep (as shown previously) might not tell us anything we did not know about sleep. Boiled down to its cognitive, truth-bearing, core, it says only that sleep "nourishes" and eases our cares. But Shakespeare embodies this truth in quite remarkable metaphors, far from trivial. Alexander Pope famously captures the poetic achievement: "What oft was thought, but ne'er so well expressed" (*Essay on Criticism*, part 2, line 298). It is surely right that the literary contribution in this and similar cases rests in the *way* something is said. Saying something aptly and tellingly is an important literary skill. There is nothing trivial or banal in Shakespeare's extraordinarily powerful expression of what "innocent sleep" is like. Strictly speaking, though, if we contrast the *mode* of expression with *what* is expressed, then it might seem that truth—bare propositional truth—again takes a step back.

Truth and Argument in Literary Works

Other concerns are sometimes raised about the explicit or derived "universal" truths in propositional form. For example, they are seldom *defended* or *argued* either in the literary works themselves or in the critical works that uncover them (the point is emphasised in Olsen 1978, 69f; see also Carroll 2002, 6f). This makes the literary context seem very different from the philosophic or scientific one, in which reasoning and evidence are paramount. This concern is the basis for the rationalist suspicion felt by Plato against the seductive charms of poetry. If an existentialist novel, one by Camus, say, or Sartre, or indeed Dostoevsky, "shows" a world in which choice is inescapable, this can hardly count as an *argument* for free will, even if the novels strike readers as powerfully persuasive. Likewise, a Kafka novel, or perhaps a Greek tragedy, that rejects free will in place of metaphysical determinism or implacable "fate" could not be said to "contradict" existentialism, much less "refute" free will. These works are not pitted against each other as rival theories but justifiably embraced as powerful alternative visions of human life. But care should be taken in the weight given to the lack of argument in fictional literature. It would beg the question against the special contribution of imaginative literature to insist that it employ the very methods of truth advancement found in science and philosophy. Literary works, the defender of truth might reasonably insist, simply have different rhetorical strategies and different means of support from other truth-promoting modes of discourse; that's what's special about them.

Thematic Reflection and Authorial Assertion

A more serious concern is with the status of the thematic propositions. Their propositional form and their truth-aptness can be deceptive. It would be wrong to suppose that every such proposition is being *asserted* as a *worldly truth*. In fact, these notions can be taken separately. It is a conventional assumption in reading poetry that sentiments expressed are not directly asserted by the poet but, at most, issued by a "dramatic speaker". When Keats in his poem "Lamia" writes, "Philosophy will clip an Angel's wings, / Conquer all mysteries by rule and line", we should not take this as an *assertion* by Keats, expressing his considered view on philosophy, any more than we suppose he is expecting an answer to his (rhetorical) question a few lines earlier: "Do not all charms fly / At the mere touch of cold philosophy?" Literature has been defined as "discourse whose sentences lack the illocutionary forces that would normally attach to them" (Ohmann 1971, 14; see also Beardsley 1978, Beardsley 1981a), and that idea captures the distance between a poet *in propria persona* and a dramatic speaker. Again, though, care must be taken in how the point is generalised. There is no reason in principle why a work of fiction should not be used to make assertions, and indeed didactic uses of fiction are common enough. Telling a story can be a good way of drumming home a point, as everyone, from Plato with his myths to Christ with his parables, knows well.

Derived Themes and Assertion

If caution is needed in attributing a belief to an author, equal care must be taken in how to assess thematic hypotheses advanced by critics. When the critic discussing *Crime and Punishment* states, "[T]he criminal must . . . accept retribution for the act that expresses the metaphysical self-determination of his free will", this is not an assertion about the *world*, an assertion in moral philosophy; it is rather a claim about the novel, an interpretation and reconstruction of one of the novel's central themes. To state a theme in a work, as part of an interpretation of the work, and to make a statement about the world at large are utterly different enterprises. There is no reason to infer that the critic supports the ethical stance in the theme; that is not needed for the exercise at hand. Significantly, there is no further attempt in the critical discussion to debate that stance independently of its role in the novel. The critic is not a moral philosopher. A derived thematic proposition might be true of the work but not true, or not uncontroversially so, of the world at large. The primary focus of the critic is to make sense of a work, to identify its major themes and characterise them in an illuminating way. Although some of the derived themes can look like general propositions in philosophy and psychology, their formulation in response to the work, in an attempt to understand what is going on in the work, occurs in a context in which a different kind of assessment is in order. It would change the context, and thus the focus of attention and evaluation, to appropriate the ideas from the novel into a wider philosophical debate.

Thematic Propositions Taken out of Context

The distinction between being *about the world* and being *about the work* applies also to universal "truths" found explicitly in works themselves. The trouble with the examples offered earlier—the trouble with the whole quotation industry—is that propositions are wrenched out of context. If we are looking to make a speech or reflect more deeply on some subject or merely impress with our literary knowledge, we might well appropriate "sayings" from great works. That is what dictionaries of quotations can offer. Taken out of context, we can propound these sayings as worldly truths. But none of this has much relevance to literary value as such. If literary works are to be valued for their truth, then the truths had better be integrally connected to the works.

Our examples show how easy it is for quotations to become cut off from the context. The lines (mentioned previously) from Wordsworth's "Valedictory Sonnet to the River Duddon" suggest (blandly) man's mortality and an attitude to it of calm acceptance. But consider the complete context:

> I THOUGHT of Thee, my partner and my guide,
> As being past away.—Vain sympathies!
> For, backward, Duddon! as I cast my eyes,
> I see what was, and is, and will abide;
> Still glides the Stream, and shall for ever glide;
> The Form remains, the Function never dies;
> While we, the brave, the mighty, and the wise,
> We Men, who in our morn of youth defied
> The elements, must vanish;—be it so!
> Enough, if something from our hands have power
> To live, and act, and serve the future hour;
> And if, as toward the silent tomb we go,
> Through love, through hope, and faith's transcendent dower,
> We feel that we are greater than we know.

The sonnet itself offers far more than the abstracted lines suggest and perhaps even contradicts them, hinting at a kind of immortality "[t]hrough love, through hope, and faith's transcendent dower". It offers a complex reflection on "Form" and "Function" in nature and a suggestion of the eternal: "I see what was, and is, and will abide". Any supposed triviality vanishes in the wider context. But so perhaps does a concern for *truth*. Is it *true* that "the Stream . . . shall for ever glide" (the capital letter implies something greater, more god-like, than the river itself). Is it *true* that "the Function never dies", that there is something eternal in nature and in man? There is no way of knowing, for this is not verifiable truth, it is not science. Propositional truth on the scientific paradigm seems hopelessly irrelevant. Our thoughts are not bound up with verification but with poetic reflection, with the imagination, with the vision that the poem proposes. This again is opacity.

Contextualisation weakens but also makes more interesting the truth status of the other quotations. Claudio in the lines from *Measure for Measure* is pleading with his sister Isabella to spare his own life by giving up her chastity to the odious Angelo. Are his remarks about the horrors of death not tinged with self-pity? Does their eloquence not conceal self-serving exaggeration? Is Claudio, as Isabella wails, not a "faithless coward"? Is there not irony in the fact that his characterisation of "[t]he weariest and most loathed worldly life" which he prefers to death fails to mention defilement and loss of purity (Isabella's fate)? When Macbeth describes "innocent sleep", only moments after murdering Duncan, his lines are resonant with the wider assault on innocence. What he says about sleep is, in the context of the play, as telling about his own guilt and state of mind as it is effective as a general reflection on sleep itself. More often than not, when explicit universal propositions crop up within works, it can be more rewarding to reflect on them not just as abstractable quasi-philosophical observations about the world but also as inwardly directed characterisations of events and persons helping to structure an artistic vision.

Worldly Content and the Function of Propositional Description

The defender of literary truth is perhaps overimpressed by a feature of all literary works, fiction and nonfiction alike, that their content is inevitably and deeply implicated in "real-world" concerns, at both subject and thematic levels. At the subject level, particularities of plot and character will be presented in world-familiar ways, and at the more universal thematic level, concepts involved (free will, innocence, desire, despair, etc.) will be those that figure in world-focused discourses like philosophy or psychology. But although worldly truth is often available, it is not always sought or even relevant in this context. Propositions can be found or formulated, but there is a fundamental distinction between a proposition used to *characterise an organising principle in a literary work* and a proposition (which might be expressed by the very same words) used to *state a truth about the world at large*. These quite different aims should not be conflated. In fact, the propositional form itself can be misleading in this regard. What a work is *about*, in the sense of its literary thematic content, need not be propositional. Works can be about pride and prejudice, unrequited love and social responsibility, the conflict of duty and desire, without expressing or implying propositions on these. Monroe Beardsley's distinction between theme and thesis (1981b,

404) is not really a distinction between a theme and something else but between two ways in which themes can be characterised. The propositional way is not obligatory.

Thematic Truth-Valuation and Value

What about falsehood at the level of thematic propositions? In contrast to factual background, it is hard to see how authors might *make mistakes* when proposing a general vision of the world. The vision might be uninteresting, incoherent, undeveloped, uninspired, clichéd, far-fetched or generally unappealing. It might also be insincere, but it is hard to see how it could be *mistaken*. One reason, as we saw with the Wordsworth example, is that the universal "truths" characteristic of literary works are often unverifiable: they are too general, they have an essential value component, they are grounded in a highly personal outlook and so forth. Of course, that is not to say that readers might not disagree with the point of view propounded or implied in a work. Existentialists might disagree with the implied determinism in Kafka, social realists might reject the nihilistic individualism in Beckett, atheists might be unsympathetic to Donne's religious sonnets. But it would be odd for any of these critics to describe the authors as *mistaken*. The critics are making a value judgement, but not one comparable to objections against writers who get their facts wrong. Usually serious readers of literature are remarkably tolerant towards outlooks different from their own, and often value works in spite of these differences. For example, even someone of a naturally optimistic disposition could admire the despairing vision in Matthew Arnold's "Dover Beach":

> the world, which seems
> To lie before us like a land of dreams,
> So various, so beautiful, so new,
> Hath really neither joy, nor love, nor light,
> Nor certitude, nor peace, nor help for pain;
>
> And we are here as on a darkling plain
> Swept with confused alarms of struggle and flight,
> Where ignorant armies clash by night.

A reader does not have to believe it is *true* that the world has "neither joy, nor love, nor light, / Nor certitude, nor peace, nor help for pain" to appreciate and value Arnold's poem. Such simple cases, easily multiplied, illustrate how thematic truth or falsity can be irrelevant to literary value. Hilary Putnam remarks of Celine's *Journey to the End of the Night*, "I do not learn that love does not exist, that all human beings are hateful and hating. . . . What I learn is to see the world as it looks to someone who is sure that hypothesis is correct" (1978, 89).

EMPATHETIC KNOWLEDGE AND CLARIFICATION

There are close relatives of literary truth that shift away from truth per se, or propositional truth, towards other "cognitive" benefits: what it is like to see the world from a certain perspective (as in the example from Putnam), what it is like to be in a certain predicament, changing our outlook on life, educating our emotions. Jenefer Robinson, for example, associates a kind of emotional learning, a "sentimental education", with certain novels. This involves more than just acquiring beliefs: "[T]he idea that learning emotionally through fiction consists primarily in the acquisition of beliefs does not do justice to the experience of reading a novel" (2005, 155). She elaborates,

> The emotional education of . . . readers . . . takes place via a series of emotional episodes in which *beliefs* are less important than such things as unexpected physiological responses, non-cognitive affective appraisals, shifts in focus of attention, the perception of new aspects of situations, and the revelation of previously hidden wants and interests. (157)

Often, Robinson believes, a reader's emotional education will be paralleled by that of certain characters. As the characters confront their predicaments and seek ways to understand and overcome them (through the controlling hands, of course, of the author), so a reader empathetically follows their path. David Novitz in this context has spoken of "empathetic knowledge" arising from fiction:

> If the problems which confront fictional characters are seen to arise in the actual world, any reader who has acquired empathetic beliefs pertinent to such problems may well be more aware of, and hence more sensitive to, the difficulties involved in solving them. . . . [If so,] we are justified in saying that the fiction has imparted empathetic *knowledge* of the situation, that it has given readers a "pretty good idea of", or enabled them to know something about, what it feels like to be ensnared in such a situation. (1987, 135–36)

Thus "knowing what it is like" becomes a cognitive payoff, related to, but not identical with, the acquiring of true beliefs.

Cognitive Strengthening

A similar view, which has gained currency in recent years, might be called *cognitive strengthening*. Again, the emphasis is away from the acquisition of newly found worldly truths towards "clarification" (Carroll 2001) or an "enriched understanding" (Graham 1997) or an "acknowledgement" (Gibson 2003) of beliefs readers are likely to hold already. As Noël Carroll puts it, "[I]n mobilising what we already know and what we can already feel, the narrative artwork can become an occasion for us to deepen our understanding of what we know and what we feel". It can do this by "reorganis[ing] the hierarchical orderings of our moral categories and premises" or "reinterpret[ing] those categories and premises in the light of new paradigm instances and hard cases" or "reclassify[ing] barely acknowledged phenomena afresh" (2001, 283). The idea is that literary works—notably narratives—do not educate readers merely by imparting truths that the readers had not thought before but by "clarifying" or "enriching" or giving fresh impetus to beliefs that readers already possess but rarely attend to. Perhaps on a small scale, something similar occurs in reflecting on Macbeth's observations about sleep. Shakespeare's powerfully expressive metaphors might not *inform* us about sleep but they provide a unique perspective for re-conceiving only vaguely considered aspects of sleep.

The idea of cognitive strengthening identifies an important and familiar phenomenon in the reading of novels and other literary works. It is a further question, though, how far it boosts the pro-truth case about literary value. By moving away from beliefs and propositional truth, it becomes distanced from paradigmatic cases of truth. In addition, it might seem to weaken certain kinds of pro-truth accounts by in effect conceding the triviality objection. Why would literary works need to "clarify" or "enhance" truths if these were already substantial in themselves (as they might be in a philosophical treatise)? And is it characteristically the case that the "clarification" or "enrichment" offered by literature merely builds on beliefs that readers already possess? Is it so rare for new beliefs to be in the offing?

AN ENDURING CONTRAST: PHILOSOPHY AND LITERATURE

The debate about truth in literature—the debate over whether truth is a fundamental value in literary works—is not, as noted from the start, one that affords any final or easy resolution. Novels, poems and plays offer numerous instances of truths and can be the occasion for learning and acquiring beliefs. They afford other cognitive payoffs as well, as shown. But is a didactic function a central achievement or aspiration of such works? Do those works that fail to teach fail as literature? Must the reading of novels always strive for self-improvement or education? The spectre of Plato still haunts the debate.

Those sceptical that truth is a fundamental value of literature like to emphasise a contrast between paradigmatic literary works (poetry and fiction) and what can be called *constitutively cognitive* discourses, such as philosophy. Philosophy, they will insist, *essentially* aims at advancing understanding and is valued accordingly. The core focus of interest in a philosophical work is on the claims it makes and the arguments in support of them. Ill-supported, poorly argued or unoriginal works are devalued for that reason.

To read philosophy is to read for truth. In contrast, to read and value a work *from a literary point of view* seems quite different. For one thing, literary works that are too overtly didactic are seldom valued highly. For another, one of the pleasures of a literary reading is to notice different ways that the content can be imaginatively construed, not necessarily focused on a single "message" or "thesis" to be conveyed.

Additionally, the expectations readers have in coming to a novel or poem for the first time are seldom cognitive expectations: readers are not commonly motivated to read by the thought that they will learn something. They might learn something and might value that learning, what they learn might even change their lives (for the better), but all that seems like a bonus gained, not a demand made. More characteristically, readers seek a distinctive kind of pleasure from their reading. The very process of reading a novel or poem is quite unlike that conventionally associated with philosophical or historical works. Readers like to be imaginatively involved with the narrative or subject content; they like to find coherence and interest at a broader thematic level; they enjoy and look out for formal qualities of structure and design. Do they seek truth as well? Some might. But that, I suggest, is not at the heart of literature.

Chapter Eight

Thought, Opacity and the Values of Literature

In this chapter, I am going to explore the idea of the opacity of narrative by weaving together threads from earlier work of mine, notably so-called thought theory (Lamarque 1981; the label "thought theory" comes from Carroll 1990, 79ff) and the perennial debate about literature and truth (Lamarque and Olsen 1994). If the view defended in chapter 7 is right—that the appraisal of a work's truth, in any literal sense of the term, is not an indispensable focus for what gives interest to literary works appreciated as literature—then we need some other account of where the values of literature lie. My claim will be that certain elements of thought theory combined with the conception of narrative opacity will provide the framework for just such an account.

THOUGHT THEORY

Thought theory is a response to an apparent paradox connected with emotional responses to fiction. The paradox arises from a tension between two intuitions: first, that people do sometimes respond to fiction with genuine emotions like fear and pity, but, second, that such emotions presuppose beliefs that just don't seem to be present in the standard contexts of responding to fiction. Thought theory seeks to resolve the paradox by weakening or at least relocating the belief condition on emotions. The claim is that while people might not believe that the fictional events they perceive are real, nevertheless they bring to mind those events or entertain them in thought. In turn, such thoughts, derived from the fictional work itself and made suitably vivid by description or image, can bring about (i.e., cause) the disputed emotions like fear and pity. If we are terrified watching the movie of the green slime, then, according to thought theory, what frightens us is the thought of the green slime as brought to mind by images in the movie; we are frightened *by* the thought, but we are not, in normal cases, frightened *of* the thought. To say we are frightened *of the slime* is to say only that it is the relevant slime-thought that causes our fear.

In what follows, I shall not be defending thought theory, as applied to emotions, but developing certain aspects of it. Five core elements serve to characterise the theory. The first is the distinction between thought and belief. Bringing a thought to mind, reflecting on it as a thought, is not the same as believing a proposition to be true. One can entertain a thought without being disposed to assert its content as a world-directed truth. Furthermore, a second point is that thoughts in the appropriate sense might encompass merely images or ideas and thus need not take the form of fully articulated propositions—for example, that *a* is *F* or that some *x* is *G*. As such, they need not even be candidates for truth.

A third element is that of a thought-cluster. Here, the idea is that it is not likely to be isolated thoughts that cause significant emotional reactions. On its own, the thought, say, that Othello killed his innocent wife Desdemona in a fit of jealousy—or, even less so, the generalised thought of a jealous husband killing his innocent wife—is unlikely to elicit strong emotion. The intense and growing emotion in our response to Shakespeare's play arises out of the precise delineation of this event, and events leading up to it, within a complex dramatic structure. It is the development of thought-clusters around the characters and around the fictive events—and the precise way those thought-clusters are constituted or formulated—that makes these episodes vivid and moving.

A fourth element from thought theory seeks to account for the specificity or directedness of the elicited emotions. Given that the characters are fictional, what determines that it is specifically Othello that we fear and Desdemona that we pity in responding to the play rather than other individuals who might be in a similar predicament? The suggestion in my original paper (Lamarque 1981) is that again we need to appeal to thought-clusters, but more precisely that we need to ground the directedness of the emotions in both a causal and a content-based connection between the thoughts brought to mind and the descriptions and images in the work itself. Even if we learn of Othello and Desdemona from a secondary source without having read or viewed Shakespeare's play, there must be a causal chain (perhaps of a Kripkean kind) traceable in principle from our thoughts to the play itself in order to ground our emotional responses (i.e., to show the responses to be directed to those particular characters). But a causal link is not sufficient; there must also be an intentional content to the emotions, a way of characterising the objects of the emotions (what they are directed at), that connects them to the intensional content or meaning of the play (e.g., the characters might come to mind under the original descriptions of them).

One final aspect of thought theory was merely hinted at in my original presentation of the theory: that there are likely to be some kinds of isomorphism between the structure of a literary work—or at least parts of a work—and the structure of thoughts that the work elicits and which generate the emotional responses.

It is this last element that is the starting point for what I want to propose now. Using the notion of narrative opacity, I shall argue that the cognitive benefits of literature are best explained through exploring the distinctive ways in which a work's content is presented and the ways readers engage with the particularities of that content. To understand how the great works of literature can, speaking metaphorically, *reshape our minds* or *change our inner landscape* in a positive manner, we can appeal to the very elements of thought theory just outlined. It is not just that we come to think new thoughts when we engage with literary works—that is obvious—but what is of more interest is how we acquire those thoughts and how they can re-order our minds in subtle ways. *How* we think becomes as salient as *what* we think, just as *how* the content is presented can help determine exactly *what* that content is.[1]

Thought and Belief

So let us see how such a view might be supported. First we need to go back to that distinction between thought and belief, at the core of thought theory. The simple idea is this: that it is possible to entertain a thought without believing it to be true—that is, without a disposition to assert it. I can hold in mind the thought that there is a lion next door without believing that there is such a lion. This is often associated with the imagination: I can imagine such a thing without believing it to be true. However, an important qualification is needed with regard to the thought-versus-belief distinction in the case of fiction. Sometimes, the relevant thoughts do not always stand in contrast to beliefs, as there are beliefs in the context of fiction that are intimately connected to the thoughts: these are, of course, beliefs about the fictional world itself. When we read Kafka's famous opening sentence, "As Gregor Samsa awoke one morning from uneasy dreams he found himself transformed . . . into a gigantic insect", there are ample clues, both internal and external (the sheer improbability of it), that we are not to take this as an assertion of fact. We have no inclination to believe it as fact. But we do, of course, bring to mind this striking scenario, and there is nothing at this stage which stops us from believing that what we have read is true in the fiction.

Many of the beliefs we acquire when reading fiction—and need to acquire if we are to gain understanding—are beliefs about a fictional subject matter. We come to believe what Gregor Samsa or Madame Bovary or Barchester are like. Acquiring these beliefs (at least true beliefs) is not always straightforward and can call for discernment, attention to detail and judgement. We are not always good at it, and it is a skill comparable to acquisition of (true) beliefs elsewhere. The knowledge we acquire of fictional characters—fully aware that they are fictional—lodges in our minds alongside other knowledge and interacts with it. When we think about or get to know real people, images and beliefs from the fictional realm can play a central part. We recognise elements of Madame Bovary in a friend; we think about love or jealousy or desire or ambition through the lens of our knowledge of fictional cases. This itself is a kind of cognitive benefit.

Several points are worth remarking here. First of all, these beliefs about what is true in the fiction share content with the thoughts we entertain in reading the fiction. At the same time that we hold in mind the thought that Othello killed Desdemona, we also believe that in the Othello world this is what happened. However, the thoughts, even the propositional thoughts, brought to mind do not map one-to-one with the beliefs, for there might be thoughts connected to fictional content that we have no desire to assert even as beliefs about the fiction. These might be thoughts that are mere suppositions or hypotheses about the content. Thus we might entertain the thought that Iago's wife Emilia has slept with Othello (Iago raises the idea himself: "it is thought abroad that 'twixt my sheets / He's done my office" [1.3.386–87]); other passages could be construed as supporting the supposition.[2] But most readers (or audiences), one suspects, would at best keep an open mind on the matter rather than positively believe it to be true.

The most important consideration, though, one we will pursue in more detail, relates to opacity. Fictional content is *perspectival*, given not transparently (pointing to a fictional world somehow independent of its presentation) but from a point of view, that is, essentially, not merely contingently, through the perspective of the descriptions constituting the content (the point is introduced in chapter 1). This opacity constrains the fittingness of the relevant beliefs or thoughts. Should there be a marked discrepancy between the mode in which the content is represented in the minds of the readers and its mode of representation in the narrative text itself, dangers of misrepresentation (even misunderstanding) arise.

A RETURN TO OPACITY

In our book *Truth, Fiction, and Literature*, Stein Haugom Olsen and I remarked on a certain kind of opacity in reports about fictional narrative content (Lamarque and Olsen 1994, 126f). One example we used focused on the name "Canterbury" in Geoffrey Chaucer's *The Canterbury Tales*.

Here is a relevant passage from the *Tales*:

> And specially, from every shires ende
> Of Engelond, to Caunturbury they wende,
> The hooly blisful martir for to seke,
> That hem hath holpen whan that they were seeke.
> Bifil that in that seson, on a day,
> In Southwerk at the Tabard as I lay
> Redy to wenden on my pilgrymage
> To Caunterbury with ful devout corage,
> At nyght were come into that hostelrye
> Wel nyne and twenty in a compaignye
> Of sondry folk, by aventure yfalle
> In felaweshipe, and pilgrimes were they alle,
> That toward Caunterbury wolden ryde.
> (Prologue, lines 15–27 [Chaucer 1957, 17])

The modern city of Canterbury contains both a cathedral and a university—the former medieval in origin, the latter founded in the 1960s. The cathedral that exists today in Canterbury is the very one in which Thomas Becket was murdered (in 1170) and that became the site for later pilgrimages. While it would be entirely accurate to report that Chaucer's pilgrims were travelling to a city with a cathedral, it would seem at least misleading to report that the pilgrims went to a city with a university (or even one that would later have a university). Having a university is a modern aspect of Canterbury that has no place in Chaucer's narrative. No doubt one might be able to formulate an appropriate *de re* report about the contents of *The Canterbury Tales* to the effect that it is true of Canterbury itself, under any description, that it was the destination of the pilgrims. But it does not seem right, without suitable qualification, simply to substitute the definite description "the city in Kent with a university" for the name "Canterbury" in the report "Chaucer's pilgrims went to Canterbury". The sentence "Chaucer's pilgrims went to the city in Kent with a university" seems, again without qualification, to be false, or certainly misleading. But what interested Olsen and me was less the preservation of truth in the substitution (*salva veritate*) so much as the preservation of the narrative (which we, in our own coinage, called *salva fictione* [Lamarque and Olsen 1994, 126]).

One inference that we drew from this was that the name "Canterbury" in *The Canterbury Tales* is not used in a purely transparent manner. Although the name has a referential function in the poem, its use does not licence just any substitution of co-designative names (or singular descriptions) if the narrative is to be preserved. A further consequence of this—going beyond the merely semantic—would be to say that only certain aspects of the city of Canterbury (roughly speaking, those aspects contemporaneous with the tales themselves) are relevant in the picture readers are invited to form of the narrative content. To bring to mind aspects of the modern city of Canterbury—like its having a university—is at best a distraction in reflecting imaginatively on the goings-on of Chaucer's pilgrims. Similarly, although the expression "The hooly blisful martir" clearly refers to St Thomas Becket, it would be a move beyond Chaucer's narrative to substitute the definite descriptions "the saint whose shrine at Canterbury was destroyed by King Henry VIII" or "the saint whose assassination was the subject of a play by T S Eliot", although these descriptions might quite appropriately figure in critical commentaries on Chaucer's narrative.

What the example shows is that the kind of opacity Olsen and I had in mind is apparent in three related but distinct occurrences: in certain kinds of narrative itself; in reports of narrative content; and in propositional attitudes (such as thinking, imagining, believing) taken towards narrative content. As far as narrative itself is concerned, it should be noted that the relevant species of opacity is not a feature of narrative per se but only of certain kinds of narrative, notably (but not exclusively) those of fiction or literature, and even in those narratives the opacity is not *intrinsic* but reflects a certain kind of interest taken in the narratives. Only where the mode of narration is salient—in other words, where the form in which a story is told matters in the appraisal of the narrative—will substitutions be blocked. Those narratives primarily concerned with imparting information—from homely conversational narratives to those of history or biography—will normally invite a transparent construal of their proper names or other referential devices. Of course, the expression "mode of narration" recalls the Fregean "mode of presentation", and there will be cases even in information-imparting narratives in which mode of narration is significant. Simple Fregean cases establish this; a narrative that states "Hesperus is Phosphorus" is unlikely to licence substitution to "Hesperus is Hesperus" where information content is lost. We will see later how important mode of narration is to literary narratives.

The opacity of narrative *reports* follows largely from the opacity of narrative. Where it matters to a narrative what form the narration takes, it will likewise matter to a report about the narrative that it treats its references opaquely (and indeed, as we shall see, preserves sense in other ways as well). But the general constraints on narrative reports are less those deriving from features of narrative than those deriving from features of speech and the reporting of speech. The principles of *oratio obliqua* and *oratio recta* apply in parallel fashion to the reporting of narrative. As we have seen, it is often entirely permissible, in the right context, to report narratives under *de re* or transparent formulations. And it might be appropriate in critical commentaries to invoke supplementary information about the subjects of narratives to enhance understanding or appreciation.

Of most interest for the present enquiry is the effect of narrative opacity on the psychological attitudes that bear on narrative content. What is it to reflect on, hold in mind, imagine or even make believe the content of a fictional narrative? To what extent are those mental states themselves subject to a corresponding opacity, limited, one might say, to *de dicto* rather than *de re* formulations?

It is time to look at some cases.

CASE STUDIES

It seems an anodyne truth that a reader's engaging with a fictional narrative involves, at least partially, the reader bringing to mind thoughts that relate to the propositional content of the narrative. Chapter 3 of F Scott Fitzgerald's novel *The Great Gatsby* begins with this sentence: "There was music from my neighbour's house through the summer nights" (1967, 45). A reader would have little difficulty entertaining the thought of—indeed, imagining—music coming from a neighbour's house through summer nights. That thought is entirely general with little specificity of detail and involving no singular reference. But, of course, the quoted sentence itself is grounded in a context, and it does contain singular reference in the form of a definite description, "my neighbour's house". The possessive pronoun "my" needs to be negotiated. In fact, as we know, it is a reference to the narrator, Nick Carraway, who has already introduced himself into the narrative, not, of course, a reference to the author Scott Fitzgerald writing in propria persona. This knowledge must inform the thought. Even the phrase "my neighbour's house" needs attentiveness if the right image is to be conjured. The reference is to Jay Gatsby's house, and there had been a passing description of it in an earlier part of the novel:

> The [house] on my right was a colossal affair by any standard—it was a factual imitation of some Hôtel de Ville in Normandy, with a tower on one side, spanking new under a thin beard of raw ivy, and a marble swimming pool, and more than forty acres of lawn and garden. (11)

This description somehow needs to inform the imagining when a reader brings the relevant thought to mind about "my neighbour's house". Finally, there is the reference to music. Although unspecific in this sentence, it soon acquires specificity. A page or so later, we are told what kind of music to imagine:

> By seven o'clock the orchestra has arrived, no thin five-piece affair, but a whole pitful of oboes and trombones and saxophones and viols and cornets and piccolos, and low and high drums. . . . playing yellow cocktail music. (46)

This simple example tells us much about what is involved in "bringing a thought to mind" in reading a literary narrative. The sentence under discussion, "There was music from my neighbour's house through the summer nights", seems quite unexceptional; however, the surface conceals the complexity in responding to literary fiction. Merely appealing to entertaining thoughts, imagining or making believe does not itself do justice to those complexities. A great deal of scene-setting—the fictional mode, narrative voice, reference (implicit and explicit), textual connectedness—must be in place for the appropriate thought and imagining to be grounded: "appropriate" in the sense of being adequately informed by the relevant surrounding context.

The presence of metaphor or imagery can make matters even more complicated. Consider, for example, the very next sentence at the beginning of chapter 3: "In his blue gardens men and girls came and went like moths among the whisperings and the champagne and the stars". Why "blue gardens"? (Artificial, unnatural, feeling blue?) Why "moths"? (Attracted by the light? Short-lived? Creatures of the night?) Is it enough merely to say that readers make believe or imagine *that men and girls came and went like moths among the whisperings and the champagne and the stars*? The literal propositional content, in isolation from a complex thought-cluster, seems inadequate to capture the full nuance of the thought that the literary context invites.

Before we pursue these additional complexities, let us return once again, and briefly, to the relation between thought and belief. We observed that a reader can entertain a thought, in the imagination, without believing it to be true. This imagining is imbued with a kind of opacity—through which what is imagined is constituted by the descriptive modes under which it is presented—and is also deeply contextual. The same is true of beliefs. Belief formation is important in the fictional context because beliefs about what is true within the fiction form the backbone of a reader's conception of the world of the fiction. But it is arguable that although important at this basic level, belief formation is not as important as the formation of thought-clusters. The level at which beliefs about a fictional world have any kind of stability is indeed pretty basic. Beliefs formed about characters, attitudes, values and meanings are much less secure and, being subject to hypothesis, supposition and interpretation, are always liable for revision.

The basic level is what might be called fact. In the description of Gatsby's parties, the narrator relates this: "[O]n Mondays eight servants, including an extra gardener, toiled all day with mops and scrubbing-brushes and hammers and garden-shears, repairing the ravages of the night before" (45). In entertaining this thought, a reader will no doubt conjure images of mops and scrubbing and hammers and shears. What about beliefs? No doubt the context invites certain low-key beliefs: that Gatsby has at least eight servants and more than one gardener, that his weekend guests leave a trail of mess and damage, that the clearing up is a lengthy process ("toiled all day") and so forth. But are even those beliefs secure? Should we not be more cautious and believe only that these are things the narrator wants the reader to take as true? And does it matter if we believe this or merely hold it in mind?

The narrator is painting a picture of Gatsby that we have every reason to treat with caution. The ambivalence Nick Carraway shows towards Gatsby (which he announces in the first couple of pages)—his contradictory attitudes of envy, repulsion, awe, grudging admiration, pity, puzzlement and compassion—suggests not only that readers are not getting an unbiased (or straightforwardly truthful) account but also that their beliefs about Gatsby are already coloured with these same attitudes.

At the heart of narrative opacity is the idea that a reader's attention to textual nuances, implicit evaluations, narrator reliability, symbolic resonance, humour, irony, tone, allusions or figurative meanings in the textual content will help give precise shape to the thoughts and beliefs that the content brings to mind. Similarly, the very ordering of the material, the manner in which information is imparted in a narrative and the setting up and fulfilment of expectations, can structure the reader's perspectives. Thought-clusters, then, are densely opaque when formed with a literary interest in mind.

Consider the development of thought-clusters around the character of Gatsby himself, pursuing this example for a final time. The unfolding characterisation takes shape slowly in the novel. Crucial information about Gatsby's true background (his criminal activities, his modest upbringing, his obsession with Daisy) takes time to emerge. Early in the novel, he is a mysterious, aloof figure attending, but not participating in, the lavish parties at his house. We are told that people turn up uninvited: "Once there they were introduced by somebody who knew Gatsby, and after that they conducted themselves according to the rules of behaviour associated with an amusement park" (47). What is the narrator conveying here? There is no escaping the evaluative resonance with the implication that "behaviour associated with an amusement park" is not that of civilised or cultivated people, and it can only be ironic that the narrator should speak of "rules" governing such unsophisticated behaviour. The partygoers gossip about Gatsby:

> "He's a bootlegger," said the young ladies, moving somewhere between his cocktails and his flowers. "One time he killed a man who had found out he was the nephew to Von Hindenburg and second cousin to the devil. Reach me a rose, honey, and pour me a last drop into that there crystal glass." (67)

The juxtaposition of those last two sentences suggests that the idea of killing a man is to these guests of no more significance than topping up a glass—

a fact borne out later by their seeming indifference to Gatsby's own murder (none of them turn up at his funeral). The crystal glass might be sophisticated but the freeloaders who drink from it are not, or at least not in the eyes of Nick Carraway.

In general, the narrator is torn in his attitude to the fabulous opulence of Gatsby's world, and indeed to Gatsby himself, an ambivalence running throughout his narration. At times, the hollowness of it strikes home—for example, in reflecting on the atmosphere around Gatsby's house when the guests leave:

> A wafer of a moon was shining over Gatsby's house, making the night fine as before, and surviving the laughter and the sound of his still glowing garden. A sudden emptiness seemed to flow now from the windows and the great doors, endowing with complete isolation the figure of the host, who stood on the porch, his hand up in a formal gesture of farewell. (62)

As Gatsby's doomed relationship with Daisy emerges, a more tragic and thus sympathetic figure develops, shaping the reader's own attitudes as mirrored in those of the narrator. At the fateful reunion of Gatsby and Daisy, Gatsby's vulnerability and the hopelessness of his quest are captured in this somewhat wistful description:

> As I went over to say goodbye I saw that the expression of bewilderment had come back into Gatsby's face, as though a faint doubt had occurred to him as to the quality of his present happiness. Almost five years! There must have been moments even that afternoon when Daisy tumbled short of his dreams—not through her own fault, but because of the colossal vitality of his illusion. It had gone beyond her, beyond everything. He had thrown himself into it with a creative passion, adding to it all the time, decking it out with every bright feather that drifted his way. No amount of fire or freshness can challenge what a man can store up in his ghostly heart. (102–3)

In the final meeting between the narrator and Gatsby, the narrator's ambivalence is out in the open:

> "They're a rotten crowd," I shouted across the lawn. "You're worth the whole damn bunch put together."
>
> I've always been glad I said that. It was the only compliment I ever gave him, because I disapproved of him from beginning to end. First he nodded politely, and then his face broke into that radiant and understanding smile, as if we'd been in ecstatic cahoots on that fact all the time. His gorgeous pink rag of a suit made a bright spot of colour against the white steps, and I thought of the night when I first came to his ancestral home, three months before. The lawn and drive had been crowded with the faces of those who guessed at his corruption—and he had stood on those steps, concealing his incorruptible dream, as he waved them goodbye. (160)

Here, then, is a character whose very being is given, as we might put it, opaquely—that is, actually constituted by the points of view embodied in the narrative descriptions. The narrator's shifting attitude towards Gatsby determines the reader's own shifts in thought and imagining. The thought-clusters that develop while reading the novel are not just a succession of propositions held in mind. They are shaped, manipulated and given structure through the linguistic resources of the narrative prose. This is narrative opacity. The psychological attitudes are complex. Yes, the reader acquires beliefs about Gatsby, but they are troubled or unstable beliefs reaching out to an objective fact that is ultimately not available beyond the perspectives of multiple narrative attitudes. Gatsby as a character is an artefact of the text, a reader's construct that can vary under interpretation but is not answerable to a world viewed transparently in which truths are waiting to be discovered. In a sense, the beliefs cannot reach through to Gatsby himself, whatever that might mean, because it makes no sense to speak of *de re* beliefs about a character of this kind.

It is important to recall that no narrative is intrinsically opaque—we read for opacity when we take a certain kind of interest in a narrative. If our interest is simply in plot and character broadly delineated, then we read more transparently than if our interest is in the fine-grained modes in which the content is presented, the latter being an interest characteristically taken in works of literature. Literary interest dictates that far more is going on in the reader than just an amassing of facts about a fictional world. That world, viewed in its fine-grained aspects, is constituted by both the descriptions given and the images evoked. It is shaped in other ways as well—for example, in the case of *The Great Gatsby*, by the strong undercurrent of wider themes that inform the thought-clusters and provide literary significance: themes regarding the American Dream, illusion, wealth and happiness, new money and old, style, status, cynicism, hope and loss. Recurrent symbols—the eyes of Doctor T J Eckleburg, the green light at the end of Daisy's dock—give further structure to the developing thoughts. Gatsby and his world lodge in the mind not as mere character and plot but as a far more complex constellation of ideas and images.

Let me end this section with a further reflection on what is involved in a reader's changing perspectives on narrative content. So far, I have emphasised the many ways these perspectives are shaped by the opaque quality of narrative descriptions—in the Gatsby case, as informed by the shifting attitudes of the narrator himself. Within narratology, there have been sophisticated analyses of the phenomenology of reading, not least by reader response theorists. This is not the occasion to explore these in detail, but it is worth noting a convergence of interests with at least one aspect of these theories. Wolfgang Iser has much to say about the complexity of reading and the ways in which a reader's perspectives can change:

> [T]he activity of reading can be characterised as a sort of kaleidoscope of perspectives, preintentions, recollections. Every sentence contains a preview of the next and forms a kind of viewfinder for what is to come: and this in turn changes the "preview" and so becomes a "viewfinder" for what has been read. This whole process represents the fulfilment of the potential, unexpressed reality of the text, but it is to be seen only as a framework for a great variety of means by which the virtual dimension may be brought into being. The process of anticipation and retrospection itself does not by any means develop in a smooth flow. (1984, 54)

He also adds, "We look forward, we look back, we decide, we change our decisions, we form expectations, we are shocked by their nonfulfilment, we question, we muse, we accept, we reject; this is the dynamic process of recreation".

This familiar shifting of perspectives in the reading process is at least partially connected to the embedded perspectives in the literary text itself. After all, an author can manipulate a reader's expectations, reactions and questionings. Intriguingly, Iser draws a conclusion from this shifting dynamic of "anticipation and retrospection" to a view about fiction's lifelikeness:

> In the course of a novel . . . we sometimes find that characters, events, and backgrounds seem to change their significance; what really happens is that the other "possibilities" begin to emerge more strongly, so that we become more directly aware of them. Indeed, it is this very shifting of perspectives that makes us feel that a novel is much more "true-to-life". Since it is we ourselves who establish the levels of interpretation and switch from one to another as we conduct our balancing operation, we ourselves impart to the text the dynamic lifelikeness which, in turn, enables us to absorb an unfamiliar experience into our personal world. (62)

Part of the thinking here is that the "shifting of perspectives" in reading mirrors the process by which we get to know people in the real world. If reading a novel were just a matter of accumulating beliefs about fictional characters in a linear manner, not only would it weaken our engagement with the characters, but, apart from anything else, it would also make it less likely that the resulting thought-clusters would induce any strong emotional response.

FORM AND CONTENT

In the context of poetry, the thought that form and content are somehow intimately connected is a commonplace in the literary community, even if it can be formulated in different ways.[3] But the lesson for narrative must be carefully applied. In Thomas Hardy's dour poem "After the Burial", there is a narrative of sorts depicting a bereaved family numbed by their grief and seemingly oblivious to the more cheerful peals of bells in the neighbourhood:

The family had buried him,
  Their bread-bringer, their best:
They had returned to the house, whose hush a dim
  Vague vacancy expressed.

There sat his sons, mute, rigid-faced,
  His daughters, strained, red-eyed,
His wife, whose wan, worn features, vigil-traced,
  Bent over him when he died.

At once a peal bursts from the bells
  Of a large tall tower hard by:
Along the street the jocund clangour swells.
  And upward to the sky.

Probably it was a wedding-peal,
  Or possibly for a birth,
Or townsman knighted for political zeal,
  This resonant mark of mirth.

The mourners, heavy-browed, sat on
  Motionless. Well they heard,
They could not help it; nevertheless thereon
  Spoke not a single word,

Nor window did they close, to numb
  The bells' insistent calls
Of joy; but suffered the harassing din to come
  And penetrate their souls. (1994, 813)

The structure of the poem is tight. The first two stanzas and the last two express the gloom and lethargy of the family; the middle two stanzas inject a tone of brightness, even humour, describing the pealing bells with their "jocund clangour" and offering the slightly mischievous explanation of a "townsman knighted for political zeal". Yet, returning to the family, we find no brightness in their reaction to these "insistent calls / Of joy". The bells become only a "harassing din" that "penetrate[s] their souls". The juxtaposition of moods in the different stanzas, if anything, darkens the overall tone. The heaviness of grief hangs over it, the "mute, rigid-faced", "strained, red-eyed", "wan, worn", "heavy-browed" people unresponsive to any "mark of mirth". For a reader merely to form the thought that a family in mourning is disturbed by outside bells would be to miss entirely the perspective from which the scene is observed (the mood, the tone of the descriptions, even the insistent metre and rhyme). This perspective is integral to its very nature.

Form-content identity in poetry is sometimes explained in terms of unparaphrasability, but that is inadequate. Hardy's lines could be paraphrased easily enough, with varying degrees of precision for different purposes. In a school lesson, for example, it might be entirely legitimate (and helpful) to summarise in different words what is going on in each stanza. What seems clear, though, even truistic, is that the summary, or paraphrase, is not *equivalent* to the poem; it is not a matter of indifference if a reader reads the poem or the paraphrase. Part of the reason for this is that if one is taking an interest in the poem *as a poem*, then one should be receptive to the overall *experience* that the poem affords, and that experience is partially determined by the very words and structures themselves. There is always more to a poem than just a core meaning that could be expressed in other ways. In this respect, poems are different from other modes of discourse—including conversation and even philosophy—in which alternative expressions can be just as effective in imparting an idea or message. When Cleanth Brooks (1968) coined the phrase "Heresy of Paraphrase" in relation to poetry, he was not saying that paraphrase of poetry is impossible or pointless—he acknowledges it might be useful in certain contexts—but rather that it should never be deemed substitutable for the poem itself. A poem never just makes a statement in which *what* is stated is indifferent to *how* it is stated.

It might be thought that form-content indivisibility is a peculiarity of poetry in which fine-grained attention to language is integral to the kind of experience that poetry offers, and for which it is valued. But narrative opacity also shows how form helps determine content in prose narrative. In a literary novel, it is not a matter of indifference how scenes are depicted, as if *the very same* scenes might have been described in any other manner. The point, as with poetry, is not about the possibility or otherwise of paraphrase. Paraphrase of scenes in novels is entirely possible and occurs in "plot summaries", but once again few would hold that a plot summary is as good as, or equivalent to, the original narrative form. Note that this is true for anything that might be classed as a literary narrative. Again, there are other kinds of narrative—perhaps stories for children made up by parents or someone recounting the day's events—that are not so bound to precise modes of narration. It is sometimes thought that the mark of the unparaphrasability of poetry is that no substitutions can be made—even synonyms for synonyms—while retaining the identity and integrity of the whole. But, it is said, such a strict rule does not hold for narrative prose. Synonyms in many cases could be substituted without any loss of work identity.

However, the status of this claim is obscure. Perhaps all the vital meaning in a literary narrative could indeed be preserved through such (small, intermittent) substitutions, and that might show that form is not so tightly tied to content in prose cases. But the idea that this might somehow licence rewording of literary works is absurd at many levels. A Jane Austen or Charles

Dickens novel, let's say, gets its identity, and through that its literary value, in the precise words—give or take minor issues of textual corruption and so forth—written by the author. Wilful changes, even preserving sense, would be unacceptable and undermine work identity. Even more significantly, it could never be said with confidence that any given synonym substitution is "harmless" to a literary narrative. To read a literary work seriously is always to attend to, or be on the lookout for, linguistic nuance.

A small example. Here, a critic notices the recurrence of the word "peep" in Dickens's *Bleak House*:

> The word "peep" echoes through the book, neatly conveying the partial and fragmented view of things which people usually achieve. Esther, for example, after her arrival at Bleak House, watches the dawn prospect from her window change "at every new peep" and then decides to "take a peep at the garden". Mrs Snagsby, curious about Tulkinghorn's business with her husband . . . "peeps at them through the window-blind"; and, shortly afterwards, at Nemo's death-bed, Miss Flite "peeps and trembles just within the door". It is obviously no coincidence that the youngest member of the Jellyby family, a relentlessly curious and peripatetic child, should be named "Peepy".
>
> The term "peep" suggests a childish inquisitiveness, or a timid and old-maidish activity. But in *Bleak House* curiosity can quickly take less innocuous forms. (Ousby 1977, 978)

A single word in so long a novel might seem of marginal significance—and thus easily substitutable—but the lesson from narrative opacity is that there is a standing assumption that form of narration *counts* in the characterisation of content. The word "peep", in this example, is not accidental; it has a function and salience in the narrative: it connects scenes, it holds nuances ("childish inquisitiveness"), it contributes to an atmosphere ("a partial and fragmented view of things"). Part of the pleasure of reading Dickens is savouring his use of language; the distinctive features of his characterisation and scene depiction are determined by their precise linguistic delineation. In that sense, form and content are indivisible even in novelistic narrative.

Consider another seemingly minor passage, also from *Bleak House*:

> My Lady Dedlock (who is childless), looking out in the early twilight from her boudoir at a keeper's lodge, and seeing the light of a fire upon the latticed panes, and smoke rising from the chimney, and a child chased by a woman, running out into the rain to meet the shining figure of a wrapped-up man coming through the gate, has been put quite out of temper. (Dickens 1977, ch. 2, 11)

Here are the critic Ian Ousby's observations about this passage:

> When the reader encounters that passage for the first time the parenthetical phrase serves adequately to account for her [i.e., Lady Dedlock's] apparent detachment and her concealed chagrin. Childless herself, she can only be a silent and distant spectator of such domestic scenes. But when the passage is read in the light of the novel's denouement it takes on a more precise reference to her fate. The spectacle of the child "chased by a woman" recalls Lady Dedlock's separation from her illegitimate daughter, Esther Summerson. One further notes in chapter 18 that the lodge is actually the scene of Lady Dedlock's first interview with Esther. (1977, 976–77)

What the critic is noticing is a resonance in the passage with other parts of the novel and the way a reader's perception shifts as more information accrues. The description bears poignancy well beyond its surface meaning. It does so much more than merely relate a fact in the fictional world. The "fact" described—the parenthetical "who is childless" even shows that it is not strictly factual—is heavy with significance. Such a simple-seeming passage confirms once again how wrong it is to view narrative prose (in literature) as merely offering a window transparently onto a world, as if all that matters is that facts about that world be placed before us, however described. Perhaps David Lewis's account of a fictional world, as a world in which the fiction is "told as known fact", might have these consequences.

According to thought theory, the strength of an emotional reaction to fiction is likely to increase as thought-clusters take shape. But more needs to be said about the formation of these clusters; we have seen from earlier examples, endorsed by the observations from Iser, that the process cannot be seen as merely passive or even linear. To consolidate the core thesis that works of literature can serve in some sense to reshape our minds, we must focus on the role of distinctively literary modes in the construction of the relevant thoughts.

NARRATIVE VOICES

We saw from the example of *The Great Gatsby* how the thought-clusters that a reader forms, for example, about the character of Gatsby himself are shaped by the narrator's own ambivalent attitudes. There seemed to be no neutral stance for the reader to occupy, nothing that might count as a purely "objective" view of the character. And this is not a purely epistemological claim. Narrative opacity suggests something stronger—that the character's very identity is grounded in these opaque perspectives. This again is the power of narrative to constitute as well as to characterise or to characterise through constitution.

The attitude of the narrator infuses a narrative in many subtle ways, and part of the pleasure of literature is noticing how these attitudes give colour and form to the thoughts a reader brings to mind.

In the opening scene of Dickens's *Great Expectations*, in which the young Pip first encounters the convict Magwitch, their conversation includes the following:

> "You young dog," said the man, licking his lips, "what fat cheeks you ha' got."
>
> I believe they were fat, though I was at that time undersized for my years, and not strong.
>
> "Darn me if I couldn't eat 'em," said the man, with a threatening shake of his head, "and if I han't half a mind to't!"
>
> I earnestly expressed my hope that he wouldn't, and held tighter to the tombstone on which he had put me; partly to keep myself upon it; partly, to keep myself from crying. (1959, 16)

There are many layers to the narrative voice in this snippet of conversation, and the tone is rich with humour, irony and menace. The narrator is Pip, who, of course, knows far more about Magwitch as he relates the incident (looking back to his childhood) than he will reveal at this stage in the narrative. To impart too much information early on—that Magwitch will become his wealthy benefactor, is the father of Estella and so forth—would ruin the story and the suspense of the scene. (Re-reading the scene in full knowledge of the novel offers a different experience from a first-time reading, when much remains mysterious.) Intriguingly, the old and the young Pip are both present in the narrative voice—this is the genius of Dickens the storyteller. Magwitch's appearance undoubtedly frightens the young Pip, and yet the old Pip is recollecting the scene against the background knowledge of his later fraught relations and final reconciliation with Magwitch. There is humour, as well as fear, in the passage. It is hard to take seriously the threat that Magwitch might actually start eating Pip and Pip's own response is curiously formal and detached ("I believe they were fat", about his cheeks; "undersized for my years"; "I earnestly expressed my hope that he wouldn't"). To miss the humour in the writing, as well as the underlying menace in the events described, and to miss the double attitudes of the narrator, in youth and age, would be to miss crucial elements in the scene. What is it for a reader to bring these events to mind? There is the basic scene to be pictured, an atmosphere felt, but also to be savoured is the complex tone in the narrative descriptions. There is a multi-layered and rounded experience here that if appreciated will linger in the mind and lodge as a memory.

We have looked at two cases of first-person narration in which the narrators are characters in the story, interacting with other characters and imbuing the characterisation with attitudes of their own, which, in turn, encourages thoughts both about them and about the characters they are describing. Not all narration is of this kind.

Sometimes narration is from a third-person point of view. But the narrative voice need not be disinterested. Narrative attitudes can emerge in "free indirect style".[4] A fascinating example can be found in the opening lines of Iris Murdoch's novel *The Book and the Brotherhood* (1987):

> "David Crimond is here in a *kilt*!"
> "Good God, is Crimond here? Where is he?"
> "Over in that tent or marquee or whatever you call it. He's with Lily Boyne."
> The first speaker was Gulliver Ashe, the second was Conrad Lomas. Gulliver was a versatile, currently unemployed, young Englishman in his early thirties, pointedly vague about his age. Conrad was a more gorgeously young young American student. He was taller than Gulliver who was rated as tall. Gulliver had never hitherto met Conrad, but he had heard of him and had addressed the remark which caused such excitement to, jointly, Conrad and his partner Tamar Hernshaw. The scene was the so-much-looked-forward-to Commem Ball at Oxford, and the time about eleven p.m. It was midsummer and the night was not yet, and was indeed never entirely to be, dark. Above the various lighted marquees, from which various musics streamed, hung a sky of dusky blue already exhibiting a few splintery yellow stars. The moon, huge, crumbly like a cheese, was still low down among trees beyond the local streamlets of the river Cherwell which bounded the more immediate territory of the college. Tamar and Conrad had just arrived, had not yet danced. Gulliver had confidently addressed them since he knew, although not well, Tamar, and had heard who her escort was to be. The sight of Tamar filled Gulliver, in fact, with irritation, since *his* partner for the momentous night was to have been (only she had cried off at the last moment) Tamar's mother Violet. Gulliver did not particularly like Violet, but had agreed to be paired with her to oblige Gerard Hernshaw, whom he usually obliged, even obeyed. Gerard was Tamar's uncle, or "uncle", since he was not Violet's brother but her cousin. Gerard was considerably older than Gulliver. Gerard's sister Patricia, who was to have had Jenkin Riderhood as her partner, had also not turned up, but had (unlike Violet who seemed to have no reason) a good reason, since Gerard's father, long ill, had suddenly become iller. (1987, 1f)

Those who know Iris Murdoch's novels (this was her twenty-third) will recognise they are being plunged straightaway, reassuringly, humorously, into a familiar Murdochian world. The setting is Oxford—more specifically, a Commem Ball run by one of the colleges. Commem Balls are grand formal occasions. The characters we are being introduced to have unusual, even exotic, names, like Gulliver, Conrad, Tamar, Violet, Gerard and Jenkin. Already from the names alone we know that these are typical denizens of the Murdochian world in which people are upper middle class and comfortably well off, seldom need to work for a living (Gulliver is "currently unemployed") and are self-consciously intellectual. Typically, they also have complex relationships, and this opening passage already hints at stresses and strains within the group. As we read, we are acquiring beliefs about who's who, who likes or dislikes whom, who is related to whom and so on. The complexity of all this is emphasised by the rapid accumulation of detail and the piling on of new names and new facts one after another. The single paragraph from which this quotation is taken goes on for another two pages, unremittingly adding details and new characters.

Few readers would have the ability to hold in mind so much detail or recall exactly who each character is, so we might suppose there is a "master-thought" of confusion disrupting the flow of constituent thoughts which are held fleetingly and then fade. The beliefs that readers form and retain might vary considerably from reader to reader as attention is diffused. That, we can assume, is a deliberate ploy of the narrative; confusion is integral to the presented scenario; we are being introduced to a tightly knit in-group (the "brotherhood" of the book's title), and the overwhelming detail creates a claustrophobic atmosphere of an intricate, web-like complexity, almost a conspiracy or intrigue, an interlocking group of people whom we, as outsiders, will take a while to get to know.

The narratorial voice is prominent, almost intrusive. The descriptions are not given, as it were, neutrally. They are deeply imbued with attitudes and values, with opacity, and are to be pondered and enjoyed in themselves not merely as vehicles for information. Conrad is introduced as a "gorgeously young young American student"; the Commem Ball itself is "so-much-looked-forward-to"; the moon is "huge, crumbly like a cheese", the sort of cheese one might eat at an Oxford ball. The narrator's voice is here complicit; the gorgeousness of Conrad is a description offered from the perspective of someone in the midst of it all, not an impartial observer. The syntax is broken in several places: "addressed the remark which caused such excitement to, jointly, Conrad and his partner Tamar" ("jointly" is out of place); "Gulliver . . . knew, although not well, Tamar"; "Patricia . . . had (unlike Violet who seemed to have no reason) a good reason". This fractured syntax is at best untidy, at worst illiterate. Why? The speaker is breathless, rushing through the details, entranced by the occasion, careless of grammatical proprieties. Semantics are awry as well: the words "musics" and "iller" are not in the lexicon. We are getting the information from an insider's point of view, from someone over-excited, swept away by the glamour, spilling out details in an incoherent rush, not wanting to miss anything, lingering on insignificant details like the fact that someone is taller than someone else.

So what happens to our accumulating thought-clusters? Once again, a peculiar narratorial manipulation controls our thinking. The descriptions are freighted in further ways besides. Those who know Iris Murdoch's work in general, the settings of her novels, as well as standard conventions of novel reading, will have their thoughts enlivened by this wider background. Thus knowledge of Murdoch's characteristic fictional worlds; her humour; her novelistic quirks; Oxford Commem Balls, with their sense of occasion, snobbism, somewhat precious participants; and also conventions of the novel, in which detail matters and irony always lurks, will combine to generate a remarkable complexity of thought in response to the cited passage. The result is a curiously seductive kind of "gestalt" of impressions and attitudes.

SECOND-ORDER THOUGHTS

So far, I have concentrated on thoughts directly related to character and incident in fiction, thoughts, we might say, at a first-order level. I have sought to emphasise that belief acquisition even at this level is perspectival. We come to believe what is the case in the narrative world by developing thoughts that are shaped in our minds by how the fictional content is presented. The considerable potentialities here can be overlooked if too simple a model of responding to fiction is followed. But there is another level of thought-development in response to fiction that is even more complex and sometimes thought to be at the heart of the cognitive yield of works of literature. This concerns thoughts that arise out of, or through reflection on, the first-order thoughts. The particularities of a work of fiction can coalesce into a second-order overview in which broader thoughts of a thematic kind relating to the whole work take shape. We are still in the realm of thoughts and thought-clusters, but they seem to be of a higher order and, for many people, are associated with just the kinds of insights or truths commonly attributed to literature as its principal cognitive payoff.

For our first example, let us return to Thomas Hardy's novel *Tess of the d'Urbervilles* (1891). The novel is often thought to epitomise a nihilistic philosophy, a conception of the universe as bleak, pitiless and without meaning, in which human life is subject to the cruellest fate, without hope and without redemption. It is a story of unrelenting misfortune, unhappiness and tragedy. Nearly everything goes wrong for the unfortunate, though entirely sympathetic and likeable, protagonist, Tess. She comes from an impoverished peasant family, not, as for a time seemed possible, related to the baronial d'Urbervilles. She is raped; her illegitimate baby dies; she marries a man who, upon hearing of her past, disowns her; she toils remorselessly at hard physical labour in the fields; eventually, out of sheer desperation, she kills (although without premeditation) the man who raped her and threatened to ruin her life a second time; and just after she is reconciled with her husband, she is arrested for the murder, convicted and hanged at the local prison. A more bleak story is hard to imagine.

Many readers, of course, have found in the novel far more than just the tragic story of a country girl brought low by ill fortune. They have brought to mind, one might say, conceptions that bring significance to the particularities. The critic Dorothy van Ghent, for example, sees a kind of "mythology" in the novel:

> The dilemma of Tess is the dilemma of morally individualizing consciousness in its earthy mixture. The subject is mythological, for it places the human protagonist in dramatic relationship with the nonhuman and orients his destiny among preternatural powers. The most primitive antagonist of consciousness is, on the simplest premise, the earth itself. It acts so in *Tess*, clogging action and defying conscious motive. (1979, 431)

Other critics have seen something more historical or social in its primary meaning. Thus the Marxist critic Arnold Kettle writes that *Tess* has

> the quality of a social document. It has even, for all its high-pitched emotional quality, the kind of impersonality that the expression suggests. Its subject is all-pervasive, affecting and determining the nature of every part. It is a novel with a thesis . . . and the thesis is true. The thesis is that in the latter half of the last century [i.e., the nineteenth century] the disintegration of the peasantry—a process which had its roots deep in the past—had reached its final and tragic stage. (Quoted in Howe 1979, 452f)

What are we to make of interpretative claims of this kind? I am not concerned in this context with questions of validity, or the kinds of evidence that is appropriately cited in support of such claims (e.g., in relation to authorial intention). I am more concerned with any implicit suggestion that by extracting these generalisations from the novel, we are entering the realm of the cognitive contribution that novels can afford. We learn from novels, it is sometimes said, because the novels offer truths that perceptive interpretations uncover (a view examined in chapter 7).

My own view of literary interpretation is rather different (Lamarque 2002). Again, a kind of perspectivalism is in evidence. On this view, the role of interpretation (or one role) is that of broadening the perspectives through which the particulars can be envisaged. The function of interpretation is not to extract some generalised truth which can be applied to the nonfictional world but precisely to make sense of the fictional world and to heighten our experience of that world. Again, my earlier metaphor of a novel *reshaping our minds* or *changing our inner landscape* comes into play. Dorothy van Ghent's mythological reading of the novel is not intended to convey something that has relevance outside the novel but is a way of casting the particularities of the novel into a new light. Van Ghent recognises this herself:

> When [the philosophical vision] can be loosened away from the novel to compete in the general field of abstract truth . . . it has the weakness of any abstraction that statistics and history and science may be allowed to criticize;

> whether true or false for one generation or another, or for one reader or another, or even for one personal mood or another, its status as truth is relative to conditions of evidence and belief existing outside the novel and existing there quite irrelevant to whatever body of particularized life the novel itself might contain. But as a structural principle active within the particulars of the novel, local and inherent there through a maximum of organic dependencies, the philosophical vision has the unassailable truth of living form. (1979, 429)

The truth of the philosophical vision, in other words, is its truth as an active "structural principle" applied to the fictional particulars. This seems entirely right. Certainly, in reading the novel, we might enrich our thoughts about the particulars by reflecting on the vision identified in van Ghent's reading, and this is part of the "reshaping" of our thoughts, but there is nothing in the reading that demands that we force the novel, in van Ghent's terms, "to compete in the general field of abstract truth". Perhaps Arnold Kettle's Marxist reading, which sees the novel as an expression of a thesis about "the disintegration of the peasantry" in nineteenth-century England, does demand such an application, but nothing could be more plain than that even if this thesis is true, it does scant justice to the power of the novel's particulars. And there are many other, probably better, ways that the thesis could be established.

The critic Irving Howe locates the power of the novel, quite naturally, in the character of Tess herself. He reaches for descriptions of Tess that are designed to reinforce our sense of where the fascination with the novel resides and where our attention to the particularities should be focused. It is not with some abstract philosophy:

> Tess as she is, a woman made real through the craft of art, and not Tess as she represents an idea. Marvellously high-spirited and resilient, Tess embodies a moral poise beyond the reach of most morality. Tess is that rare creature in literature: goodness made interesting. She is human life stretched and racked, yet forever springing back to renewal. . . . the novel may have a strong element of the pessimistic and the painful, but Tess herself is energy and joy, a life neither foolishly primitive nor feebly sophisticated. Though subjected to endless indignities, assaults and defeats, Tess remains a figure of harmony—between her self and her role, between her nature and her culture. (1979, 454)

By reflecting on these supplementary descriptions by the critic, we can further filter the thoughts we ourselves recovered in responding to the novel. Reading in this sense is a collaborative process.

A final example will help consolidate and expand these points. Let us consider George Meredith's novel *The Egoist* (1879). The title indicates one focus of attention and contrasts with the title of Hardy's novel, with its focus on the central character. In highlighting an abstract conception like "egoism",

Meredith seems to invite us early on to engage the second-order level of interest.

The plot of *The Egoist* is fairly convoluted, but the central theme, indicated in the title, is clear enough throughout. At the core of the novel are two main protagonists, Sir Willoughby Patterne ("The Egoist") and the beautiful and resourceful Clara Middleton, to whom he is engaged to be married. As it becomes evident to Clara just what demands Sir Willoughby will make of her in the marriage, drawing her into his egoistic world and allowing her no independence of thought, she grows more and more concerned and seeks to escape from the engagement. He refuses this and constantly misinterprets her motives. Eventually, she tries to run away, even at the cost of losing everything, but gets no further than the railway station. Meanwhile, Clara becomes acquainted with Laetitia Dale, who had once herself been courted by Sir Willoughby and seems not to have Clara's concerns about his "egoism"—indeed, is still in love with him. Clara contrives to reignite this relationship, which she believes would suit both parties as well as releasing herself. The novel ends with Clara finally managing to get out of her engagement with Sir Willoughby, who has been persuaded to pursue Laetitia instead, even though the latter is more open-eyed now about his egoism. A double marriage concludes the novel, between Sir Willoughby and Laetitia (after laying down some conditions of her own) and Clara and Vernon Whitford, a cousin of Sir Willoughby and a literary scholar who had been living at Patterne Hall. Meredith called the novel a "comedy in narrative" and the "happy" ending suggests just such. But the themes of egoism and, in particular, the plight of women in Victorian society are powerfully drawn and seriously meant.

The critic Robert M Adams writes this of Clara Middleton, illuminating both the character and the core theme:

> She appeals to us not on the basis of legal or ethical technicalities, but as a human being caught in an inhuman system of commodity relationships. By her father, by Willoughby, by "right-thinking society" as a whole, she is valued for her purity, her docility, her serviceability to men. Meredith's intuition of the suffocating web that can be woven about a young woman by playing on these "virtues" of hers is a tremendous imaginative achievement. What makes her struggle so exasperating is that breaking the net would be so easy for her, if only she would forfeit her fragile reputation. How she guides herself surely, instinctively, without calculation or crudity, through a labyrinth of blinding dilemmas to safety is the heart of Meredith's book. (1997, viii)

Certain images run through the novel, helping to illustrate Clara's predicament and her relation to Sir Willoughby:

> Clara as an *objet d'art* is one of the central images. She will ornament Sir Willoughby's house and his life. She will be static, at home; Sir Willoughby

> pictures her awaiting his return from masculine pursuits; it is the classic Victorian male image of the wife. Closely linked with this is the image of possession, of enslavement, which recurs varied and insistent throughout. . . .
>
> A second group of images sharpens the focus. These are images of hunting, prey and sacrifice. Meredith describes Clara running like a hare pursued by hounds. She is also "a victim decked for the sacrifice". This particular phrase returns us to the ornament image for she goes on to describe herself as "the garlanded heifer you see on Greek vases". (Calder 1979, 476–77)

These images have a literary function in connecting scenes, elaborating the character of Clara and, of course, giving vitality to the more abstract themes of egoism and the oppression of women. In fact, the idea of egoism is more complicated, and nuanced, than might be supposed when simply tied to the selfishness of Sir Willoughby:

> The egoist we understand to be Sir Willoughby, yet Clara describes herself as an egoist, and it is her "egoism" that prompts her rebellion, her awareness of herself as an independent, individual woman. This idea of egoism, which runs through practically everything that Meredith wrote, is double-edged. Egoism is on the one hand the core of selfish, limited, self-aggrandizing behaviour; on the other it is the spur to what Meredith calls insurrection. A sense of oneself is vital. An ignorance of self in others is disastrous. Sir Willoughby and Clara demonstrate the two facets of the same idea. (474)

Meredith subscribed to an evolutionary conception of human behaviour, in which modern behaviour often recalls or reverts to our primitive ancestry. The theory is presented explicitly in the novel:

> The Egoist is our fountain-head, primeval man; the primitive is born again, the elemental reconstituted. Born again into new conditions, the primitive may be highly polished of men, and forfeit nothing save the roughness of his original nature . . . he has become the civilized Egoist; primitive still, as sure as man has teeth, but developed in his manner of using them. (Meredith 1979, 324–25)

There is a close connection between the themes of *The Egoist* and John Stuart Mill's essay "On the Subjection of Women" (1869), which Meredith had read and admired. Indeed, it has been claimed that "what Meredith has done in *The Egoist* is to dramatize the ideas of Mill" (Hill 1979, 523). Here, some connections are spelt out:

> Mill describes the legal dependence of women as "the primitive state of slavery" which has not lost "the taint of its brutal origin". Women are in the situation of bond-servants, educated to accept their captive state. "Men do not want solely the obedience of women, they want their sentiments," Mill writes, expressing the thesis of *The Egoist* precisely. "How many are the forms and gradations of animalism and selfishness, often under an outward varnish of

> civilization and even cultivation!" he exclaims in a voice that could as well be Meredith's. "There is nothing which men so easily learn as this self-worship", he is observing a little later, and to all that Mill has to say about the effect upon men and women alike, and upon the harmony of their relations in the state of marriage, which the inferiority imposed on women is bound to produce, Meredith is in fullest accord. (523–24)

The novel, then, offers themes of a serious kind that bind together the particularities of character and plot and give them higher-order significance. As noted earlier, it is often supposed that it is at this thematic level that we enter the realm of the truth-telling contribution that novels can afford. *The Egoist* has literary value on this view, at least partially, because it reinforces Mill's arguments about the subjection of women, offering insights into both that debate and an analysis of egoism as a manifestation of primitive human behaviour.

No doubt there are contexts in which Meredith's novel can count as a powerful contribution to analyses of the role of women in Victorian society and to philosophical and sociopsychological debates about egoism. But it should not be thought that the primary role of literary interpretation is to extract social, moral or political truths that have general application to a wider field of enquiry. Of course, no adequate response to *The Egoist* could fail to reflect on the themes identified. But the themes can be seen as providing another perspective through which the thoughts and images arising from the novel's particulars take shape. They give depth and further interest to the thought-clusters secured at the first-order level. In assessing the distinctive contribution of the novel, we could debate whether Meredith is right to try to explain the selfish behaviour of Victorian men as a throwback to primitive ancestral dispositions. But that leads away from the novel into sociology and social history. It does better justice to the literary standing of the novel to ask instead how effective the concept of the primitive is in organising and making sense of the material presented in the novel itself. To view Sir Willoughby, so archetypical of a certain kind of Victorian male, through the prism of the "primitive", and to reflect on Clara as an *objet d'art* and as "a victim decked for the sacrifice", gives added richness to the characters as they lodge in the mind. We might get a far deeper and more lasting "insight" into these themes by calling them to mind *through the particulars* (the characters, the dialogue, the scenes) than by seeking to formulate generalised truths suitable for extra-literary debate. This is where the "vision" of the novel lies. Its power is in the particulars, not the generalities.

CONCLUSION

Let me end by drawing some of the threads together. I have argued that the content of literary fictional narrative is infused with a kind of opacity. The content is given and thus constituted, as we might say, "under a description". This is true not just for the fictional characters and fictional incidents described in the narrative, which acquire their nature and very existence from the modes of their presentation, but also for any real-world setting, both material and moral, which itself is presented under a perspective. What I have called opacity runs deep in narrative representation: tone, irony, humour, connotation, allusion, narrative voice and other aspects of representation colour all narrative that aspires to literary status. Or, more accurately, one should say that readers come to literary works with an expectation that narrative perspective of this kind is salient, that the modes of representation are significant. I have shown how the relevant kind of opacity occurs in narratives themselves—as well as in thoughts about narrative content. Only with these complications in place can we give any credence to the orthodox view that fictional narratives prescribe imaginings. But it focuses attention on the constraints under which that imagining takes place.

I have concentrated on the thoughts and thought-clusters that readers form in responding to works of literature under the expectation of what might be called literariness. My emphasis has been on the way that narrative can shape the thoughts of those attending to it, not merely by imparting beliefs about narrative worlds but also by informing the thoughts with the unique perspective through which the worlds are given. Although we do form beliefs when we read works of literature, beliefs about both narrative worlds and the world at large, I do not think these are as important in our response to the works as are the thought-clusters; additionally, I think the beliefs, too, are infused with a kind of opacity which makes them potentially unstable and subject to revision if only because they are linked so intimately to the descriptive modes that give rise to them. Although I have not developed the idea here, I still hold that by emphasising thoughts over beliefs, and perspective-imbued thoughts in particular, we can go some way towards explaining how and why we respond emotionally as well as cognitively to narrative. This is where I hold that thought theory can contribute to the problem of emotional response as well as to the problem of literature and knowledge.

The cognitive benefits of literature, such as they are, rest not principally on the acquisition of beliefs or the revelation of truths but in the way that narrative content lodges in the mind, imagistically or propositionally, under the very perspectives that inform the content itself. Attending to fictional particulars under the perspective of authorial and textual control, subject always to genre or cultural conventions, can shape the mind by inducing and guiding thoughts and thought processes. The building up of thought-clusters, of the kind that according to thought theory elicit emotional responses, can reconfigure our minds, usually, although not inevitably, in positive ways. Novels, we say, leave their mark on us. The great ones stay with us forever. This is what makes the experience of reading a novel valuable and valuable for its own sake. What we go on to do with the thoughts thus accumulated is another matter altogether. They might affect our subsequent actions and attitudes or they might re-order our conception of ourselves. They might have no practical effect whatsoever. But any effects they do have will be contingent and largely dependent on local psychological dispositions of individual readers. This is why one should be careful in proposing too ambitious a truth-revealing capacity for works of fiction over and above the capacity to present particularities perspectivally and literally in thought-provoking ways.

NOTES

1. I hope what I have to offer goes some way towards meeting the challenge laid down by John Gibson: "What literary aesthetics desperately needs is to find a way of talking about works of imaginative literature that can acknowledge, and in the same breath, the fictionality and the worldliness of literary content" (2007, 175).
2. For an illuminating discussion of the case, see Pettersson (2002), 220f.
3. For a classic statement, see Bradley (1926); for a recent reformulation (and defence of Bradley), see Lamarque (2009a).
4. The idea is explored in Wood (2008) and in Goldie (2012). Wood's characterisation of free indirect style, "[W]e inhabit omniscience and partiality at once" (2008, 11), fits well with the case described here.

Chapter Nine

Aesthetics and Literature

A Problematic Relation?

Among philosophers of art, it is simply taken for granted that literature falls within the purview of aesthetics. My aim is not in the end to challenge this assumption but to show, first, that it is not as obvious as might be supposed; second, that it does not presuppose, and should not rely on, reductive accounts of either literature or aesthetics; third, that it entails a conception of literature not always fully acknowledged; and fourth, that, when properly characterised, it converges with familiar principles of literary criticism.

RESISTANCE TO THE AESTHETIC

It is worth noting at the outset that literary critics on the whole show a marked reluctance to acknowledge the relevance of aesthetics to literature. This in itself ought to be more surprising than it is to philosophers of art for whom, as noted, the matter is barely controversial. Of course, there could be many reasons for this reluctance, not least a narrow view of what counts as aesthetics. An insight into the kind of worries that literary critics have with the aesthetic comes from an exchange between three prominent critics, Frank Kermode, Geoffrey Hartman and John Guillory, in a volume entitled *Pleasure and Change: The Aesthetics of Canon* (2004), which gives the text of Kermode's Tanner Lectures at Berkeley with comments by the other two. Kermode's aim is precisely to relocate at least some notion of the aesthetic—specifically the idea of "aesthetic pleasure"—in the vacuum left by the decline of "theory" since the turn of the twenty-first century. The ostensible focus is on canon formation and the extent to which judgements of aesthetic quality, apart from what Kermode calls "collusion with the discourses of power", could validly be thought to underlie the shaping of the canon.[1]

Although the critics Hartman and Guillory are happy to move with Kermode beyond the simplistic ideological analyses of 1990s cultural critics, they both express scepticism about aesthetic pleasure. Guillory notes "the pervasive embarrassment with the subject of pleasure [in the critical community], and the ease with which pleasure has been neutralized as the merely contingent effect of reception" (Kermode 2004, 66). His own unease with aesthetic pleasure stems from suspicion about "higher pleasures" and the traditional elevation of poetry among the literary arts. Although he accepts—more readily than Kermode himself—the specificity of aesthetic pleasure among other kinds of pleasures, he is inclined, against Kermode, to reject the link between pleasure and canonicity. Hartman finds the very concept of pleasure, in the literary context, "problematic" and "descriptively poor" and speaks of its "onomatopoeic pallor". To the extent that pleasure is indeed at the heart of the aesthetic—a point to which we shall return—the scepticism voiced by Guillory and Hartman about the bearing of aesthetics on literature is probably widely shared. However, Kermode is not completely isolated. The critic Harold Bloom, for example, famously led an attack on fashionable literary theory at its very height in the 1990s in the name of the "autonomy of the aesthetic" (1994, 9). Like Kermode, Bloom defends the canon on the grounds of aesthetic value while recognising that "the flight from or repression of the aesthetic is endemic in our institutions" (22).

To compress the debate drastically and crudely, the "flight from the aesthetic" among critics seems to stem from several sources: the broad politicisation of criticism in the heyday of theory and the emphasis on instrumental values of literature as against more purely intrinsic values;[2] the thought that appeal to aesthetic quality is already tainted with unwelcome ideological accretions (Bourdieu 1984; Eagleton 1990); a shying away from value judgements of any kind; a belief that reference to pleasure or emotion or experience or even a phenomenology of reading is marginal to the critical enterprise; and, by implication, the thought that the very vocabulary of aesthetics, as exemplified in Frank Sibley's famous list of aesthetic concepts—*unified, balanced, integrated, lifeless, serene, sombre, dynamic, powerful, vivid, delicate, moving* and so forth—is itself peripheral to substantial critical discourse.

What is curious, however, is that philosophical aestheticians, who readily accept a place for literature within aesthetics, often share many of the reservations found among literary critics. Aesthetic pleasure is not a prominent topic for aestheticians who write about literature, nor is much serious effort made to promote an aesthetic vocabulary in describing literary works. What place, then, does literature hold within contemporary aesthetics?

First of all, it finds a natural place in philosophy of art, which is often treated, mistakenly, as identical with aesthetics. Few aestheticians doubt that literature should count as one of the arts. After all, when the fine arts were initially characterised in the early eighteenth century, poetry was included along with painting, music, sculpture and dance, and indeed the idea of an "ars poetica" goes back beyond Horace to the ancient Greeks. There is little dispute that poetry is one of the high art forms and the artistry of poetry is not hard to discern. Yet it is a curiosity of current discussions of literature within aesthetics that almost nothing is written about poetry per se. Most attention is given to narrative fiction in the novel or drama, but it is at least not obvious that there is a unified conception that conjoins poetry and prose fiction under the label "fine art".

Among the cluster of issues that do occupy philosophers writing about literature, questions about cognitive and ethical values still rank high (as they did for the ancient Greek philosophers), as do debates about authorial intention in criticism, and about fiction and emotion. Yet it is a characteristic of these debates that they seldom focus on specifically *literary*, much less *aesthetic*, features. The question about emotional responses to fiction has been dominated by examples from film, mostly genre varieties like horror. Other issues about fiction—reference, truth-value and ontology—apply indifferently to non-literary as well as literary narratives and usually are focused in theories of meaning or metaphysics. It is perhaps for this reason that they have never caught the attention of literary critics. The key debates about intention, cognition and ethics also arise, indiscriminately, for other art forms, and the core arguments do not rest crucially on the nature and status of literature. All in all, it is far from obvious that when philosophers turn their attention to literature they are really engaged in *aesthetics* at all, as opposed to philosophy of language, metaphysics, ontology, epistemology, moral philosophy and, at best, a broadly conceived philosophy of art.

FINDING A SUITABLE GROUNDING IN AESTHETICS

So if literary critics are sceptical and philosophers only marginally interested, what future is there for an aesthetics of literature? More precisely, what might be involved in supposing literary works to be appropriate objects of aesthetic attention and aesthetic appraisal? Kermode and Bloom are no doubt right that some conception of *aesthetic pleasure* is integral to such an approach, but their literary critical opponents are also right to be suspicious of this. Kermode gets off on the wrong foot by seeking to naturalise the pleasures of literature via Freud and Roland Barthes, identifying them with a heady mix of sexuality (Barthes's *jouissance*), transgression and what he calls "dismay". Apart from the fact that this simplistic psychologising is hopelessly vague and open to counter-example, the highly implausible idea that there is a distinct phenomenology associated with reading literature can only discredit the enterprise that Kermode is engaged in. A characterisation of the aesthetic pleasure that literature can afford is not some empirical datum with which the enquiry starts but at best a destination reached from quite other premises.

If aesthetics is to be at all relevant to literature, it must deploy recognisable features of aesthetic appraisal as applied more widely, but it must also capture something distinctive about literature as an art form. This is by no means an easy task or even one that the subject matter obviously demands. After all, aesthetic appraisal in most other contexts is connected in some way with perception or sensory experience or the "appearance" of objects, and it is often supposed that this already distances literature from other art forms (and indeed from aesthetics). Is there anything sufficiently analogous to the experiential side of aesthetic response to make the literary case worth considering in this context? The answer, I believe, is "yes", but it will not be found in reductive accounts of *jouissance* or transgressive pleasures. The key is in a suitably qualified conception of *appreciation*.[3] If it can be shown that there is a distinct mode of appreciating literature *as literature* or *as art*, then the first crucial step will have been taken to establish that an aesthetics of literature is possible and worthwhile.

We should look, I suggest, to Frank Sibley, rather than Immanuel Kant and the idea of disinterested attention, for inspiration on how to proceed. The Sibleyan tradition of aesthetics suggests important constraints on how an aesthetic approach might be developed, although we need not be committed to all of Sibley's specific claims. Sibley identified a range of concepts (noted previously) which serve to characterise aesthetic aspects of art or other objects. Setting aside the question of how useful such concepts are to the literary critic, it is important to acknowledge some benefits of the lists he assembled.

One benefit is to show that aesthetics is not exclusively confined to beauty, as it seemed to be in the eighteenth century. To speak merely of the "beauty" of literary works is as anodyne as speaking merely of the "pleasure" they afford. Sibley showed that aesthetic appraisals, thus aesthetic interests, are considerably wider than that. Another benefit is his recognition of the subtly different ways in which descriptive and evaluative elements can interact in aesthetic concepts (Sibley 1974). Aesthetic characterisations are not always or only ways of evaluating works; they also have implications for how the work *appears*, what *impact* it has, what is *salient* in it, what merits aesthetic *attention*. Aesthetic descriptions bring such matters to light.

There are also three more substantive theses in Sibley that seem especially pertinent. The first is the view that aesthetic properties are emergent or *gestalt* properties that require something more than merely sensory perception for their discernment. Sibley maintains that only people possessing a certain kind of "sensitivity" or "taste", itself subject to training and improvement, will be able to apply aesthetic terms appropriately and engage in aesthetic appreciation. Something parallel is true in the literary case—namely, that mere grasp of the language is not sufficient to appreciate a work aesthetically. Whether a particular sensibility is called for might be open to question (see Olsen 1987, 7), but that some skill is involved beyond linguistic competence seems certain. Literary appreciation is not a natural but rather a trained mode of discernment.

The second Sibleyan thesis relates to this—namely, that there is no logical or even inductive relation between an object's non-aesthetic properties and its aesthetic ones. No list of non-aesthetic—physical, structural, perceptual—properties entails (or makes probable) the presence of an aesthetic property. The idea that no aesthetic concepts are condition-governed has been challenged (e.g., Kivy 1973), but there is no need to engage that debate here. There is at least a case for saying in the literary application that a work's emergent aesthetic features, of a kind that will be exemplified later, are not deducible from textual features alone.

Thirdly, Sibley's aesthetic particularism has an application in the literary context. This is the view that aesthetic judgements are not generalisable. From the fact that in this work this combination of non-aesthetic features contributes to this aesthetic effect, it does not follow that there is a generalisable principle stating that whenever that or a similar combination occurs the same effect will follow (2003, 133). For example, the use of the "same" poetic imagery—love as a rose, time as a tyrant—in different works never ensures sameness of aesthetic effect.[4]

One of the principal lessons from the Sibleyan tradition is that aesthetic qualities, while related to non-aesthetic qualities, are not reducible to them. The temptation to reduce literary works to instances of more familiar or more tractable kinds is the biggest obstacle to a successful characterisation of literary aesthetic appreciation. Only if literary works can be shown to be objects of a distinctive kind of aesthetic appraisal, and to promote and reward such appraisal, will it be possible to set apart the literary sphere as a subject worthy of its own treatment within aesthetics. But the tendency to "naturalise" literature is strong—for example, to see works of literature as no more than pleasing pieces of language.

If the aesthetics of literature has any hope of finding a coherent, central and defensible place for *aesthetic pleasure*, for *aesthetic features* distinct from merely textual features, for a *sui generis* mode of *aesthetic appreciation* and for some conception of *aesthetic value*, then it needs to avoid the temptation of reduction on several fronts: to any one literary form (e.g., poetry alone); to purely linguistic properties (semantic, syntactic or rhetorical); to formal properties (e.g., style or structure); to purely hedonistic conceptions of pleasure; to intuitive, "natural" or untutored "responses"; and to aestheticism.

In what follows, I will focus principally on three kinds of reduction, which I see as obstacles to an aesthetics of literature, each of which has its adherents. One is to *form*, one is to *meaning*, and one is to a certain kind of *narrative realism*.

FINE WRITING AND ITS LIMITS

A prominent temptation in trying to characterise literature in aesthetic terms is to reduce literature to "fine writing" or "belles lettres". In itself, the idea is not implausible, for there is indeed a generic sense of "literature" in which it means just that. Fine writing is exemplified across nearly all modes of discourse: history, philosophy, biography, letter writing, political speeches, as well as throughout the more narrowly defined literary arts of drama, poetry and the novel. And it is not uncommon to describe such discourses, when well written, as "literary".

Fine writing is easier to recognise than to define. David Hume's philosophical writing frequently exhibits literary or aesthetic qualities, as when he describes his philosophical journey in the *Treatise*:

> Methinks that I am like a man, who having struck on many shoals, and having narrowly escap'd shipwreck in passing a small frith, has yet the temerity to put to sea in the same leaky weather-beaten vessel, and even carries his ambition so far as to think of compassing the globe under these disadvantageous circumstances. (2007, 172)

It is not only the metaphorical figure that contributes to the literary effect but also the phrasing, structure, cadences and choice of words. Nevertheless, we should probably look to rhetoric rather than aesthetics to characterise the effectiveness of writing of this kind. Perhaps surprisingly, I am not inclined to build the aesthetics of literature on the base of "fine writing" or on a belles-lettrist conception of literature.

For one thing, giving focus to fine writing affords no principled way to distinguish between "literature" in the generic sense and "literature" in the narrow sense of literary art. The label "imaginative literature" for the latter is not entirely satisfactory, for it is not as if the imagination has no role in other discourses. If imaginative means fictional, then that seems to favour certain kinds of literary works, such as novels, over others, such as lyric poetry. It is better, as we shall see, to draw the distinction between literary artworks and works of history, philosophy or biography, independently of "fine writing", in terms of practice-based modes of attention and appreciation. Fine writing might be a sufficient condition for literature in the generic sense, but it is not sufficient for literature as art and arguably not even necessary. Those novels, for example, that are written in the first person through the narrative voice of a child (e.g., *Catcher in the Rye*) or someone uneducated (e.g., *True History of the Kelly Gang*, Peter Carey's novel) might not exemplify fine writing as that is normally understood, even if the writing is described as clever, effective, moving or realistic. Other reasons altogether qualify the writing as literature or as art.

It might seem perverse to set aside fine writing when addressing the aesthetic qualities of literature so a further word needs to be said on this. Of course, aesthetic pleasure is to be had in good writing wherever it appears. Nor is it uncommon for critics to use aesthetic concepts—expressive, moving, powerful, resonant, striking—to characterise poetic usage. But good writing in literary art is seldom an end in itself, rather a means to some further end or effect. Mellifluous prose or delicately nuanced imagery will not always be appropriate in every literary context, say, in a dialogue (in a novel) between drunken members of street gangs. Rhetorical or formal devices, like figurative language, imagery, alliteration, rhyme schemes, repetition, metre, do not have intrinsic aesthetic value but gain their effectiveness by the contribution they make to a desired end, be it emotional impact, realistic depiction, humour or poetic insight. The use of alliteration, rhyming couplets or enriched figuration affords no aesthetic pleasure, for example, if used to convey bad news.[5]

The important theoretical point, though, is that formal or rhetorical devices are in themselves *textual* features, identifiable independently of discursive aims and often subject to learnable rules. They acquire aesthetic significance only when assigned a function within an artistic structure. Here is an example. Consider a critic's observations on certain rhetorical features in these well-known lines from Wordsworth's "Tintern Abbey":

> . . . a sense sublime
> Of something far more deeply interfused,
> Whose dwelling is the light of setting suns,
> And the round ocean, and the living air,
> And the blue sky, and in the mind of man:
> A motion and a spirit, that impels
> All thinking things, all objects of all thought,
> And rolls through all things.

> Some of the sweep of this passage is also to be explained by the repetition of "and": "*And* the round ocean, *and* the living air, / *And* the blue sky, *and* in the mind of man". In conventional prose "and" would normally signal the end of a list, but here, no sooner has Wordsworth thought to end it than some other facet of nature's multitudinouness occurs to him. The list is apparently endless, and Wordsworth's profligate way with connectives all adds to the sense of amplitude and prodigality. This impression is strengthened by a similarly

> extravagant use of "all": "*All* thinking things, *all* objects of *all* thought, / And rolls through *all* things". The omnipresence of the "a"-sound is also worth noting: seven consecutive lines in this section begin with it, and all the singular elemental words—"man", "and", "am", "all", "a"—contain it. When this ubiquitous sound is coupled with the way every aspect of the universe is merged together with connectives and embraced by repeated "all"s, we have the impression that man, language and the universe are merging together in a paean of ecstatic oneness. (Rowe 2004, 174–75)

What is striking about this passage is that it highlights a textual feature—the repetition of "and" and "all"—which might in other contexts be thought a defect, far less a mark of fine writing. But the critic identifies an aesthetic function for this rhetorical feature and assigns both significance and value to it. The aesthetic significance of the repetition *emerges* from the particularities of the poetic context and the construction put upon it. The example demonstrates a fundamental aspect of literary aesthetic effect: the consonance of means to end. The critic's aesthetic appreciation of the passage lies in perceiving a consonance between the formal means and the further poetic purpose of expressing "nature's multitudinousness" and the "ecstatic oneness" of man and universe. The appreciation does not rest on the rhetorical feature (the *textual* feature) alone.

MEANING: A SUBSIDIARY ROLE

Just as it is wrong to reduce literature—and the aesthetic qualities of literature—to fine writing, so it is wrong to seek a reductive explanation of literature in terms of language or meaning per se. Literary works are not simply strings of sentences to be assigned meaning—in a word, they are not simply *texts*. Extreme textualists in effect dismiss the idea that there is anything distinctive about literary works among other kinds of texts. They hold, with Roland Barthes, that texts are undifferentiated "writing", or *écriture*, waiting for readers to fashion into their own meanings (Barthes 1977), or, with Richard Rorty, that "the coherence of the text . . . is no more than the fact that someone has found something interesting to say about a group of marks and noises" (1992, 97). It is not just the aesthetic interest in literature that gets lost under such reduction but also literature itself as a meaningful category.

A more subtle form of linguistic reductionism, short of textualism, takes literary works to be contextualised utterances akin to utterances in any form of communicative exchange. Noël Carroll is well known for promoting the analogy between literary writing and conversation (2001, pt. III), and Robert Stecker identifies what he calls "work meaning" with "utterance meaning" (2003, 59). On this view, there is no difference *in principle* between writing a novel, writing a letter, having a conversation or making a political speech.

All manifest the same desire to convey meaning. All invite the same goal of understanding, and success is judged on whether the meaning is conveyed. It is no wonder that the debate about intentions is so prominent among philosophers who start with this premise about literature. The primary questions become what kind of meaning is conveyed and what are the constraints in grasping that meaning: is it the explicitly intended meaning of the author, is it the contextualised meaning of the words used, is it the meaning of an utterance combining intention and convention, and so forth?

I suggest that this framework is utterly misconceived; the emphasis on conveying and grasping meanings distracts attention from more fundamental issues about what literary works are and what they are valued for.[6] Significantly, there is no intention debate about aesthetic description. If we are to pursue the possibility of an aesthetics of literature, it will be necessary to move beyond a focus on utterances and their meanings. A radical shift is needed from the picture of an author producing a *text*, communicating a *meaning* and inviting *understanding* to that of an author creating a *work*, engaging a *practice* and inviting *appreciation* (see Olsen 1987; Lamarque 2009b). It is the latter that must underpin any coherent, non-reductive aesthetics of literature.

There is no denying, of course, that literary works are associated with texts and meanings nor that the question of what a particular phrase or sentence means will inevitably arise. This is sometimes called "explication". The mistake is to suppose that explication is a model for literary interpretation or literary appreciation. Consider this example: Edmund Spenser's poem *Epithalamion*, written in 1594, demands a great deal of explication, at least for modern readers. Here is part of stanza 9:

> Loe where she comes along with portly pace,
> Lyke Phoebe from her chamber in the East,
> Arysing forth to run her mighty race,
> Clad all in white, that seemes a virgin best.
> So well it her beseemes that ye would weene
> Some angell she had beene.
> Her long loose yellow locks lyke golden wyre,
> Sprinckled with perle, and perling flowers a tweene,
> Does lyke a golden mantle her attyre,
> And being crownéd with a girland greene,
> Seeme lyke some mayden Queene.

The meanings of Elizabethan words—"portly" (stately), "seemes" (suits), "weene" (expect), or "perling" (winding)—need to be recovered, as do the classical or mythological references to the likes of Phoebe (goddess of the moon). The expression "mayden Queene" must be recognised as an allusion to Queen Elizabeth I. A scholarly edition will make such matters clear with the aim of aiding understanding. There is little need to refer to Spenser's intentions, as the recovered facts rest on shared contemporary knowledge.

However, the pursuit of textual or utterance meaning in this vein is a bare preliminary to an appreciation of Spenser's poem as a literary work. Such appreciation only begins with the recognition that the poem belongs in the conventionalised "epithalamic" tradition popular in the Renaissance but dating back to the Roman poet Catullus. Epithalamia are celebrations of weddings, following strict conventions of versification, imagery, epithets and temporal structure, with a conventional progression through the religious rites, the processions, the banqueting, the singing and revelry, the retreat of bride and groom to the bedchamber and the final consummation.

What becomes salient in appreciation of Spenser's poem is not the way he follows convention or uses conventional imagery but rather how he departs from convention to produce something unusual and unique. Unusually, for example, the poem is about the poet's own wedding, fusing the role of bridegroom and poet-speaker. References to the bride's beauty take on a personal not merely conventional colour. Another unconventional motif is, in the words of a critic, the recurring

> ominous associations of darkness . . . [for example] where the stars are described as torches in the temple of heaven
>
> that to us wretched earthly clods
> In dreadful darkness lend desired light . . .
>
> Here it is not only the marriage but the whole of human experience which is menaced by the night's sad dread. Thus the threat of disaster, the irrational fear of vaguely specified suffering, hovers faintly over the poem, lending particular urgency to the concluding prayers. (Greene 1968, 648–49)

Literary critical observations of this kind move some distance from a search for utterance or conversational meaning. The exploitation of and departure from specific poetic conventions already provides a richer context for appreciation than afforded by any effort merely to understand the poem's meaning. That the "threat of disaster . . . hovers faintly over the poem" is a fact, if a fact at all, not about meaning but about tone and mood.

The appreciation of Spenser's poem arises not only from recognition of its embeddedness in a poetic tradition but also from wider expectations of literary art per se. Appreciating the poem involves locating it both in the specific context of the epithalamic tradition and in the context of poetic art more widely conceived. It is integral to the practice of reading a poem *as a work of art* that interest is given to structural and thematic unity. Again, the focus is not on what the poem *means*—beyond textual explication—but on how the poem *works*, how its effects are achieved. Here is a critic noticing such aspects in *Epithalamion*:

> The world of the poem may be seen as a series of concentric areas. In the center is the couple, always at the dramatic focus; about them lies the town, the "social context"—the merchants' daughters, the young men who ring the bells, the boys who cry "Hymen" with "strong confused noyse"; beyond lies the natural setting, the woods that echo the jubilation with an answering joy . . . vaguely outside of this is the world of classical figures, the Muses and the Graces, Maia and Alsmena, Hera, Cynthia, and Hymen . . . finally above all these realms stretches the thinly disguised Christian Heaven, the "temple of the gods", lending light to wretched earthly clods. The poem begins and ends with the widest perspective; at the center of the poem, during the ceremony, the focus has narrowed to the couple itself. Immediately before and after the ceremony the focus includes the "social context". The opening, with its perspective into the past, is balanced by the concluding perspective into the future. Thus, structurally as well as thematically, the amplitude is complemented with an elegant symmetry and an intricate harmony. (Greene 1968, 648–49)

It is not fortuitous that the critic ends this analysis by using aesthetic terms like "elegant symmetry" and "intricate harmony", for what the analysis has identified is an aesthetic feature, not merely a textual feature, of the poem. The idea of there being concentric circles unifying the work structurally and thematically, with the couple at the centre and the Christian heaven around the perimeter, is not "given" in the text, implied by semantic content, but is an "emergent" feature imaginatively reconstructed by a reader seeking a distinctive kind of appreciation from the work. That readers of literary art should seek symmetries and unity and connectedness of this kind (both formally and through any generalised vision that a work embodies) is not a merely contingent aspect of particular interests, but rather it is essential to the mode of response demanded by the very practice of literature. Literary works are defined as works that invite and reward such a response. This is at the heart of what makes literature a suitable object for aesthetic appraisal and is not reducible to facts about linguistic meaning.

FICTIONAL WORLDS

The examples I have offered so far are from poems, and it might be thought that in focusing on poetry I have made the case for an aesthetics of literature too easy. Few would disagree that poetic art exhibits aesthetic features, even if, as I have tried to show, there is not clear agreement on what such features are. But what about literary works in prose: the novel or narrative fiction?

In fact, I don't believe that from an aesthetic point of view there is a difference in kind or that prose fiction is any less susceptible to aesthetic appraisal or appraisal as art. One problem is that narrative fiction, more so than poetry, encourages a bifurcation of interest that in one form or another runs through all literary criticism: interest, on the one hand, in structures, devises, narrative styles and modes, narrators and implied authors and, on the other, interest in the human dramas depicted, the people, the conflicts, the politics, the emotions and the sociological and psychological implications. The latter interest, especially when turned into ideology, can seem remote from aesthetics, but the former can seem remote from what matters about the novel.

The aesthetic interest in the novel as an art form should not, again, be reduced to formalistic considerations. Surprisingly, though, when philosophers turn to the novel it is not that kind of reduction that tempts them but another kind that sees narrative art primarily in terms of plot and character and "world". A great deal has been written about fictional worlds, truth in fiction and the status of fictional characters but little of that, however intrinsically interesting, has much to do with aesthetics. It is reductive to the extent that it takes fictional description to be transparent, to depict people in fictional worlds exactly as a historian or biographer might depict real people. To read and understand a fictional narrative, according to reductive views, is to grasp the "facts" about a fictional world either through "make believe" or by projecting, in some other way, worlds, in David Lewis's terms, in which the fiction is "told as known fact". What such attention to narrative misses is precisely what makes narratives a focus for aesthetics—namely, the modes by which the "world" is presented and the lack of transparency in fictional description.

The "world", for example, of Dickens's *Bleak House* is not merely Victorian London, or even Dickensian London drawn as a more or less realistic backdrop for the action of the novel; it is itself an elaborate imaginative construct built on a wealth of fine-grained description and infused throughout with symbolic significance. The critic J Hillis Miller characterises this world as follows:

> The world possesses an immanent tendency toward decomposition which only the most delicately and resolutely applied constructive force can counteract. And it is just this force which is almost totally absent in *Bleak House*.
>
> The world of the novel is already, when the story begins, a kind of junk heap of broken things. (1977, 948)

In describing the "decay and disintegration" that is a defining feature of this world, the critic notes "the great number of disorderly, dirty, broken-down interiors":

> The Jellyby household is "nothing but bills, dirt, waste, noise, tumbles downstairs, confusion, and wretchedness". At the time of the preparations for Caddy Jellyby's marriage "nothing belonging to the family, which it had been possible to break, was unbroken . . . nothing which it had been possible to spoil in any way, was unspoilt". . . . Skimpole's home too is "in a state of dilapida-

> tion", Symond's Inn, where Richard Carstone's lawyer, Vholes, lives, has been made "of old building materials, which took kindly to the dry rot and to dirt and to all things decaying and dismal", and Richard himself lives in a room which is full of "a great confusion of clothes, tin cases, books, boots, brushes, and portmanteaus, strewn all about the floor". The "dusty bundles of papers" in his room seem to Esther "like dusty mirrors reflecting his own mind". (948–49)

After citing evidence of this kind from across the novel, the critic draws a thematic conclusion: "[O]ne of the basic symbolic equations . . . is the suggested parallel between . . . two forms of disintegration", "physical or spiritual": "either the destruction of the individual through his absorption in the impersonal institution of 'law and equity', or the dissolution of all solid material form in 'that kindred mystery, the street mud'" (952).

Here we see the typical practice of the critic, making connections and finding generalised descriptions to characterise a recurrent theme. The very identity of the "world" rests on the mode of its presentation in the novel. There is no independent perspective on this world—the decay and disintegration are not contingent features but help determine what the world is—and the symbolic significance borne by its characterisation is essential to its identity. This is precisely the "opacity" of narrative discussed in chapter 1 and chapter 8. The same is true of the modes of presentation of the fictional characters for how they are presented is likewise indivisible from what they are. Characters are "perspectival" entities whose very identity is given "under a description" (again, see chapter 8). When the character Krook dies of spontaneous combustion, his horrific demise symbolises another return to the basic elements of disintegration, the fog and the mud, manifested in the "thick yellow liquor" on the window sill. His death, "inborn, inbred, engendered in the corrupted humours of the vicious body itself" (Dickens 1977, 403), is not just an event in the world but also an image through which to imagine that world.

These quasi-ontological points about fictional worlds and characters are crucial to understanding the contribution of aesthetics to literature. They show that appreciation of narrative content is not (merely) a factual investigation into what is true in a possible world but an imaginative reconstruction of an artefact of language. Grasp of the propositional content of the narrative sentences is not enough to apprehend the "world" and characters presented. Something more like a Sibleyan gestalt is needed to appreciate the significance of the fine-grained descriptive content and the interconnectedness of its elements. A principle of functionality operates that is not applicable to fact-based narratives—namely, that for any element of the narrative (a phrase, a sentence, a passage, as well as an incident, a character or a description of place) it is always legitimate to ask what function that element is performing (see chapter 4). An answer to the question—an interpretative judgement locating the element within a broader perspective—will help to indicate not the *meaning* of the work but how it *works* and where its interest lies.

The appreciation of fictive narrative in prose is not fundamentally different from the appreciation of poetry. In both, a special kind of discernment is called for which goes beyond mere comprehension of the text and presupposes initiation into a distinctive practice of reading. A reader approaching a text from a *literary* point of view has expectations about what rewards will flow from giving it that kind of attention. The expectation is of a value-experience. A work that affords little by way of internal connectedness, thematic unity, complexity of structure and a generalised vision giving significance to the particularities of the subject will not reward literary attention and will be open to, at best, limited aesthetic appreciation.

CONCLUSION

Maybe none of this would persuade Geoffrey Hartman or John Guillory that applying aesthetics to literature is a worthwhile activity. Yet the aesthetic pleasure that I have called "appreciation" is very unlike the reductive sensual pleasures that Frank Kermode promoted and they rejected. In fact, we seem to have come full circle, for the response to literature *as literature* or *as art* that I have outlined is in essence familiar to literary critics. It has not elevated one mode of literature over another, poetry or narrative, and it has discarded formalism and the belleslettrist conception of literature. It has also repudiated a tendency among philosophers, alienating to critics, to see narrative fiction as a mere window into alternative worlds, peopled by facsimiles of ourselves. Not only do critics reject the assumption of realism but, rightly, they are also suspicious of the implied conception of realism as transparency.

My argument has been that a substantial aesthetics of literature must avoid misplaced emphasis in three areas: on intrinsic textual properties, on the priority of meaning and on reductive views of plot and character. That need not be uncongenial to literary critics. The argument has promoted various distinctions not universally acknowledged by critics but not at odds with basic critical principles: between texts and works, specifically textual features and aesthetic ones; between appreciation and understanding; and between what something means and how something works. The aesthetic elements identified in literature are not simply well-crafted turns of phrase or expressive images—although everyone agrees such things exist—but rather emergent qualities that become salient when appropriate attention is directed to works. There is a kind of perception involved in discerning such qualities and ultimately it is a source of pleasure. In that sense, there need be no watering down of aesthetics when applied to literature.

NOTES

1. For further arguments in favour of "aesthetic quality" over "ideology" in canon formation, see van Peer (1996).

2. Criticisms of the instrumental attitude to literature within theory appear in Attridge (2004), 7–10.

3. It should be noted that the conception of appreciation developed in this chapter is distinct from an alternative conception, which I do not have space to consider but should not be left unmentioned, advanced by Susan Feagin (1996). Feagin's conception principally concerns affect or feeling, although it includes elements of interpretation and meta-reflection. She offers a sophisticated account of the psychology of our responses to literary fiction—notably, our emotions of empathy and sympathy—and explores the multiple ways that literary works stimulate and manipulate feelings, which in turn ultimately ground value judgements. Much of this is highly illuminating, but there are doubts about its centrality to *aesthetics* and indeed to *literary criticism*. One might suppose that critics like John Guillory would take affective response, like pleasure, to be "neutralized as the merely contingent effect of reception" (see previously). There are worries, too, that emphasis on localised affects cannot account for a work's overall aesthetic unity. For a discussion, see Lamarque (2000).

4. The singularity of the work is often remarked. Hence Malcolm Budd:

> The value of poetry is singular or non-substitutable; poetry has an importance it could never lose by being replaced by something else that achieves the same end; for what we value is the experience of the poem itself, a specifically linguistic expression of a complex of thought, desire and sentiment. (1995, 85)

It is notable that Budd makes the point by reference to the "experience" of poetry.

5. Hume has noted the inappropriateness of powerful rhetoric on such occasions:

> Who could ever think of it as a good expedient for comforting an afflicted parent, to exaggerate, with all the force of elocution, the irreparable loss, which he has met with by the death of a favourite child? The more power of imagination and expression you here employ, the more you increase his despair and affliction. (2008, 132)

6. Gregory Currie has criticised me for rejecting the conversational model, on the grounds that the pragmatics of "communicative utterance" are "indispensable" in literary reading as in any other kind of communication (2010, 17–18). Maybe some simple pragmatic inferences from what is said in a literary work to what is meant are legitimate. But the constraints imposed by the practice of literary interpretation (look for connecting themes, ask what an action symbolises, be on the lookout for allusion and so forth) are radically different from the standard constraints in, at least, conversational exchange (where themes, symbols and allusion have no natural place). If Currie wants to extend "pragmatic inference" right into these highly conventionalised responses, that's fine, but it weakens the thought that literary "utterances" are somehow on a par with other kinds, notably conversational ones.

Chapter Ten

On Keeping Psychology Out of Literary Criticism

All human practices are amenable to psychological description—description in terms of motives, desires, beliefs, emotions or expectations—and many are open to psychological explanation as well. The making up and telling of stories, the construction of poems, the reading and enjoying of literary products of all kinds, as activities in a practice or set of practices, are no exception. There is plenty of scope for psychological investigation of the literary realm. Empirical studies into what actually goes on when writers write or readers read can yield informative and unexpected results.[1] None of that is being questioned in what follows.

The question I want to pursue is not whether participants in the practices of literature do manifest distinctive psychological states, in individual cases or systematically as a class, but whether the occurrence of such states—in particular, affective states—plays a significant role in literary critical judgements of meaning or value. My argument will be that they do not and that they should not, at least if literary criticism is to retain its focus on literature as art. My discussion will centre on emotions in both authors and readers, but I take my conclusions to range more widely over psychological states. My thesis indeed is that psychology should be kept out of literary criticism. Empirical facts about the psychological states of actual people and empirical theories about such states will not illuminate what is of value in individual works of literature.

MODERNISM AND ROMANTICISM

There have been uneasy relations between psychology and literature for over a hundred years. Of course, one could go back two and a half thousand years when Plato was denigrating poetry for its dangerous play with emotions, but it is not much more than a hundred years since criticism established itself as a serious academic pursuit. In the early days, it was thought that linking criticism to a science like psychology would add to its respectability. This was perhaps partly behind the development of the psychological theory of criticism presented by I A Richards in his *Principles of Literary Criticism* of 1926. Armed with the distinction between referential and emotive functions of language and convinced that poetry deals paradigmatically with the latter, Richards postulated a complex isomorphism between poetic structure and affective response. What makes literature valuable, on Richards's account, is that it can arouse and organise emotion to a degree that is not available in everyday life. In effect, it is psychologically valuable in what it can do for the psychological well-being of those exposed to it.

Yet, curiously, at just that time in the development of criticism, there was a striking move away from psychology and emotion (or at least emotion centred on the author). Indeed, T S Eliot's essay "Tradition and the Individual Talent", which was first associated with that move, was published in 1919, seven years before Richards's *Principles*. It was here that Eliot made his famous pronouncement about the "extinction of personality" in poetry:

> [T]he poet has, not a "personality" to express, but a particular medium, which is only a medium and not a personality, in which impressions and experiences combine in peculiar and unexpected ways. Impressions and experiences which are important for the man may take no place in the poetry, and those which become important in the poetry may play quite a negligible part in the man, the personality. (1972, 75)

This is a passage remarkable for its anticipation of many powerful currents of critical theory that came to dominate the twentieth century, from New Criticism to structuralism to poststructuralism. Eliot goes on:

> It is not in his personal emotions, the emotions provoked by particular events in his life, that the poet is in any way remarkable or interesting. His particular emotions may be simple, crude, or flat. The emotion in his poetry will be a very complex thing, but not with the complexity of the emotions of people who have very complex or unusual emotions in life. . . . Poetry is not a turning loose of emotion, but an escape from emotion: it is not the expression of personality but an escape from personality. (76)

So began a modernist criticism, which emphasised poetry as linguistic medium, in direct challenge to a romantic criticism which dwelt on poetry as personal expression and emotional resonance.[2] The romantic vision had dominated the previous century, and it had become a commonplace to endorse Wordsworth's sentiment that "all good poetry is the spontaneous overflow of powerful feelings". Idealist philosophers like Benedetto Croce and R G Collingwood built their own expression theories of art around such an intuition.

The two camps, the romantics and the modernists, jostled repeatedly through the century with some notable exchanges. One such exchange was between E M W Tillyard and C S Lewis in their book *The Personal Heresy: A Controversy* from 1939. Lewis takes the modernist line in attacking the "Personal Heresy". He writes, "[W]hen we read poetry as poetry should be read, we have before us no representation which claims to be the poet, and frequently no representation of . . . a personality at all" (Tillyard and Lewis 1939, 4).

By the time that W K Wimsatt and Monroe C Beardsley wrote their two essays "The Intentional Fallacy" and "The Affective Fallacy" in 1946 and 1949, respectively, most of these ideas had already been well aired, if not universally accepted, in the critical community. I will not say much about intention per se—it is an overworked topic—but it is worth recalling that the explicit target of "The Intentional Fallacy" was romanticism, particularly the expression theory of Benedetto Croce. The aim was to distinguish what the authors called "criticism of poetry" from what they called "author psychology"—in other words, to keep author psychology out of criticism properly so called. Famously, their own credo, in contrast to Wordsworth's, proclaimed that a "poem . . . is detached from the author at birth . . . belongs to the public . . . [and] is embodied in language". But less often quoted is a wider rejection of author psychology: "[T]here is a gross body of life, of sensory and mental experience, which lies behind and in some sense causes every poem, but can never be and need not be known in the verbal and hence intellectual composition which is the poem" (Wimsatt and Beardsley 1972a, 340). This is the autonomy view of poetry at its most striking. I will come back to the expression theory and its critics later.

In many ways, the other paper, "The Affective Fallacy", is more interesting for our purposes. This, as is well known, is an attack on "trying to derive the standard of criticism from the psychological effects of the poem" and, among other things, directly challenges I A Richards's emotive theory of meaning. But again, it is primarily an attack on importing psychology into criticism, this time from the perspective of the reader's responses: "The report of some readers . . . that a poem or story induces in them vivid images, intense feelings, or heightened consciousness, is neither anything which can be refuted nor anything which it is possible for the objective critic to take into account" (Wimsatt and Beardsley 1972b, 353). The critic should attend not so much to the emotion induced by a poem but to "the reasons for emotion, the poem itself", and such attention "will talk not of tears, prickles, or other physiological symptoms, of feeling angry, joyful, hot, cold, or intense, or of vaguer states of emotional disturbance, but of shades of distinction and relation between objects of emotion". They go on:

> It is precisely here that the discerning critic has an insuperable advantage over the subject of the laboratory experiment and over the tabulator of the subject's responses. The critic is not a contributor to statistically countable reports about the poem, but a teacher or explicator of meanings. (354)

In other words, no psychological experiments about how readers respond emotionally to poetry will reveal what the critic can reveal about a poem's meaning and achievement. This, to anticipate, strikes me as right, but in recent years philosophers—notably, among others, Susan Feagin (1996) and Jenefer Robinson (2005)—have wanted to introduce the tears, prickles and physiological symptoms, the anger and joy and emotional disturbance, back into criticism, so the affective fallacy is on the agenda again. Of course, merely stating that there is such a fallacy is not an argument, but I believe there are arguments in defence of Wimsatt and Beardsley and I shall come back to them.

However, no survey of the pro- and anti-psychology dialectic in twentieth-century critical theory can quite end there. There would be a huge and deplorable gap without mentioning psychoanalysis. For a sizeable chunk of the twentieth century, the branch of psychology most closely associated with literature and criticism was psychoanalysis in its various manifestations. Many current psychologists might lament this influence, but like it or not, here was a systematic attempt to apply psychological theory to literature. Furthermore, it was based on a deceptively simple premise, as stated by the erstwhile psychoanalytic critic Frederick Crews: "The simple fact that literature is made and enjoyed by human minds guarantees its accessibility to study in terms of broad principles of psychic and social functioning" (1970, 1). In his seminal paper "Creative Writers and Daydreaming" (1908), Freud had sought to identify some general motivation behind creative writing:

> A strong experience in the present awakens in the creative writer a memory of an earlier experience (usually belonging to his childhood) from which there now proceeds a wish which finds its fulfilment in the creative work. The work itself exhibits elements of the recent provoking occasion as well as of the old memory. (S. E. 1908, IX, 151)[3]

This postulated link between writing and wish-fulfilment epitomises many of the dangers of appeal to psychology in criticism. It looks reductive, speculative, indifferent to the particularity of the work and difficult to verify. In fact, to be fair to Freud, he was much more cautious in *The Interpretation of*

Dreams, from 1900, when he first mooted the connection between Hamlet and Oedipus: "[A]ll genuinely creative writings", he stressed, "are the product of more than a single motive and more than a single impulse in the poet's mind, and are open to more than a single interpretation" (S. E. 1900, IV, 206). In his essay "Psychopathic Characters on the Stage" (1905), Freud reflected on what we now know as the paradox of tragedy—why tragedy gives pleasure: tragic portrayals, he thought, are "based on an illusion"; the viewer's "suffering is mitigated by the certainty that, firstly, it is someone other than himself who is acting and suffering on the stage, and, secondly, that after all it is only a game" (S. E. 1905, VII, 306).

The appeal, such as it is, of psychoanalysis lies in its aim to provide a general explanation across the board, not just of why works are written but of why readers enjoy certain genres—notably tragedies and romances—and also why particular works have an enduring value. Interestingly, such overarching explanations in the arts have been sought in recent years through evolutionary theory.[4] But it is precisely this appeal to generality that also displays the weakness of such accounts. Could we really expect there to be a unified explanation for why Homer wrote the *Iliad*, Milton *Paradise Lost*, Trollope the Barchester Chronicles, and Philip Larkin "The Whitsun Weddings", and is there any substantial psychological explanation of why these works continue to be enjoyed (an explanation beyond the fact that they possess unique literary qualities)? More on that as we proceed.

Psychoanalytic criticism is an extension, although not an exemplary case, of romantic theories, at least in its appeal to the states of mind of authors and readers. Even if these states are unconscious, they are nevertheless real and thought to be determining factors in what is produced and what is valued. Anti-romantic attacks came not just from New Criticism, with its general rejection of psychologising, but also from an unholy alliance of Marxism and poststructuralism. For Marxists, social determinants on literary production and literary value are more important than psychological ones. The Marxist idea that appealed to poststructuralists was that the autonomous self is largely a fiction or social construct. Literary works cannot be thought of as products of pure mental processes, conscious or unconscious, on this view, because mental life is not an autonomous sphere but rather a site of conflicting social forces—or discourses, for the poststructuralists—lacking any kind of unity or anything that could count as the romantics' seat of personality or individual genius. For the poststructuralists—just as for the Marxists in a slightly different context—the extinction of personality that T S Eliot had spoken of becomes an ontological fact, not just a postulate for criticism.

I take it that in a broad sense, this attack on autonomy is a further manifestation of modernism in its fight against romanticism. The unity or autonomy of the self, under this conception, becomes an illusion, so no reference can be made to it in any genuinely informative account of literary practice. If psychology, like liberal humanism in general, presupposes a self, sufficiently coherent to engage in expression or reception, then, on such a view, there can be no psychology-based criticism. The death of the author is indeed the death of psychology in criticism, but it is not, as Roland Barthes predicted, the birth of the reader in any recognisable sense, for, in following through the consequences, the reader, too, has no psychologically real point of view from which to respond to a text.[5] In so radical a scenario, even meaning itself becomes a victim of depersonalisation, at which point meaning strictly vanishes altogether.

Against this background, any anti-romantic stance about literary criticism, such as the one I am inclined to support, must tread a delicate path. It could scarcely be more important that different strands of anti-romanticism should be distinguished. It is all too easy to be trapped in guilt by association. My own position is not at one with any of those so far advanced. It is far from that of Marxist criticism, which has never quite shaken off the charge of reductivism, and in any case relies on externalist or causal accounts of literary practice, as does, typically, psychoanalytic criticism. It is equally far from poststructuralism, which, in certain forms, needlessly and groundlessly rejects the very bases of any coherent kind of criticism such as the self, meaning, objectivity and aesthetic value. Nor, finally, is it very close to New Criticism, which overemphasises linguistic meaning in criticism, based on notions like "semantic density" or "irony", and thus gives undue weight to debates about the sources of meaning, notably intention, which I, like many literary critics, think is not of central importance. Some of the arguments for the affective fallacy are more relevant, as I will show, but to reject all notions of reader response is clearly a mistake.

EXPRESSION

To develop and defend my own point of view, I am going to focus the remainder of the discussion on certain arguments in Jenefer Robinson's book *Deeper than Reason* (2005), partly because I believe it is a very good book and rewarding to get to grips with, but partly because by examining the disagreements between us—some of them deep—in relation to literature our respective positions should become clearer. Robinson explicitly calls her theory, particularly her theory of artistic expression, a "romantic" one and much of what she says about the role of emotion in literature will be congenial to those who think psychology has something to contribute to literary criticism. (Or at least it might *seem* congenial. I wonder, in fact, when the details are examined just how congenial it is to psychologists.)

Let us look first at Robinson's defence of expression theory. Her discussion of Collingwood and Alan Tormey's attack on Collingwood is exemplary and should be required reading for anyone studying expression in art. It brings out the issues with perfect clarity. I will not have anything to say on her expository and exegetical analysis. I am interested, though, in her own position. She calls this a "new romantic theory of expression", but I do wonder if it really is a theory of expression at all. Here are the five necessary conditions she identifies for an artist to express an emotion in a work of art:

1. [T]he work is evidence that a persona (which could but need not be the artist) is experiencing / has experienced this emotion;
2. the artist intentionally puts the evidence in the work and intends it to be perceived *as* evidence of the emotion in the persona;
3. the persona's emotion is perceptible in the character of the work;
4. the work articulates and individuates the persona's emotion; and
5. through the articulation and elucidation of the emotion in the work, both artist and audience can become clear about it and bring it to consciousness. (2005, 270)

The first striking thing about these conditions is the insistence that possession of the expressed emotion is attributed not to the artist—except entirely contingently—but to a "persona". In other formulations, Robinson speaks of an "implied author". There is thus no implication that the author has any real emotion to express, and indeed the only reference to any actual person's real psychological state, if such it be, is to the author's *intention* to put "the evidence [of a persona's experiencing an emotion] in the work" and for that evidence "to be perceived *as* evidence of the emotion in the persona". There is little here that the anti-romantic need take issue with. Of course, we expect a work that genuinely expresses an emotion to be the product of an intention that that should be so. It also seems exactly right, directed by caution and readerly protocols, that any emotion expressed in a work be attributed first and foremost to a persona or dramatic speaker. This is a literary critical commonplace, even if not always acknowledged by philosophers.

However, a reader of Robinson's account of artistic expression and her elaboration of it might well detect a sense of discomfort on her part with this distancing of author and emotion, even though she remains consistent in the account itself. After all, the book is about real emotions as psychological states of real people—on which she offers a penetrating and insightful analysis—and she sees a clear parallel between people expressing their emotions through actions, gestures or facial expressions, and artists expressing emotions in their work. She writes, for example, "The person's or persona's emotional state is expressed in the character of the artwork, just as the expressive character of a person's face or gestures or tone of voice may express the emotional state of that person" (2005, 270–71). Note the use of "person's or persona's", as if there were little difference. More importantly, is there not an obvious disanalogy between the artistic and non-artistic cases? When we see someone expressing their unhappiness or depression in their gestures and tone of voice, we have no inclination to attribute the emotion to a persona or anything analogous to an implied author; we attribute it directly to the person concerned (unless, of course, we think they are dissembling, but then there is no genuine expression). In the literary case, though, Robinson warns us not to make that direct connection.

The paradigm cases that Robinson refers to, quite naturally, in the literary context are romantic lyric poems, and she uses examples like Keats's "Ode to a Nightingale". One of the emotions she identifies in this poem is a "yearning for a timeless world of art and beauty". It is significant, though, that in the page immediately following that in which she insists this emotion be attributed to a persona and not to Keats himself, she writes:

> [W]e should not be too quick to assert that it doesn't matter whether it is the author or his persona who is expressing his emotions in a poem. . . . [W]e are often quite interested in the fact that Keats himself probably yearned for a timeless world of art and beauty, and that it is perfectly appropriate to identify the poetic voice with that of Keats himself. . . . It is not unreasonable to enjoy the feeling that one is engaging with the actual emotions of a great poet. (255)

This is no doubt right, for we do have interests in the personality of poets. But if true, it is a biographical, not a literary, interest. From a literary point of view, it is the emotion attributed to the persona that is the focus of attention. That is where the expression lies. A psychologist interested in the psychopathology of a poet might well go to the poem with the biographical focus in mind. But no one seeking to engage with the poem as a work of art need seek help from a psychologist. Why? Because the emotion expressed is not an occurrent emotion—only an emotion attributed to a dramatic speaker constructed in the text. To understand the emotions expressed in lyric poetry, we need to know not about psychology but about poetry, its conventions and powers. The emotions we examine are not psychological but poetic; any intensity or power they exhibit is a property of the work explicable through the rhetorical devices employed not through the mind that created them. This is the insight of modernism over romanticism, and it does seem to be an insight that Robinson endorses, in spite of designating her theory "romantic".

Take another type of case, poems written about the death of a child, in which one might suppose the emotion to be both real and especially intense. Robert Bridges's "On a Dead Child" (1890) starts like this:

> Perfect little body, without fault or stain on thee,
> With promise of strength and manhood full and fair!
> Though cold and stark and bare,
> The bloom and the charm of life doth awhile remain on thee.

Thy mother's treasure wert thou;—alas! no longer
 To visit her heart with wondrous joy; to be
 Thy father's pride;—ah, he
Must gather his faith together, and his strength make stronger.
(Bridges 1914, 267)

It is likely that Bridges wrote the poem when working as a doctor at the Great Ormond Street Hospital for Children in London, where the death of a child would have been common, and it is not implausible to suppose he had a particular case in mind. However, the specific occasion is deliberately obscured—in spite of a hint of the physician's role, "To me, as I move thee now in the last duty"—in the interests of a more universal treatment of the theme. There is plenty of emotion in the poem, but it is far from an uncontrolled outpouring of grief tied to an occurrent emotional state. In fact, the speaker, as is common in elegies of this kind, goes on to reflect more generally on death, searching for some consolation—"Death, whither hath he taken thee? / To a world, do I think, that rights the disaster of this?"—but finds nothing to mitigate the sorrow:

Ah! little at best can all our hopes avail us
 To lift this sorrow, or cheer us, when in the dark,
 Unwilling, alone we embark,
And the things we have seen and have known and have heard of, fail us.

Of course, on a theme of this kind the dangers of sentimentality, indulgence and cliché are ever-present. Gerard Manley Hopkins found all these faults in the poem, writing to Bridges, "The diction is not exquisite as yours can be when you are at ease. No, but you say it is severe: perhaps it is bald. But indeed [here he is citing the fifth stanza: 'So I lay thee there, thy sunken eyelids closing,— / Go lie thou there in thy coffin, thy last little bed!— / Propping thy wise, sad head, / Thy firm, pale hands across thy chest disposing'] 'wise, sad head' and 'firm, pale hands' do not strike me as severe at all, nor yet exquisite. Rather they belong to a familiar commonplace" (cited in Stanford 1979, 88).

Terry Eagleton is equally harsh about a better-known poem on the death of a child, Dylan Thomas's "A Refusal to Mourn the Death, by Fire, of a Child in London" (1946):

> The child is a mere occasion for baroque image-spinning. . . . The whole piece is flagrantly opportunistic. . . . When the piece finally gets round to the girl . . . it manages to make indifference sound like wisdom. . . . "I shall not murder / The mankind of her going with a grave truth" sounds impressively candid and tough-minded. Other[s] may perfume this death with their moral platitudes, but Thomas himself . . . defiantly refuses to play along with this hypocritical bombast. The only problem is that the very language in which he rejects this posturing is itself rhetorical posturing. "Grave truth" is a cheap pun. (Eagleton 2007, 75–76)

Perhaps it is impossible to avoid either "rhetorical posturing" or sentimentality in writing on this subject. But in the end, judgements of this kind are directed not to any felt emotion but to the articulation of an emotion. It is rhetoric, not psychology, being judged. Alan Tormey, developing his anti-Romantic argument, makes this point: "[S]tatements about the expressive qualities of an art work remain, irresolutely, statements *about* the work, and any revision or rejection of such statements can be supported only by referring to the work itself"; they are "not subject to falsification through the discovery of any truths about the inner life of the artist" (Tormey 1971, 105).

Ben Jonson's "On My First Son" is also expressive of grief, even more poignantly so in speaking of the death of the poet's son, aged seven. Its directness and surface simplicity are often admired, the lines quietly but powerfully intense:

> Farewell, thou child of my right hand, and joy;
> My sin was too much hope of thee, lov'd boy.
> Seven years thou wert lent to me, and I thee pay,
> Exacted by thy fate, on the just day.
> Oh, could I lose all father now! For why
> Will man lament the state he should envy?
> To have so soon 'scaped world's and flesh's rage,
> And if no other misery, yet age!
> Rest in soft peace, and, ask'd, say here doth lie
> Ben Jonson his best piece of *poetrie*.
> For whose sake, henceforth, all his vows be such
> As what he loves may never like too much.
> (Jonson 1616, XLV)

Laurence Lerner notices the "subtle rhythms, capturing the broken but controlled voice of the sorrowing parent" and insists, surely rightly, that we distinguish "the meaning of the poem when written, and the meaning of the act of writing it" (Lerner 1992, 354). Barbara Herrnstein Smith argues that the final couplet "yields emotion, which is not stable, over to wisdom, which is" (Herrnstein Smith 1968, 204). For all its seeming simplicity of metaphor, the poem develops a line of thought, both controlling and making sense of the emotion:

> The poem builds not towards one, but towards two climactic affirmations, manifesting on different levels the insight to which Jonson's grief has led him. On the purely human level, Jonson's close identification with his son is given new force by the metaphor in line ten, which dramatically merges his identity as poet and as father in the recognition that the child is his best creation. This tribute, however, is itself placed in perspective by the final line, which is not so much a new comprehension of human relationships as it is a realization of the limits fixed upon them. It may be taken as the reaffirmation of the belief in man's imperfection and his dependence on the Divine Good which has

> strengthened Jonson throughout his bereavement but which has acquired a new impact at the moment of his last farewell. (Kay 1971, 129)

What survives in these poems is the expression of grief, not the grief expressed. While the titles in the Thomas and Jonson examples indicate the specificity of the originating cause, the content in all three poems points beyond this. How do such examples bear on Robinson's expression theory? First, as she admits, the articulated emotion of grief *in the poems*—in contrast to whatever psychologically real emotion of grief lay behind their composition—is attributable to a persona, not directly to the authors (whatever the biographical circumstances). Of course, as with her Keats example, we might have an interest in the actual feelings of the poets but that interest is of a different kind and can only involve speculation. The poems readily satisfy her conditions: they are "evidence that a persona . . . is experiencing / has experienced this emotion", the "persona's emotion is perceptible in the character of the work" and "the work articulates and individuates the persona's emotion". The reader's attention is directed not to any real psychological state (however intense the originating cause) but, in all the cases, to tightly, at times claustrophobically, structured linguistic artefacts. To understand the poems *as poems*, the reader need not explore the poets' states of mind—only the linguistic expression in the poems themselves, recognising paradigmatic features of the elegiac lyric, both realised and challenged. The power and interest of the poems lie not in what they tell us about an individual on a particular occasion—why should that be of interest so many years later?—but in how they portray an emotion, one might say a poetic emotion, in a timeless fashion.

The relation between the poets' actual states of mind and the poems is radically unlike the relation of a person suffering from grief and that person's overt behaviour. Indeed, it is really only here that reservations arise about Robinson's expression theory—namely, in its emphasis of the analogy between poetic expression and ordinary behavioural expression. Otherwise, the theory seems right in its distancing of author and emotion, even if this makes the evocation of "romanticism" problematic. My concern, as it were, from her point of view, is only that the theory sits oddly in a general account of emotional expression precisely because it has so little to do with real psychological states or with psychology *tout court*.

EMOTION AND UNDERSTANDING

Turning now to the other aspect of Robinson's account of literature, we do find real psychological states—not states attributed to fictional personae—taking centre stage. Here, my disagreements are deeper. Robinson's view is that for at least some literary works, it is necessary for a reader to experience real emotional responses in order to understand the works. This view is developed in a chapter of *Deeper Than Reason* aptly entitled "The Importance of Being Emotional". As a theory of literary understanding or literary interpretation, the account offered does not seem persuasive. Unlike in her expression theory, with its emphasis on implied authors, Robinson, in her emotion theory of understanding, seems to be significantly at odds with mainstream literary critical practice. That might not worry her, but it is at least noteworthy that, broadly speaking, academic critics tend to give little attention to (psychologically real) emotional responses to literature. No doubt there are a number of reasons for this: partly just that such critics are wary of responses that might seem subjective, variable and unmeasurable; partly, and perhaps more deeply, because if you study a work in detail, with repeated re-readings, perhaps doing fine-grained analysis of particular passages or exploring social, political and cultural forces at work, any strong emotional responses associated with a first-time reading are likely to have worn off.

There are two parts to Robinson's theory. The first affirms the appropriateness, even the inevitability, of responding emotionally to some works of fiction; the second affirms the necessary role of such responses in literary understanding. Thus, speaking of a scene in Tolstoy's *Anna Karenina*, Robinson writes, "[W]e feel an intense urge to help Anna, an intense distress and sorrow at her predicament, an intense desire and hope that her predicament will be resolved. The passage is so poignant indeed that it easily provokes tears and other physiological symptoms of sadness and distress" (2005, 110–11). The emphasis is on strong and "intense" emotional responses. But who is the "we" referred to in this quotation, the "we" who feels intense urges, intense distress, intense desires and hopes? What do we say of readers who do not respond with such intensity? Is it taken to be just a fact of the matter that readers will respond this way? Or true of sensitive readers? Or readers properly informed about literature? Robinson knows enough about emotions to know that they are not always easy to predict and depend on complex sets of circumstances both in the psychology of individuals and in surrounding conditions.

What is significant is that Robinson is here talking about actual psychological states of actual readers. There is an asymmetry then between readers and authors. In the case of authors, their own personal emotions are bracketed off from the emotions expressed in the work. But if we need an *implied author* for expressed emotions, why should we not postulate an *implied reader* for response emotions? Why insulate a work from authorial emotions but not from readers' emotions? Might we not say that the passage from *Anna Karenina* is intensely moving without implying that any reader must feel some intense emotion? Some readers might, others might not. These seem to be just contingencies. All of the emotions that Robinson mentions could be attributed to the passage rather than to the reader. It is a passage that is sad, distressing, of the kind to give someone an urge to help and so on. These are characteristics of the work, not necessarily of any actual person.

This brings us to the second strand of Robinson's theory, the idea that a reader who does not have these strong affective responses has failed to understand the work. Robinson has several arguments for this view, but they all relate back to a master argument, which is this:

> Understanding character is essential to understanding the great realist novels . . . understanding character is relevantly like understanding real people, and . . . understanding real people is impossible without emotional engagement with them and their predicaments. (2005, 126)

The argument looks deceptively simple and persuasive, but the trouble lies with the middle proposition, "understanding character is relevantly like understanding real people". Realistically drawn characters, like Anna Karenina, are indeed similar in certain respects to real people. We imagine them to be real people and in filling out the narratives of their lives we make inferences based on common assumptions about what people of that kind are like. But the notion of "understanding character" is equivocal; it can mean understanding characters as imagined people and it can mean understanding them as elements in a literary work (the difference is explored in chapter 4). Perhaps—although I am not entirely convinced—to understand them in the first sense, as imagined people, readers need to engage emotionally with them. But understanding them in the second sense, as elements in a literary work, surely does not require any actual emotional response. It is the second sense that concerns the critic attending to the works *as* literature or *as* art. The point about the first sense, concerning merely imaginary people, is that the manner of their presentation in a narrative is of only contingent significance. Your recounting to me the story of Anna Karenina in your own words—or anyone's retelling of the story—would be just as likely to stir my emotions as the account in the novel. All that matters is that the imaginary person—Anna—is recognisably the same character in each case.

But when Anna is thought of as an element in Tolstoy's novel or, in the terms of chapter 1, when the work is read *opaquely*, the manner of the presentation is not contingent but essential. Now we attend to the character as an integral part of a linguistic artefact, in which the fine-grainedness of the presentation informs our response to it. Other elements, literary elements, come into play. To understand Anna, within this conception, is to understand the thematic, symbolic and meaning-laden relations that the character-as-described enters into with other characters and other incidents in the novel. On this conception, emotional engagement from a reader is at best a contingent by-product of reading, not an integral part of a literary response and as likely to cloud understanding as to illuminate it.

Yes, the scene with Anna's son Seryozha must be recognised as poignant, distressing and sorrowful. It must be recognised as an emotional scene. That is the way it is presented to us. If we read it as humorous or ironic, we would be misunderstanding the passage. But from a literary perspective, we must view it as an element in the construction of Anna's character, as resonating with other scenes in the novel, as elaborating on the desperate state of Anna's predicament, even perhaps as expressive in the sense that Robinson proposes for the lyric poem. We must locate the emotion in the scene, just as we did with the poetic expressions of grief. When Robinson says, "[I]f I laugh and cry, shiver, tense, and relax in all the appropriate places, then I can be said to have understood the story", she is not speaking with a literary interest in mind but as someone simply reflecting on an imaginary person in an imaginary world.

This takes us back to the affective fallacy and the passage in which Wimsatt and Beardsley instruct us to "talk not of tears, prickles, or other physiological symptoms, of feeling angry, joyful, hot, cold, or intense . . . but of shades of distinction and relation between objects of emotion". A final example is shared by both Robinson and Wimsatt and Beardsley, and it reveals what might be meant by "objects of emotion". It is the example of Macbeth. Robinson tells us that when attending to the scene in the play in which Macduff is told that his wife and all their children have been murdered on Macbeth's orders, she responds with horror and disgust "by shuddering, turning cold, and tensing [her] muscles" (2005, 111). Many readers or viewers might feel the same. But for Robinson, it is only with some such response that a reader or viewer could genuinely *understand* the scene. But that, I have argued, is not *literary* understanding, not least because it does not depend on specific features (what we have called fine-grained features) of the work as a linguistic artefact. After all, hearing of any premeditated murder of a whole family will induce a similar sort of revulsion.

When Wimsatt and Beardsley discuss the murder of Duncan in the play, they do offer a literary understanding that draws on literary specifics: "Set in its galaxy of symbols—the hoarse raven, the thickening light, and the crow making wing, the babe plucked from the breast, the dagger in the air, the ghost, the bloody hands—this ancient murder has become an object of strongly fixed emotive value" (Wimsatt and Beardsley 1972b, 357). One implication seems to be, in contradiction to Robinson's view, that any emotive response to this scene far from being a precondition of understanding actually *presupposes* understanding. Without first grasping the embeddedness of the action in a "galaxy of symbols", no reader will be able to respond appropriately to the specific object identified, for the event described is not just the cold-blooded murder of a king but also a literary scene of considerable complexity. An emotional response to an object of *that* kind will be quite unlike an emotional response to any real-life event.

THE LIMITS OF PSYCHOLOGY

Let me end by drawing out some conclusions. The specific, albeit negative, view I have defended is that the actual psychological states of authors and readers, notably affective states like emotions, do not and should not play a significant part in literary critical practice. Intense emotions can be expressed in works, particularly lyric poetry, but these emotions are ultimately properties of the works and not of actual people; they are attributable to personae or implied authors or they are a characteristic of described scenes and actions. Authors and readers might well have emotions in producing and responding to works, but this will always be a contingent matter inessential to an appreciation of the works themselves.

We can broaden out this conclusion to reflect on empirical studies by psychologists or cognitive scientists interested in the literary domain. Take the work that cognitive scientists have done on the mechanisms for responding emotionally to fictional characters (e.g., Meskin and Weinberg 2003; Weinberg and Meskin 2006). Some is illuminating[6] and some even reinforces ideas that I came up with a long time ago a priori. But I don't think it has much to contribute to literary criticism, to the analysis and appreciation of particular literary works. The theories themselves are neutral as to literary value and apply equally to fictional narratives of all kinds. Likewise, empirical studies that examine—as did psychoanalysis—motives for writing fiction or the satisfactions of reading will not illuminate critical practice. Critical practice is concerned with literary works of art, how they work, what they achieve, what values they exemplify. Responding to a literary work *as literature* is a distinctive, broadly normative, activity.

A few years ago, the *Journal of Aesthetics and Art Criticism* published a forceful exchange between the cognitive scientist Laura Sizer and the philosophers Peter Kivy and Noël Carroll on music and emotion (Sizer 2007; Kivy 2007a; Carroll and Moore 2007; Kivy 2007b). In the debate, Sizer claims that experiments in cognitive science have shown that a certain version of arousal theory is true—in particular, the view that music arouses moods in its listeners. Kivy takes issue with this on the grounds that the experiments fail to attend to the right kinds of listeners in the right kinds of circumstances (e.g., listening in the appropriate manner). I admit to being sympathetic to Kivy's scepticism. Listening to music merely as a stimulus in a laboratory and listening to it in an informed, serious and engaged manner in, say, a concert hall are not the same. I extend that analogy to literature. One could read canonical works of literature simply to emote over love stories or tragic endings, just as one could read lyric poetry to dig out biographical insights into poets' minds. But neither is a good basis for literary study, nor do they take seriously the peculiarities of literary appreciation. Literary criticism that focuses on literature as art is not a branch of psychology, and psychological explanations concerning states of mind are the wrong kind of explanation to shed light on it.

NOTES

1. For example, the psychological work on "transportation" in narrative in Gerrig (1993) and Green and Brock (2000), or the studies of reading strategies in Zwaan (1994), den Broek et al. (2001), and Wolfe and Woodwyck (2010). Whether these studies of narrative can cast much illumination on the distinctive practices of reading works of *literature* (*as* literature or *as* art) is debatable. Part of the aim of this chapter is to show that what matters here are not so much empirical facts about how readers do read literary works or what states of mind they are in (that will depend crucially on the class of readers chosen), but rather normative issues about what the best or most fruitful reading strategies are for discovering and appreciating literary values.

2. Elisa Galgut has pointed me to another passage from Eliot, from many years later, which appears in tension with his earlier statement (a tension he himself acknowledges):

> There are two forms of impersonality: that which is natural to the mere skillful craftsman, and that which is more and more achieved by the maturing artist. . . . The second impersonality is that of the poet who, out of intense and personal experience, is able to express a general truth; retaining all the particularity of his experience, to make of it a general symbol. And the strange thing is that Yeats, having been a great craftsman of the first kind, became a great poet in the second. It is not that he became a different man, for, as I have hinted, one feels sure that the intense experience of youth had been lived through—and indeed, without this early experience he could have never attained anything of the wisdom which appears in his later writing. But he had to wait for a later maturity to find expression of early experience; and this makes him, I think, a unique and especially interesting poet. (Eliot 1940)

It is significant, though, that Eliot still uses the term "impersonality", and, although alluding to facts about the origins of the poems in experience, he is not making inferences to the meanings of the poems. Also, his original image of the mind as a "catalyst" "storing up . . . feelings, phrases, images" can apply in this new context.

The passage has something in common with a comment made by F R Leavis about a poem by Thomas Hardy: "It is a poem that we recognize to have come directly out of life; it could, that is, have been written only by a man who had the experience of a life to remember back through" (Leavis 1952–1953, 98). But Leavis, too, in spite of this remark, is anxious to show how poetic analysis itself (rather than biography or psychology) will reveal the value of the poem.

3. All references to Freud's work will be to Freud 1953–1974. In the text, the date of the work will be given, followed by the volume in the Standard Edition (S. E.), and the page reference.

4. See Dutton (2009).

5. It seems that Barthes noticed this himself when he characterises the reader as "without history, biography, psychology; he is simply that *someone* who holds together in a single field all the traces by which the written text is constituted" (1977, 148).

6. Reservations are expressed well in Stock (2011b).

Bibliography

Adams, Robert M. 1979. "Preface". In George Meredith, *The Egoist*, edited by Robert M. Adams. New York: W. W. Norton.

Aristotle. 1984. *Poetics*. Translated by Ingram Bywater. In *The Complete Works of Aristotle: The Revised Oxford Translation*, edited by Jonathan Barnes, vol. 2. Princeton, NJ: Princeton University Press.

Attridge, Derek. 2004. *The Singularity of Literature*. London: Routledge.

Baker, G. P., and P. M. S. Hacker. 1985. *Wittgenstein: Rules, Grammar, and Necessity*. Volume 2 of an Analytical Commentary on the Philosophical Investigations. Oxford: Blackwell.

Barthes, Roland. 1977. "The Death of the Author". In *Image-Music-Text*, essays selected and translated by Stephen Heath. London: Fontana.

———. 1986. "The Reality Effect". In *The Rustle of Language*, translated by Richard Howard. Oxford: Basil Blackwell.

Beardsley, Monroe C. 1978. "Aesthetic Intentions and Fictive Illocutions". In *What Is Literature?*, edited by P. Hernadi. Bloomington: Indiana University Press.

———. 1981a. "Fiction as Representation". *Synthese* 46:291–313.

———. 1981b. *Aesthetics: Problems in the Philosophy of Criticism*. 2nd edition. Indianapolis: Hackett.

Beebe, Maurice. 1975. "The Three Motives of Rasknolnikov: A Reinterpretation of *Crime and Punishment*". In Fyodor Dostoevsky, *Crime and Punishment*, edited by George Gibian. New York: W. W. Norton.

Bell, J. M. 1973. "What Is Referential Opacity?" *Journal of Philosophical Logic* 2:155–80.

Blackburn, Simon. 2010. "Some Remarks about Value as a Work of Literature". *British Journal of Aesthetics* 50:85–88.

Bloom, Harold. 1994. *The Western Canon: The Books and Schools of the Ages*. New York: Riverhead Books.

Bourdieu, Pierre. 1984. *Distinction: A Social Critique of the Judgement of Taste*. London: Routledge.

Bradbury, Malcolm. 2000. *To the Hermitage*. London: Picador.

Bradley, A. C. 1926. "Poetry for Poetry's Sake". *Oxford Lectures on Poetry*. 2nd edition. London: Macmillan.

Bridges, Robert. 1914. *Poetical Works of Robert Bridges*, excluding the eight dramas. Oxford: Oxford University Press.

Bruner, Jerome. 1994a. *Acts of Meaning*. Cambridge, MA: Harvard University Press.

———. 1994b. "The 'Remembered' Self". In *The Remembering Self: Construction and Accuracy in the Self-Narrative*, edited by Ulric Neisser and Robyn Fivush. Cambridge: Cambridge University Press.

———. 2002. *Making Stories: Law, Literature, Life*. Cambridge, MA: Harvard University Press.

Budd, Malcolm. 1995. *Values of Art: Pictures, Poetry and Music*. Harmondsworth: Penguin Books.

Calder, Jenni. 1979. "The Insurrection of Women". In George Meredith, *The Egoist*, edited by Robert M. Adams. New York: W. W. Norton.

Carnap, Rudolf. 1956. "Empiricism, Semantics, and Ontology". In *Meaning and Necessity: A Study in Semantics and Modal Logic*, enlarged edition. Chicago: University of Chicago Press.

Carroll, Noël. 1990. *The Philosophy of Horror: Or Paradoxes of the Heart*. London: Routledge.

———. 1997. "The Film of Presumptive Assertion". In *Film Theory and Philosophy*, edited by R. Allen and M. Smith. Oxford: Oxford University Press.

———. 2001. *Beyond Aesthetics: Philosophical Essays*. Cambridge: Cambridge University Press.

———. 2002. "The Wheel of Virtue: Art, Literature, and Moral Knowledge". *Journal of Aesthetics and Art Criticism* 60:3–26.

Carroll, Noël, and Margaret Moore. 2007. "Not Reconciled: Comments for Peter Kivy". *Journal of Aesthetics and Art Criticism* 65 (3): 318–22.

Cavell, Stanley. 1987. *Disowning Knowledge: In Six Plays of Shakespeare*. Cambridge: Cambridge University Press.

Chaucer, Geoffrey. 1957. *The Works of Geoffrey Chaucer*. 2nd edition. Edited by F. N. Robinson. Boston: Houghton Mifflin.

Coleridge, Samuel Taylor. 1997. *The Complete Poems*. Harmondsworth: Penguin.

Collingwood, R. G. 1938. *The Principles of Art*. Oxford: Clarendon Press.

Craig, G. Armour. 1971. "Private Vision and Social Order in *Jane Eyre*". In Charlotte Brontë, *Jane Eyre*, edited by Richard J. Dunn. New York: W. W. Norton.

Craig, David. 1969. "Introduction". In Charles Dickens, *Hard Times*. Harmondsworth: Penguin Books.

Craik, W. A. 1972. "Emma". In Jane Austen, *Emma*, edited by Stephen M. Parrish. New York: W. W. Norton.

Crews, Frederick. 1970. *Psychoanalysis and Literary Process*. Cambridge, MA: Winthrop.

Crites, S. 1986. "Storytime: Recollecting the Past and Projecting the Future". In *Narrative Psychology: The Storied Nature of Human Conduct*, edited by T. R. Sarbin. Westport, CT: Praeger.

Currie, Gregory. 1985. "What is Fiction?" *Journal of Aesthetics and Art Criticism* 43:385–92.

———. 1990. *The Nature of Fiction*. Cambridge: Cambridge University Press.

———. 1995. *Image and Mind: Film, Philosophy and Cognitive Science*. Cambridge: Cambridge University Press.

———. 2010. *Narrative and Narrators: A Philosophy of Stories*. Oxford: Oxford University Press.

Danto, Arthur. 1987. "Philosophy as/and/of Literature". In *Literature and the Question of Philosophy*, edited by Anthony J. Cascardi. Baltimore and London: The Johns Hopkins University Press.

Davies, David. 2009. "Scruton on the Inscrutability of Photographs". *British Journal of Aesthetics* 49:341–55.

Davies, Martin, and Tony Stone, eds. 1995. *Mental Simulations*. Oxford: Blackwell.

De Man, Paul. 1986. *The Resistance to Theory*. Manchester: Manchester University Press.

Dennett, Daniel. 1978. "Where Am I?" In *Brainstorms: Philosophical Essays on Mind and Psychology*. Cambridge, MA: Bradford Books.

———. 1988. "Why Everyone is a Novelist". *Times Literary Supplement* 4459 (September 16–22): 1029.

Dickens, Charles. 1959. *Great Expectations*. London: Collins.

———. 1964. *Our Mutual Friend*. New York: Signet.

———. 1969. *Hard Times*. Harmondsworth: Penguin Books.

———. 1977. *Bleak House*, edited by George Ford and Sylvère Monod. New York: W. W. Norton.
Dickinson, Emily. 1924. *The Complete Poems of Emily Dickinson*. Boston: Little, Brown.
Didion, Joan. 1973. "Some Dreamers of the Golden Dream". In *The New Journalism*, edited by Tom Wolfe. New York: Harper & Row.
Donovan, Robert. 1973. "The Two Heroines of *Moll Flanders*". In Daniel Defoe, *Moll Flanders*, Norton Critical Edition, edited by Edward Kelly. New York: W. W. Norton. (Originally published in R. Donovan, *The Shaping Vision: Imagination in the English Novel from Defoe to Dickens*. Ithaca, NY: Cornell University Press, 1966.)
Dutton, Denis. 2009. *The Art Instinct: Beauty, Pleasure, & Human Evolution*. Oxford: Oxford University Press.
Eagleton, Terry. 1990. *Ideology of the Aesthetic*. Oxford: Basil Blackwell.
———. 2007. *How to Read a Poem*. Malden, MA: Blackwell.
———. 2012. *The Event of Literature*. New Haven, CT: Yale University Press.
Edmonds, Rosemary. 1969. "Introduction". In L. N. Tolstoy, *War and Peace*, vol. 1. Harmondsworth: Penguin.
Eliot, T. S. 1940. First Annual Yeats Lecture, delivered to the Friends of the Irish Academy at the Abbey Theatre, Dublin, in 1940. http://www.ancientsites.com/aw/Post/327817 (accessed October 24, 2013).
———. 1972. "Tradition and the Individual Talent". In David Lodge, ed., *20th Century Literary Criticism*. London: Longman.
Erlich, Victor. 1965. *Russian Formalism: History-Doctrine*. The Hague: Mouton.
Evans, Richard J. 2000. *In Defence of History*. London: Granta Books.
Ewbank, Inga-Stina. 1972. "The Structure and Pattern of the Whole Novel". In Emily Brontë, *Wuthering Heights*, Norton Critical Edition, edited by William M. Sale Jr. New York: W. W. Norton. (Originally published in Inga-Stina Ewbank, *Their Proper Sphere: A Study of the Brontë Sisters as Early Victorian Female Novelists*. Cambridge, MA: Harvard University Press, 1966.)
Falck, Colin. 1989. *Myth, Truth and Literature*. Cambridge: Cambridge University Press.
Feagin, Susan. 1996. *Reading With Feeling: The Aesthetics of Appreciation*. Ithaca, NY: Cornell University Press.
Fitzgerald, F. Scott. 1967. *The Great Gatsby*. Harmondsworth: Penguin.
Freud, Sigmund. 1953–1974. *Standard Edition of the Complete Psychological Works of Sigmund Freud*. 24 vols. Edited and translated by James Strachey. London: Hogarth.
Friday, Jonathan. 1996. "Transparency and the Photographic Image". *British Journal of Aesthetics* 36:30–42.
———. 2012. "Scruton's 'Photography and Representation'". In *Scruton's Aesthetics*, edited by Andy Hamilton and Nick Zangwill. Basingstoke: Palgrave Macmillan.
Friend, Stacie. 2012. "Fiction as a Genre". *Proceedings of the Aristotelian Society* 112 (2): 179–209.
Gaut, Berys. 2005. "Art and Cognition". In *Contemporary Debates in Aesthetics and the Philosophy of Art*, edited by Matthew Kieran. Oxford: Blackwell.
Gerrig, R. J. 1993. *Experiencing Narrative Worlds: On the Psychological Activities of Reading*. New Haven, CT: Yale University Press.
Gibson, John. 2003. "Between Truth and Triviality". *British Journal of Aesthetics* 43:224–37.
———. 2007. *Fiction and the Weave of Life*. Oxford: Oxford University Press.
———. 2011. "Thick Narratives". In *Narrative, Emotion & Insight*, edited by Noël Carroll and John Gibson. University Park: Pennsylvania State University Press.
Goldie, Peter. 2012. *The Mess Inside: Narrative, Emotion, & the Mind*. Oxford: Oxford University Press.
Goodman, Nelson. 1978. *Ways of Worldmaking*. Hassocks, Sussex: Harvester Press.
———. 1984. *Of Mind and Other Matters*. Cambridge, MA: Harvard University Press.
Graham, Gordon. 1997. *Philosophy of the Arts: An Introduction to Aesthetics*. London: Routledge.
Green, M. C., and T. C. Brock. 2000. "The Role of Transportation in the Persuasiveness of Public Narratives". *Journal of Personality and Social Psychology* 79:701–21.

Greene, T. 1968. "Spenser and the Epithalamic Convention". In *Edmund Spenser's Poetry*, edited by H. Maclean. New York: W. W. Norton.

Grice, H. P. 1957. "Meaning". *Philosophical Review* 66:377–88.

Hardy, Thomas. 1979. *Tess of the d'Urbervilles*. Edited by Scott Elledge. New York: W. W. Norton.

———. 1994. *The Collected Poems of Thomas Hardy*. Ware: Wordsworth Editions.

Hawkes, Terence. 1975. *Structuralism and Semiotics*. London: Methuen.

Herrnstein Smith, Barbara. 1968. *Poetic Closure: A Study of How Poems End*. Chicago: Chicago University Press.

Hill, Charles J. 1979. "Theme and Image in *The Egoist*". In George Meredith, *The Egoist*, edited by Robert M. Adams. New York: W. W. Norton.

Howe, Irving. 1979. "The Center of Hardy's Achievement". In Thomas Hardy, *Tess of the d'Ubervilles*, edited by Scott Elledge. New York: W. W. Norton.

Hume, David. 1963. "Of Tragedy". In David Hume, *Essays: Moral, Political and Literary*. Oxford: Oxford University Press.

———. 2007. *A Treatise of Human Nature*. Vol. 1. Edited by David Fate Norton and Mary J. Norton. Oxford: Oxford University Press.

———. 2008. "Of Tragedy". In *David Hume: Selected Essays*, edited by S. Copley and A. Edgar. Oxford: Oxford World's Classics.

Iser, Wolfgang. 1984. "The Reading Process". In *Reader-Response Criticism: From Formalism to Poststructuralism*, edited by Jane P. Tompkins. Baltimore: Johns Hopkins University Press.

Ivanov, Vyacheslav. 1975. "The Revolt Against Mother Earth". In Fyodor Dostoevsky, *Crime and Punishment*, edited by George Gibian. New York: W. W. Norton.

Johannessen, Kjell S. 1988. "The Concept of Practice in Wittgenstein's Later Philosophy". *Inquiry* 31:357–69.

Johnson, Samuel. 1905. *The Life of Milton*. In Samuel Johnson, *Lives of the English Poets*, 3 vols., edited by G. B. Hill. Oxford: Clarendon Press.

———. 1969. *Preface to Shakespeare's Plays*. London: Scholar Press.

———. 1985. *The History of Rasselas, Prince of Abyssinia*. London: Penguin Classics.

Jonson, Ben. 1616. *Epigrams*.

Kay, W. David. 1971. "The Christian Wisdom of Ben Jonson's 'On My First Sonne'". *Studies in English Literature, 1500–1900*, Vol. 11, No. 1, The English Renaissance, 125–36.

Keats, John. 2009. Letter to Benjamin Bailey, November 22, 1817. In *Selected Letters*, edited by Robert Gittings. London: Penguin Classics.

Kermode, Frank. 2004. *Pleasure and Change: The Aesthetics of Canon*. New York: Oxford University Press.

King, William. 1992. "Scruton and Reasons for Looking at Photographs". *British Journal of Aesthetics* 32:258–65.

Kivy, Peter. 1973. *Speaking of Art*. The Hague: Martinus Nijhoff.

———. 2007a. "Moodology: A Response to Laura Sizer". *Journal of Aesthetics and Art Criticism* 65 (3): 312–18.

———. 2007b. "Moodophilia: A Response to Noël Carroll and Margaret Moore". *Journal of Aesthetics and Art Criticism* 65 (3): 323–29.

Knights, L. C. 1964. "How Many Children Had Lady Macbeth?" In *Explorations*. Harmondsworth: Penguin.

Lamarque, Peter. 1981. "How Can We Fear and Pity Fictions?" *British Journal of Aesthetics* 21:291–304. Reprinted, with modifications, in Peter Lamarque, *Fictional Points of View*. Ithaca, NY: Cornell University Press, 1996.

———. 1996. *Fictional Points of View*. Ithaca, NY: Cornell University Press.

———. 2000. Review of Susan Feagin's *Reading With Feeling*. *Mind* 109:145–49.

———. 2001. "Literature". In *The Routledge Companion to Aesthetics*, edited by B. Gaut and D. Lopes. London: Routledge. (Revised entry in *The Routledge Companion to Aesthetics*, 3rd edition (2013), 521–31.)

———. 2002. "Appreciation and Literary Interpretation". In *Is There a Single Right Interpretation?*, edited by Michael Krausz. University Park: Pennsylvania State University Press.

———. 2003. "Fiction". In *The Oxford Handbook of Aesthetics*, edited by Jerrold Levinson. Oxford: Oxford University Press.

———. 2009a. "The Elusiveness of Poetic Meaning". *Ratio* 22:398–420.

———. 2009b. *The Philosophy of Literature*. Oxford: Blackwell.

———. 2010. *Work and Object: Explorations in the Metaphysics of Art*. Oxford: Oxford University Press.

Lamarque, Peter, and Stein Haugom Olsen. 1994. *Truth, Fiction and Literature*. Oxford: Clarendon Press.

Leavis, F. R. 1952–1953. "Reality and Sincerity". *Scrutiny* 29:90–98.

Lerner, Laurence. 1992. "Subverting the Canon". *British Journal of Aesthetics*. 32:347–58.

Lévi-Strauss, Claude. 1972. *Structural Anthropology*. Harmondsworth: Penguin Books.

Levinson, Jerrold. 1996. *The Pleasures of Aesthetics: Philosophical Essays*. Ithaca, NY: Cornell University Press.

Lewis, Cecil Day. 1947. *The Poetic Image*. New York: Oxford University Press.

Lewis, C. S. 1969. *The Allegory of Love*. Oxford: Oxford University Press.

Lieblich, A., and R. Josselson. 1997. *The Narrative Study of Lives*. Vol. 5. London: Sage.

Locke, John. 1979. *An Essay Concerning Human Understanding*, edited by Peter Nidditch. Oxford: Oxford University Press.

Lopes, Dominic McIver. 2003. "The Aesthetics of Photographic Transparency". *Mind* 112:433–48.

Lyas, Colin. 1983. "The Relevance of the Author's Sincerity". In *Philosophy and Fiction: Essays in Literary Aesthetics*, edited by Peter Lamarque. Aberdeen: Aberdeen University Press.

MacIntyre, Alasdair. 1985. *After Virtue: A Study in Moral Theory*. 2nd edition. London: Duckworth.

Meredith, George. 1979. *The Egoist*, edited by Robert M. Adams. New York: W. W. Norton.

Meskin, Aaron, and Jonathan Weinberg. 2003. "Emotions, Fiction, and Cognitive Architecture". *British Journal of Aesthetics* 43:18–34.

Miller, J. Hillis. 1977. "The World of *Bleak House*". In Charles Dickens, *Bleak House*, Norton Critical Edition, edited by G. Ford and S. Monod. New York: W. W. Norton.

Morawetz, Thomas. 1973. "The Concept of a Practice". *Philosophical Studies* 24:209–26.

———. 1978. *Wittgenstein and Knowledge: The Importance of "On Certainty"*. Amherst: University of Massachusetts Press.

Murdoch, Iris. 1970. *The Sovereignty of Good*. London: Routledge.

———. 1987. *The Book and the Brotherhood*. London: Chatto & Windus.

———. 1993. *Metaphysics as a Guide to Morals*. Harmondsworth: Penguin.

Nelson, William. 1973. *Fact or Fiction: The Dilemma of the Renaissance Storyteller*. Cambridge, MA: Harvard University Press.

Nietzsche, Friedrich. 1997. "On Truth and Falsity in Their Extramoral Sense". In *Philosophical Writings*, edited by Reinhold Grimm and Caroline y Vedia. New York: Continuum.

Norris, Christopher. 1985. *The Contest of Faculties*. London: Methuen.

Novitz, David. 1987. *Knowledge, Fiction and Imagination*. Philadelphia, PA: Temple University Press.

———. 1992. *The Boundaries of Art*. Philadelphia, PA: Temple University Press.

Nussbaum, Martha. 1990. *Love's Knowledge: Essays on Philosophy and Literature*. Oxford: Oxford University Press.

Ogden, C. K. 1951. *Bentham's Theory of Fictions*. 2nd edition. London: Routledge & Kegan Paul.

Ohmann, Richard. 1971. "Speech Acts and the Definition of Literature". *Philosophy and Rhetoric* 4:1–19.

Olsen, Stein Haugom. 1977. "Do You Like Emma Woodhouse?" *Critical Quarterly* 19:3–19.

———. 1978. *The Structure of Literary Understanding*. Cambridge: Cambridge University Press.

———. 1987. *The End of Literary Theory*. Cambridge: Cambridge University Press.

———. 2000. "Conventions and Rules in Literature". In *The Philosophy of Interpretation*, edited by J. Margolis and T. Rockmore, 25–43. Oxford: Blackwell.

———. 2005. "The Concept of Literature: An Institutional Account". In *From Text to Literature: New Analytic and Pragmatic Approaches*, edited by Stein Haugom Olsen and Anders Pettersson. Basingstoke: Palgrave Macmillan.
Orenstein, A., and P. Kotatko. 2013. *Knowledge, Language and Logic: Questions for Quine* (Boston Studies in the Philosophy and History of Science). Dordrecht: Kluwer.
Ousby, Ian. 1977. "The Broken Glass: Vision and Comprehension in *Bleak House*". In Charles Dickens, *Bleak House*, edited by George Ford and Sylvère Monod. New York: W. W. Norton.
Parfit, Derek. 1984. *Reasons and Persons*. Oxford: Oxford University Press.
Pettersson, Torsten. 2002. "The Literary Work as a Pliable Entity: Combining Realism and Pluralism". In *Is There a Single Right Interpretation?*, edited by Michael Krausz. University Park: Pennsylvania State University Press.
Phillips, Dawn. 2009. "Photography and Causation: Responding to Scruton's Scepticism". *British Journal of Aesthetics* 49:327–40.
Plato. 1998. *Republic*. Translated by Robin Waterfield. Oxford: Oxford University Press.
Polkinghorne, Donald E. 1988. *Narrative Knowing and the Human Sciences*. Albany: State University of New York Press.
Prado, C. G. 1984. *Making Believe: Philosophical Reflections on Fiction*. Westport, CT: Praeger.
Putnam, Hilary. 1975. *Philosophical Papers Vol. II: Mind, Language and Reality*. Cambridge: Cambridge University Press.
———. 1978. "Literature, Science, and Reflection". In Hilary Putnam, *Meaning and the Moral Sciences*. London: Routledge.
———. 1981. *Reason, Truth and History*. Cambridge: Cambridge University Press.
Quine, W. V. O. 1956. "Quantifiers and Propositional Attitudes". *Journal of Philosophy* 53:177–87.
———. 1960. *Word & Object*. Cambridge, MA: MIT Press.
———. 1961. *From a Logical Point of View*. New York: Harper Torchbooks.
Rawls, John. 1955. "Two Concepts of Rules". *Philosophical Review* 64 (1): 3–32.
Recanati, Francois. 2000. *Oratio Obliqua, Oratio Recta: An Essay on Metarepresentation*. Boston: MIT Press.
Richards, I. A. 1967. *Principles of Literary Criticism*. London: Routledge & Kegan Paul.
Ricks, Christopher. 1996. "Literature and the Matter of Fact". In *Essays in Appreciation*. Oxford: Clarendon Press.
Riffaterre, Michael. 1973. "Interpretation and Descriptive Poetry: A Reading of Wordsworth's 'Yew Trees.'" *New Literary History* 4:229–57.
Robinson, Jenefer. 2005. *Deeper than Reason*. Oxford: Oxford University Press.
Rorty, Richard. 1982. "Is There a Problem About Fictional Discourse?" In *Consequences of Pragmatism*. Brighton: Harvester Press.
———. 1986. "The Contingency of Language". In *London Review of Books*, vol. 8, no. 7, April 17.
———. 1992. "The Pragmatist's Progress". In *Interpretation and Overinterpretation*, edited by U. Eco et al. Cambridge: Cambridge University Press.
Rouse, J. 1990. "The Narrative Reconstruction of Science". *Inquiry* 33:179–96.
Rowe, M. W. 1997. "Lamarque and Olsen on Literature and Truth". *Philosophical Quarterly*, 47:322–41.
———. 2004. "Poetry and Abstraction". In M. W. Rowe, *Philosophy and Literature: A Book of Essays*. Aldershot: Ashgate.
Rudd, Anthony. 2007. "In Defence of Narrativity". *European Journal of Philosophy* 17:60–75.
Russell, Bertrand. 1956. *Logic and Knowledge*, edited by R. C. Marsh. London: George Allen & Unwin.
Schafer, R. 1981. "Narration in the Psychoanalytic Dialogue". In *On Narrative*, edited by W. J. T. Mitchell. Chicago: University of Chicago Press.
Schechtman, Marya. 1996. *The Constitution of Selves*. Ithaca, NY: Cornell University Press.
———. 2007. "Stories, Lives, and Basic Survival". In *Narrative and Understanding Persons*, edited by Dan Hutto. Cambridge: Cambridge University Press.

———. 2011. "The Narrative Self". In Shaun Gallagher, *The Oxford Handbook of the Self*. Oxford: Oxford University Press.
Scruton, Roger. 1983. "Photography and Representation". In *Aesthetic Understanding: Essays in the Philosophy of Art and Culture*. London: Methuen.
———. 2009. "Replies to Critics". *British Journal of Aesthetics* 49:451–61.
Searle, John R. 1969. *Speech Acts*. Cambridge: Cambridge University Press.
———. 1979. "The Logical Status of Fictional Discourse". In J. R. Searle, *Expression and Meaning*. Cambridge: Cambridge University Press. (Originally published in *New Literary History* 6 (1975): 319–32.)
———. 1980. "Minds, Brains and Programs". *Behavioral and Brain Sciences* 3:417–57.
———. 1995. *The Construction of Social Reality*. London: Allen Lane.
Sibley, Frank. 1974. "Particularity, Art, and Evaluation". *Proceedings of the Aristotelian Society*, suppl. vol. 48, 1–21.
———. 2003. "Aesthetic Concepts". In *Aesthetics and the Philosophy of Art: The Analytic Tradition: An Anthology*, edited by Peter Lamarque and Stein Haugom Olsen. Oxford: Blackwell.
Sizer, Laura. 2007. "Moods in the Music and the Man: A Response to Kivy and Carroll". *Journal of Aesthetics and Art Criticism* 65 (3): 307–12.
Smart, J. J. C., and Bernard Williams. 1973. *Utilitarianism: For and Against*. Cambridge: Cambridge University Press.
Stanford, Donald Elwin. 1979. *In the Classic Mode: The Achievement of Robert Bridges*. Cranbury, NJ: Associated University Presses.
Stecker, Robert. 2003. *Interpretation and Construction*. Oxford: Blackwell.
———. 2004. "What is Literature?" In *Philosophy of Literature: Contemporary and Classic Readings: An Anthology*, edited by Eileen John and Dominic McIver Lopes. Oxford: Blackwell.
Stock, Kathleen. 2011a. "Fictive Utterance and Imagining". *Proceedings of the Aristotelian Society*, suppl. vol. 85:145–61.
———. 2011b. "Unpacking the Boxes: The Cognitive Theory of Imagination and Aesthetics". In *The Aesthetic Mind: Philosophy and Psychology*, ed. Elisabeth Schellekens and Peter Goldie, 268–82. Oxford: Oxford University Press.
Stolnitz, Jerome. 2003. "On the Cognitive Triviality of Art". In *Aesthetics and the Philosophy of Art: The Analytic Tradition: An Anthology*, edited by Peter Lamarque and Stein Haugom Olsen. Oxford: Blackwell.
Strawson, Galen. 2004. "Against Narrativity". *Ratio* 17:428–52.
Taylor, Charles. 1989. *Sources of the Self*. Cambridge: Cambridge University Press.
Thompson, Hunter S. "The Hell's Angels, a Strange and Terrible Saga". In Tom Wolfe, *The New Journalism*. New York: Harper & Row.
Thomson, Judith Jarvis. 1976. "Killing, Letting Die, and the Trolley Problem". *Monist* 59:204–17.
Tillyard, E. M. W., and C. S. Lewis. 1939. *The Personal Heresy: A Controversy*. London: Oxford University Press.
Trudeau, N. A. 2002. *Gettysburg: A Testing of Courage*. New York: HarperCollins.
Van den Broek, Paul, Robert F. Lorch Jr., Tracy Linderholm, and Mary Gustafson. 2001. "The Effects of Readers' Goals on Inference Generation and Memory for Texts". *Memory and Cognition* 29:1081–87.
Van Ghent, Dorothy. 1979. "On *Tess of the d'Ubervilles*". In Thomas Hardy, *Tess of the d'Ubervilles*, edited by Scott Elledge. New York: W. W. Norton.
van Peer, W. 1996. "Canon Formation: Ideology or Aesthetic Quality?" *British Journal of Aesthetics* 36:87–108.
Vargas Llosa, Mario. 1986. *The Real Life of Alejandro Mayta*. London: Faber and Faber.
Velleman, J. David. 2003. "Narrative Explanation". *Philosophical Review* 112:1–25.
Vice, Samantha. 2003. "Literature and the Narrative Self". *Philosophy* 78:93–108.
Walsh, Richard. 2007. *The Rhetoric of Fictionality: Narrative Theory and the Idea of Fiction*. Columbus: The Ohio State University Press.

Walton, Kendall. 1984. "Transparent Pictures: On the Nature of Photographic Realism". *Critical Inquiry* 11:246–77.

———. 1990. *Mimesis as Make-Believe*. Cambridge, MA: Harvard University Press.

———. 1997. "On Pictures and Photographs: Objections Answered". In *Film Theory and Philosophy*, edited by Richard Allen and Murray Smith. Oxford: Oxford University Press.

Warburton, Nigel. 1988. "Seeing Through 'Seeing Through Photographs'". *Ratio* 30:64–74.

Watt, Ian. 1957. *The Rise of the Novel*. London: Chatto & Windus.

Weinberg, Jonathan M., and Meskin Aaron. 2006. "Puzzling over the Imagination: Philosophical Problems, and Architectural Solutions". In *The Architecture of the Imagination*, edited by Shaun Nichols. Oxford: Oxford University Press.

Weitz, Morris. 1955. "Truth in Literature". *Revue Internationale de Philosophie* 9:116–29.

White, Hayden. 1978. *Tropics of Discourse: Essays in Cultural Criticism*. Baltimore: Johns Hopkins University Press.

———. 1980. "The Value of Narrativity in the Representation of Reality". *Critical Inquiry* 7:5–27.

———. 1987. *The Content and the Form: Narrative Discourse and Historical Representation*. Baltimore: Johns Hopkins University Press.

———. 1989. "Figuring the Nature of Times Deceased". In *Future Literary Theory*, edited by R. Cohen. New York: Routledge.

———. 1999. *Figural Realism: Studies in the Mimesis Effect*. Baltimore: Johns Hopkins University Press.

———. 2010. *The Fiction of Narrative: Essays on History, Literature, and Theory 1957–2007*. Baltimore: Johns Hopkins University Press.

Wilson, George N. 2003. "Narrative". In *The Oxford Handbook of Aesthetics*, edited by Jerrold Levinson. Oxford: Oxford University Press.

Wimsatt, W. K. 1954. *The Verbal Icon*. Lexington: University of Kentucky Press.

Wimsatt, W. K., and M. C. Beardsley. 1972a. "The Intentional Fallacy". In *20th Century Literary Criticism*, edited by David Lodge. London: Longman.

———. 1972b. "The Affective Fallacy". In *20th Century Literary Criticism*, edited by David Lodge. London: Longman.

Wittgenstein, Ludwig. 1968. *Philosophical Investigations* (*PI*). 3rd edition. Translated by G. E. M. Anscombe. Oxford: Basil Blackwell.

———. 1969. *The Blue and the Brown Books* (*BBB*). 2nd edition. Oxford: Basil Blackwell.

———. 1974a. *On Certainty* (*OC*). Edited by G. E. M. Anscombe and G. H. von Wright and translated by Denis Paul and G. E. M. Anscombe. Oxford: Basil Blackwell.

———. 1974b. *Philosophical Grammar* (*PG*). Edited by Rush Rhees and translated by Anthony Kenny. Oxford: Basil Blackwell.

———. 1975. *Philosophical Remarks* (*PR*). Edited from his posthumous writings by Rush Rhees and translated by Raymond Hargreaves and Roger White. Oxford: Basil Blackwell.

———. 1978a. *Remarks on Colour* (*RC*). Edited by G. E. M. Anscombe and translated by Linda L. McAlister and Margarete Schättle. Oxford: Basil Blackwell.

———. 1978b. *Remarks on the Foundations of Mathematics* (*RFM*). 3rd edition. Edited by G. H. von Wright, R. Rhee, and G. E. M. Anscombe and translated by G. E. M. Anscombe. Oxford: Basil Blackwell.

———. 1980. *Culture and Value* (*CV*). Edited by G. H. von Wright in collaboration with Heikki Nyman and translated by Peter Winch. Oxford: Basil Blackwell.

———. 1981. *Zettel* (*Z*). 2nd edition. Edited by G. E. M. Anscombe and G. H. von Wright and translated by G. E. M. Anscombe. Oxford: Basil Blackwell.

Wolfe, Tom. 1973. *The New Journalism*. New York: Harper & Row.

Wolfe, Michael B. W., and Joshua M. Woodwyck. 2010. "Processing and Memory of Information Presented in Narrative or Expository Texts". *British Journal of Educational Psychology* 80:341–62.

Wood, James. 2008. *How Fiction Works*. London: Jonathan Cape.

Wordsworth, William. 2006. Preface to *Lyrical Ballads* [1800]. In *Romanticism: An Anthology*, 3rd edition, edited by D. Wu. Oxford: Blackwell.

Zahavi, Dan. 2007. "Self and Other: The Limits of Narrative Understanding". In *Narrative and Understanding Persons*, edited by Dan Hutto. Cambridge: Cambridge University Press.

Zwaan, Rolf A. 1994. "Effect of Genre Expectations on Text Comprehension". *Journal of Experimental Psychology: Learning, Memory, and Cognition* 20:920–33.

Index

Adams, Robert, 163
Aristotle, x, 48, 85, 100, 122, 124–125, 126, 127, 128
Arnold, Matthew, 136
Attridge, Derek, 183n2
Austen, Jane, 10, 67, 75, 131, 154

Baker, G P, 115
Barthes, Roland, 38, 74, 79, 93, 101, 123–124, 171, 176, 190, 200n5
Beardsley, Monroe, 135–136, 187–188, 198
Beebe, Maurice, 131
Beevor, Antony, 87
Bentham, Jeremy, 41, 42, 42–43
Berkeley, George, 86, 95
Bloom, Harold, 170, 171
Bradbury, Malcolm, 130
Bradley, A C, 31n10
Breslin, Jimmy, 89
Bridges, Robert: "On a Dead Child", 192–193
Brontë, Charlotte, 67, 76
Brontë, Emily, 67, 100–101
Brooks, Cleanth, 154
Bruner, Jerome, 23–24, 62, 63
Bryant, Arthur, 87
Budd, Malcolm, 183n4
Bunyan, John, 85

Calder, Jenni, 163–164
Capote, Truman, 88
Carnap, Rudolf, 44, 107–108, 111
Carroll, Noël, 66n3, 66n6, 96, 137–138, 141, 176, 199
Carter, Asa (a.k.a. Forrest Carter), 83
Cavell, Stanley, 86
Chaucer, Geoffrey: *Canterbury Tales*, 144–146
Coleridge, Samuel Taylor, 28–29
Collingwood, R G, 28, 187, 190
Craig, David, 102
Craig, G Armour, 76
Craik, W A, 75
Crews, Frederick, 188
Crites, S, 66n2
Currie, Gregory, 22, 31n1, 31n7, 32n16, 183n6

Davies, David, 22
Defoe, Daniel, 84, 90, 91, 93
De Man, Paul, 124
Dennett, Daniel, 24, 86–87
De Quincy, Thomas, 87
Descartes, René, 34, 37, 46, 55
Dickens, Charles, 67, 84, 130; *Bleak House*, 29, 73, 155–156, 180–181; *Great Expectations*, 157; *Hard Times*, 102; *Our Mutual Friend*, 70–71
Dickinson, Emily, 27
Didion, Joan, 99, 102
Donovan, Robert, 93

Dostoevsky, Fyodor, 131, 132; *Crime and Punishment*, 129–130, 133
Durrell, Lawrence, 13

Eagleton, Terry, 112, 193
Edmonds, Rosemary, 130
Eliot, George, 130
Eliot, T S, 86, 186, 189, 200n2
Evans, Richard, 18
Ewbank, Inga-Stina, 100–101

Falck, Colin, 127
Feagin, Susan, 183n3, 188
Fielding, Henry, 84
Fitzgerald, F Scott: *The Great Gatsby*, 54, 147–151, 156
Flaubert, Gustave, 70, 74, 86
Fowles, John, 10, 13
Fox, James, 88
Freud, Sigmund, 171, 188–189
Friday, Jonathan, 31n5
Friend, Stacie, 22–23

Gaarder, Jostein, 87
Galgut, Elisa, 200n2
Gibson, John, 32n17, 137, 167n1
Goethe, J W, 13, 70
Goldie, Peter, xi, 26, 30, 32n15, 32n19
Golding, William, 130
Goodman, Nelson, 36, 44, 45, 46, 66n7
Gower, John, 116
Graham, Gordon, 137
Greene, T, 178, 179
Grice, H P, 31n4
Guillory, John, 169, 170, 182, 183n3

Hacker, P, 115
Hardy, Thomas, 200n2; "After the Burial", 152–153; "The Darkling Thrush", 3–4; "I Am the One", 27–28; *Tess of the d'Urbervilles*, 72–73, 74–75, 79, 160–161
Hartman, Geoffrey, 169, 170, 182
Hawkes, Terence, 50n3
Hemingway, Ernest, 66n4, 88
Herrnstein Smith, Barbara, 194
Heyer, Georgette, 85
Hill, Charles, 7, 164
Hofstadter, Douglas, 87
Hopkins, Gerald Manley, 193
Horace, 122, 123, 171
Howe, Irving, 74–75, 162
Hume, David, 59, 86, 122, 174, 183n5

Iser, Wolfgang, 151–152, 156
Ivanov, Vyacheslav, 129–130

Jakobson, Roman, 72
James, Henry, 86
Johannessen, Kjell, 118n9
Johnson, Samuel, 122, 123, 125, 128, 131; *History of Rasselas*, 85
Jonson, Ben: "On My First Son", 194–195

Kant, Immanuel, xi, 37, 43, 44, 45, 49, 172
Kay, W David, 194–195
Keats, John, 195; "Lamia", 133; "Ode on a Grecian Urn", 127; "Ode to a Nightingale", 192
Keneally, Thomas, 83, 88
Kermode, Frank, 169–170, 171–172, 182
Kivy, Peter, 199
Knights, L C, 74

Lawrence, D H, 87
Leavis, F R, 200n2
Lerner, Laurence, 194
Levinson, Jerrold, 95
Lévi-Strauss, Claude, 54
Lewis, Cecil Day, 127
Lewis, C S, 116–117, 187
Lewis, David, 156, 180
Locke, John, 41, 43, 44, 87
Longford, Elizabeth, 87
Lopes, Dominic McIver, 6–7, 8, 31n5

MacIntyre, Alasdair, 60–61, 62, 64
Mailer, Norman, 88, 94
Marlowe, Christopher, 13, 70
McGinnis, Joe, 88
Meredith, George: *The Egoist*, 162–164, 165
Mill, John Stuart, 164–165
Miller, J Hillis, 73, 180–181
Morawetz, Thomas, 114, 118n6
Murdoch, Iris, 126, 127; *The Book and the Brotherhood*, 158–160

Nietzsche, Friedrich, 50n6, 87, 123
Novitz, David, 61, 63, 64, 137
Nussbaum, Martha, 67, 86

Ogden, C K, 41
Ohmann, Richard, 133
Olsen, Stein Haugom, 32n13, 75, 95, 118n3, 118n7, 132, 144, 145, 146
Orwell, George, 87, 88
Ousby, Ian, 155–156

Parfit, Derek, 87
Pirsig, Robert, 87
Plato, 86, 124, 125, 132, 133, 138, 186
Polkinghorne, Donald, 60
Pope, Alexander, 132
Prado, C G, 65n1
Putnam, Hilary, 50n2, 87, 136, 137

Queneau, Raymond, 13
Quine, W V O, 4–5, 9, 11, 42, 44

Rawls, John, 105, 107, 112–113, 117, 118n1
Recanati, François, 31n1
Richards, I A, 125, 186, 187
Richardson, Samuel, 84, 90, 91
Robinson, Jenefer, 137, 188–192, 195–197, 198
Rorty, Richard, 45–46, 176
Rouse, J, 65n1
Rousseau, Jean Jacques, 85
Rowe, M W, 175–176
Rudd, Anthony, 25–26
Russell, Bertrand, 41, 42–43, 44

Schafer, R, 65n1
Schama, Simon, 88
Schechtman, Marya, 23, 24, 25, 26, 32n20
Scott, Walter, 85, 87
Scruton, Roger, 7, 8, 9, 31n5–31n6, 72
Searle, John, 87, 95, 113, 118n8
Shaara, Michael, 54
Shakespeare, William, 67, 126, 132, 138; *As You Like It*, 123; *King Lear*, 76; *Macbeth*, 74, 129, 135, 198; *Measure for Measure*, 129, 135; *Othello*, 142, 144
Sibley, Frank, 170, 172–173, 181
Sizer, Laura, 199
Smart, J J C, 87
Solzhenitsyn, Alexander, 85
Spenser, Edmund: *Epithalamion*, 177–179
Starkey, David, 87
Stecker, Robert, 176
Stock, Kathleen, 32n14
Stolnitz, Jerome, 131
Strawson, Galen, xi, 24–25, 26, 29, 30

Talese, Gay, 88, 89
Taylor, Charles, 23
Thomas, Dylan, 193, 195
Thompson, Hunter, 98
Thomson, Judith Jarvis, 87
Tillyard, E M W, 187
Tolstoy, Leo: *Anna Karenina*, 99, 196, 197–198; *War and Peace*, 4, 85, 97, 130
Tomalin, Nicholas, 89
Tormey, Alan, 190, 194
Trudeau, N A, 53–54, 55–56

Van Ghent, Dorothy, 72–73, 161–162
Vargas Llosa, Mario, 38; *The Real Life of Alejandro Mayta*, 34–35, 48, 49
Velleman, J David, 81n4
Vice, Samantha, 29
Vidal, Gore, 85
Voltaire (François-Marie Arouet), 85

Walsh, Richard, 21–22
Walton, Kendall, 6, 7, 8, 22, 94–95, 96
Warburton, Nigel, 90
Watt, Ian, 90, 92, 104n1
Weitz, Morris, 127
Welles, Orson, 87
White, Hayden, 2, 15, 16–18, 19, 21, 26, 30, 32n11, 65n1, 66n2
Williams, Bernard, 87
Wimsatt, W K, 127, 187–188, 198
Wittgenstein, Ludwig, 105–118
Wolfe, Tom, 88, 89–90, 91, 92, 93, 98
Wood, James, 167n4
Wordsworth, William, 125, 128, 136, 187; "Tintern Abbey", 175; "Valedictory Sonnet to the River Duddon", 129, 134

Zahavi, D., 29